IN SEARCH OF
GOD

THE LANGUAGE AND
LOGIC OF BELIEF

Let us be worthy masters of the beautiful boats you set upon the waters. Let us find in your silence the right to love in peace. Let us sail out free to found a republic of love with your blessing, under the wings of your doves, in the ships you built for our faring-forth.

J. R. Salamanca, *Embarkation*

IN SEARCH OF
GOD

THE LANGUAGE AND
LOGIC OF BELIEF

Daniel Kolak

WILLIAM PATERSON COLLEGE

WADSWORTH PUBLISHING COMPANY
BELMONT, CALIFORNIA
A DIVISION OF WADSWORTH, INC.

Philosophy Editor: Tammy Goldfeld

Editorial Assistant: Kristina Pappas

Production: Rogue Valley Publications

Print Buyer: Karen Hunt

Permissions Editor: Bob Kauser

Designer: Scratchgravel Publishing Services

Copy Editor: Sheryl Rose

Cover: Madeleine Budnick

Compositor: Scratchgravel Publishing Services

Printer: Malloy Lithographing, Inc.

*This book is printed on
acid-free recycled paper.*

 ™

International Thomson Publishing
The trademark ITP is used under license.

Printed in the United States of America

1 2 3 4 5 6 7 8 9 10—98 97 96 95 94

Library of Congress Cataloging-in-Publication Data

Kolak, Daniel.
    In search of God / Daniel Kolak.
      p. cm.
    ISBN 0-534-19536-9 (alk. paper)
    1. God. 2. God—Proofs. 3. Methodology. I. Title.
  BT102.K55 1994
  231'.042—dc20   93-32062

CONTENTS

Contents

For Ray

PREFACE

GOD MAY BE DEAD. RELIGION DEFINITELY IS NOT. WHY? BECAUSE many, perhaps most, of the people who continue to believe or are unwilling to give up the search have been persuaded that their metaphysical needs—which, for them, swirl into one nebulous, whirlwind mystery, God— are best met by religion. What they are really looking for is a personal philosophy for dealing with ultimate questions. The problem is that they have no idea what philosophy is or that it even exists, what it is for, and how to go about getting one.

In this book I try to solve this problem in a philosophical way. Rather than discussing different philosophical views, criticizing various positions, surveying the history of thought, and so on, I begin with your own framework of beliefs, propositions, and attitudes. I show how to go about examining your belief structures by looking very closely at the language and logic of your framework. We then go on a journey of exploration into the unknown but where the landmarks are always yours: your experience, your suppositions, your assumptions, and your attitudes weighed relative to each other within your overall framework in which you exist as a conscious being in *your* world. To inquire into the existence of God is to think about that whole world, about the meaning of the existence of all things to you. In that sense, to conceive of God is to think about your world in its totality.

The mind thus thinking about its world notices itself, and in the dark reflection sees that all this might not be.

This is where the idea of God is born within us, is it not—in the realization, the thought, the insecurity, that all things might not be. Just as the thought of death (seeing the alternative to existence, the insecurity of it) gives rise to the self-conscious experience of subjectivity and the concept of self, doesn't the thought of the death of the world (seeing the insecurity of the world itself) give rise to the concept of God? The mind wonders: "Here I am, existing as a limited conscious being in the world, and when there arises within me the possibility of the negation of all this there comes at the heels of my insecurity the idea of an unlimited something beyond myself, God—is God real?" But then does the mind continue to inquire? Or does it give in to fear and shut the insecurity, the question, off?

If we are prepared seriously to address the question of God, then reality itself and everything in it, including ourselves, becomes the object of thought, hovering suspended, insecure in the mind's negation. We want to bring our full awareness to the whole of reality, to look passionately into it and ask: What are you! Who are you! What is this! To understand it we must deny it; we must allow the question to dislodge us from our answers; we must become like a river, insecure and powerful in our thirsting for the sea.

I thank the following people. My friend and former colleague Marshall Missner read the entire manuscript at two different stages; his copious and detailed comments influenced the work throughout. Another friend and former colleague, Garrett Thomson, sacrificed a good deal of his visit from Latin America to these chapters, sharing with me his uncanny brilliance and making many substantial improvements. David Goloff, a superb mathematician who has a natural gift for philosophy, with whom I am currently writing *Mathematical Thought*, was an extremely supportive friend, unselfishly contributing his intuitions and insights to several parts of this book. And the influence of Ray Martin—teacher, friend, co-author—courses throughout.

This book also owes a lot to the philosophy club, where I developed the concept of a philosophical journey with students who taught me as much as I taught them. Many ideas were first tried out at the club, where insights sprung forth easily and spontaneously. Some of the more complicated and technical matters found a much simpler incarnation thanks to the relentless stamina of the all-night brainstorming sessions, driven by students who wouldn't let me quit being a philosopher by pretending to be an authority. You all have my gratitude, especially: Hope May, now working on her doctorate in philosophy at Michigan State University; Joe Salerno, now working on his doctorate in philosophy at Ohio State University; Kevin Levin, finishing his Master's in philosophy at the University of Maryland; also Mike Russo, John Berg, and Steve Tuske as well as Jesus Ilundain, presently completing his doctorate in philosophy at the University of Illinois at Urbana-Champaign.

I thank my editors at Wadsworth for their guidance and support. Ken King, at the helm of philosophy for over twenty years, first approached me with the idea of writing this book and brought the project to fruition. *In Search of God* marks our sixth project together, now under Tammy Goldfeld's apt guidance. Thanks to the manuscript reviewers: Douglas Shrader, SUNY-Oneonta; James D. Ryan, Bronx Community College; Raymond Pfeiffer, Delta College; Jeff Jordan, University of Delaware; and Ronald Epp, University of Hartford.

To all the friends and relatives who come visiting only to find me spending most of my time writing: If you glean even a small piece of the enjoyment and nourishment this book has given me, this will more than make up for it. Finally, to my wife, Wendy Zentz, my best friend for over a dozen years, I must simply say I love you, very, very much.

Daniel Kolak

Introduction

YOU'RE WALKING DOWN A ROAD. WITHOUT THINKING, YOU'RE JUST WALK-
ing. Your mind is not anywhere else but there on that road.
There is a wholeness and beauty, an innocence, to such a walk.
One imagines that in its infancy humanity walked about like that
for many thousands of years before the first thought ever occurred, in complete inner silence. Today that is still how animals
live in the world, moving through it but silent inside, without
thinking.

Suppose you're walking down the road, thinking. What are
you thinking about? Either about the road or about something
else. If you're thinking about something else, then your mind is
not completely on the road. For instance, you might be thinking
about what happened yesterday, who your best friend is, what
you might like to have for dinner, and so on. Your attention is

not completely on the road. Part of it is off on another road, exploring imaginary paths.

Suppose, on the other hand, while walking down the road you're thinking about the very road you're on. What would that entail? Your attention is on the road. Yet you're not like the animal or the machine who moves along a given path by instinct or by programming, without thinking. What are you doing? What does it mean to think about the very road you're on? Well, you're not just attending to the road with a heightened awareness of the road and the surroundings. You could have a heightened awareness, like an owl or an eagle, without thinking. Rather, perhaps you're wondering about who built the road, how it was built, what it is made of, how you came to be walking on this road, why you're on this road rather than some other, where it leads, where it comes from, and what the alternative roads might be. In other words, you're *questioning*. Thinking about the road you're on means questioning it.

Usually in life we are in a constant hurry, rushing about, trying to get somewhere. We're always trying to pick up speed. Every day there is more and more to do and we keep getting more and more behind. "Getting nowhere fast," the saying goes. Our motto is just the opposite: *"Getting somewhere slow."* Philosophy has this in common with religion: Although their purposes are very different, they are both a sort of retreat from life's hectic pace.

To approach a question not dogmatically but philosophically, with an open mind, means first slowing down and getting very clear about what we are asking, what we are inquiring into, what we are trying to accomplish. Obscurity is but clever closed-mindedness. The many insights that can be found by looking at a question itself, at what it means, where it comes from, and various possible ways of trying to answer it, may be more important than any one answer. Our journey—the process, the method of inquiry—in and of itself, matters.

Second, to inquire philosophically means examining our beliefs about ourselves and the world, not for the purpose of reinforcing or changing our beliefs but, rather, *to see alternatives.* How, though, do we *see* alternatives? Not with our eyes. Our eyes can only, at best, show us what is directly in front of our noses. We can only see alternatives in our "mind's eye," that is, by thinking.

2

Thinking is a very special kind of questioning. When the philosopher says, "Think about it," this is not the same as "come up with an answer to a question." What you are thinking about might not even be a question. Rather, you turn the thing being examined into a question so that your attention and puzzlement can now be directed there: this thing, which you see is such and such a way, could be otherwise than the way it is. How so? Why is it like this? How else might it be? What is this? In thinking about X you're contemplating alternatives, putting models of X together, taking them apart. Animals, for instance, can't think—not yet, anyway, except perhaps at a rudimentary level—because they cannot consider things other than what is directly before them, what is given. The bird can't say to itself, "Hm, I wonder why I'm a bird rather than a dog." This would require that it model itself as something other than what it is. The tiger cannot say, "I don't want to be a tiger any more." Animals cannot question what they are because they cannot model what they are; the minds with which they perceive the world cannot conceive of alternatives. They cannot think. You can.

Among all the known species, to be able to think—to build mental models and actively focus your mind's eye on things other than what is before your physical eyes—is, as far as we know, unique to humans. Being able to think is not the same as just having an imagination or dreaming. Other animals probably dream and may even be able to imagine things. Thinking is more like guiding the conscious imagination, dreaming while awake. The real world does not disappear; possible worlds—alternative worlds, models of the real world—appear.

The danger is that it becomes easy not only to waste this ability to think, to build mental models of what is, but to use mental modeling to escape from reality through thinking, by living in our imaginations. In that sense, thinking is a sort of creative and conscious ability to lie to ourselves that something other than what is before us is before us, as if it really were there so that we can see it, attend to it. Steering ourselves using this power of conscious imagination is one thing. Manipulating ourselves, getting seduced by our own imaginations until we are caught in a dream of our own making from which we cannot escape because we can no longer consciously control it, is another. When we cannot consciously control what goes on in our own minds, it feels not like illusion but reality, because—not being under our conscious control—it feels as if we're not the ones making it the way it is. This is why dreams, which after all are of our own making, feel so real while they have us in our own grip. Philosophy uses the power of thought—the imaginative ability of making and using mental models to see in the mind's eye things other than what is given before our physical eyes—not for the purpose of losing ourselves to the world but finding ourselves, connecting us to it. The purpose of mental modeling in philosophy is to build a network of possible worlds, a framework of understanding for the real world.

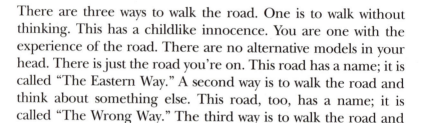

There are three ways to walk the road. One is to walk without thinking. This has a childlike innocence. You are one with the experience of the road. There are no alternative models in your head. There is just the road you're on. This road has a name; it is called "The Eastern Way." A second way is to walk the road and think about something else. This road, too, has a name; it is called "The Wrong Way." The third way is to walk the road and think about the road. This is called "The Western Way."

In walking the road without thinking, there are no alternative models, only the one road in your perception, and so you are less likely to wander off into the jungle or walk in circles or butt your head into a tree. When deer run through the woods they never hit a tree, not because their heads are empty but because in their heads there are no alternative imaginary trees, no alternative possible trees, no alternative model trees; the trees before their eyes are the only trees they see. The Eastern Way makes us more like deer but in a heightened way by freeing us from any false obstacles of our own making.

On the other hand, when we walk the road while thinking about the road we're on, we see not just where we are but also where we are not and where else we might be. Thus the Western Way too, makes freedom more possible. In this book we shall take the Western Way. But we shall take it all the way. After all, so long as we stay on the road and don't go the Wrong Way, we won't miss the Eastern Way. We'll come around to it.

CHAPTER 0

Does God Exist?

0.0 A Question of Meaning

DOES GOD EXIST? WHEN WE ASK OURSELVES THIS QUESTION, WHAT IS THE topic of inquiry? Ourselves, our beliefs, or God?

"Is there a God?" may seem very different from asking, for instance, "Is there a library in this town?" The latter has a definite answer that has nothing to do with us or our beliefs. But of course asking if God exists is not different from asking if a library exists. Whether some particular library exists has nothing to do with whether we believe it. Is the building there, are the books there? If yes, the library exists. If not, it does not exist. Likewise, God's existence or nonexistence has nothing to do with our beliefs. Whether God exists depends solely on whether such and such an entity, whatever it may be, is or is not there. If yes, then God exists. If not, then not. This is obvious but easy to forget.

5

Suppose we want to know whether Buzzard's Bay, Louisiana, an eighteenth-century town wiped out by a hurricane, had a library. Checking the history books, we find that in the ensuing flood, the whole town—citizens, buildings, records, everything— washed away into the ocean. Whether Buzzard's Bay had a library is unknowable. But in that town a library either did exist or else it did not exist. The fact that the existence of the library is unknowable does not in any way influence that town's layout. Either people could or could not go to a particular place in that town and borrow some books. It all depends on whether such a place existed.

"Does God exist?" is about God. What we believe has nothing to do with whether God exists. What, though, do we mean by "God"? People have very different conceptions of God—even whether God is a one or a many. The nature of God, however— what *sort* of God—is secondary to whether any sort of God (even a plurality) exists.

Does some sort of God exist? Let us for now choose to be somewhat ambiguous about what we mean by "God." Initially, our inquiry will extend to, but not be limited by, a broad range of widely accepted conceptions of God. In spite of differences among these various conceptions, there is enough similarity for us to agree, generally, what we are searching for. Should we discover that a creator of the cosmos exists, or an extremely powerful being in charge of the world, and so on, few of us would quibble (though some no doubt still would).

To ask whether some sort of God exists, then, is not to inquire about our own natures nor even about the nature of God. The question is not about us or what we believe, nor about any particular religion. It has to do with the way the world is, the nature of reality. Does the world have a God? Is reality ultimately created by, guided by, sustained by, someone, something—God? Is that how all this came to be? Or is the whole universe, including ourselves, an accident, a temporary interlude between nothings? *Does God exist?*

0.1 A Question of Existence

When we ask whether something—anything—*exists*, what are we asking? We have an idea of something, a concept of it, and we want to know whether there really is such a thing or whether it is just an idea, merely a concept.

Say you have the idea for a movie. You describe the scenes, the plot, and we listen with interest. Then we ask: "Does that movie exist—is it real? Or does it exist just as an idea in your head?"

On the other hand, suppose we ask Doug whether his novel exists. He begins with the first sentence and proceeds, word by word, chapter by chapter, to recite from memory the whole story. Moved, we ask Doug to recite the novel again and he does. Is the status of Doug's novel the same as the status of your movie—is his novel, because it exists "only in his head," therefore not real?

There is a difference between what it takes for a novel to be real and what it takes for a movie to be real. Doug's novel is very real—it just isn't written down. His novel might well be the greatest novel ever written. It just so happens Doug is an artist who says he's so repulsed by the levels of degeneracy to which the world of art has sunk that he refuses to soil the perfection of his creation by publishing it. He doesn't want "other novels" near his on the shelf. Doug prefers to keep his novel away from the rest of the world and reveal it to just a few individuals.

To say Doug's novel is not real would put it in the category of my opera. Even though I might whistle a few tunes and tell you my opera is about humanity's inhumanity to itself, my opera does not really exist. It is only a figment of my imagination, an idea, a concept in my head, the result of wishful thinking. If you compose a poem and then don't recite it, and I don't recite a poem because I didn't compose one, what we have is not two nonexistent things but one nonexistent thing—my poem—and one existent thing—your poem. "Where's your poem?" you ask. "My poem is nonexistent," I say. "Where's yours?" "In my mind." At this point I would be wrong to insist that your poem too, because it is only in your mind, does not exist. It does. It exists in your mind. Poetry and novels are the sorts of thing that even if they exist only in the mind can still be real. The same is true of mathematical objects; the number 3 is real, it exists. Compare the number 3 with the number "sigma." Sigma is the name of the positive whole integer between 3 and 5 other than 4. Sigma does not exist; it is a name for a nonnumber. Whereas the number 3 does exist; it is the name of a real number.

So, some things, like poems, novels, and numbers, can be real even if they exist only in the mind. Movies, cars, houses, stars, and planets cannot. Here we notice something important. We cannot proceed in our journey simply by rattling off questions, making up answers, and plunging on ahead to the next question. We have to slow down. We have to slow *way* down. In fact, it might not be such a bad idea if we grind to a screeching halt and camp for a bit.

0.2 God and Reality

To inquire into the existence of God is to think about the whole world, about the meaning of the existence of all things—to consider an alternative *everything*. Not an alternative *to* everything. An *alternative everything*. In that sense, to conceive of God is to think about the world in its totality.

So when the question of God arises within us, what is it that we want to know? Do we want to know whether God exists as a full-fledged concept, like a completed novel, a completed poem, a fully composed symphony in one's head, the product purely of thought, "real for us," or do we want to know whether this concept applies to something out there, like stars and planets, the universe itself, existing independently of thought and the creative endeavors of our imaginations, "real for itself"? Some concept or idea, X, exists in the mind and we want to know whether this idea, this concept, applies not just to our picture of reality but to reality itself. "Does X apply to the mind only, is it but a figment of the imagination, the result only of thought—or is X, in and of itself, *real?*" Isn't that what we want to know when we are curious about God?

The mind gives rise to some idea, some concept, some notion of something other than what is before the eyes, which perhaps it would like to be real independently of itself. When the mind says, "I think, therefore I am," it realizes the possibility that it might *not* be. To *think* about its own existence is to conceive *alternatives* to its own existing: nonexisting. Here the birth of self-consciousness through *thought*—seeing, in the mind's eye, the alternative to your own existing and thereby creating a mental model of yourself, an "I"—seems to go hand in hand with the awareness of death. The mind, in realizing it might not be, makes a model of itself and sees itself in the imagination—the existence of the mind reflected in the mind's eye—and says, "I exist, I am here." And then it wonders: How did I get here? Why do I exist? Did I have an origin? What is the origin of me? What is the origin of this ability to see alternatives—subjectivity—to what is—objectivity? Why does it arise? Of all the objects in the world, what is the thinking subject, me—the object of these questions—made of? If I am just made of objects, like rocks, water, and earth, then how could the objects of which I consist come to have within them a thinking subject, an alternative to objects within objects, a model of subjectivity—an *I*? How strange to think that thought originates in the presence of what is not there.

The mind looking at the world sees itself looking and in the dark reflection sees that all this might not be. This is where the idea of God is born within us, is it not, in the realization, the thought, the insecurity, that all things might not be? In other words, just as the thought of death—seeing the alternative to my existence, the insecurity of it—gives rise to the self-conscious experience of subjectivity and the concept of self, doesn't the thought of the death of the world—seeing in the alternative to there being a world, any world at all, the insecurity of the world itself—give rise to the concept of God? The mind wonders: "Here I am, existing as a limited conscious being in the world, and when there arises within me the possibility of the negation of all this there comes at the heels of my insecurity the idea of an unlimited something beyond myself, God—is God real?" But then does the mind continue to inquire? Or does it give in to fear and shut the insecurity, the question, off?

If we are prepared seriously to address the question, "Is God real?" reality itself, and everything in it, including ourselves, becomes the object of thought, hovering suspended, insecure in the mind's negation. People sometimes say, "real for you," or "real for me?" But this is not the sense in which we want to inquire into whether God is real. We want to bring our full awareness to the whole of reality, look passionately into it and ask: What are you! Who are you! What is this! To understand it we must deny it; we must allow the question to dislodge us from our answers; we must become like a river, insecure and powerful in our thirsting for the sea.

0.3 Yes-Believers, No-Believers, and Non-Believers

At one time just about all people believed the Earth was flat. Their beliefs were very strong. They were also very wrong.

The Earth is not flat for some and round for others. The shape of the Earth is what it is for everyone. It is not more round for some and less round for others. The Earth is just as round as it is, no more and no less. We might not know the shape exactly, but to a certain degree and within a certain margin of error the Earth has the shape it has independently of what anyone thinks or believes. The Earth is not triangular. It is not square. It is round.

Rocks, tables, chairs, atoms, stars, planets, and galaxies . . . these are just some of the sorts of entities we regard, within a particular comfort zone, as being real. Santa Claus, Superman, Zeus, leprechauns, and the pot of gold at the end of the rainbow are some of the sorts of things we regard, within our comfort zone, as not being real. Of course, Superman is a fictional character who "exists only in fiction." Zeus is a mythological god who "exists only in mythology." But neither Superman nor Zeus have any real existence, in the sense of the things we are prepared, within our comfort zone, to regard as being real independently of our own minds. They are purely the products of thought. We might, of course, be wrong. But presently we are merely trying to get specific about what we are asking when we ask, "Does God exist?" We want to draw full attention to the question.

"Does God exist?" means: Is some particular sort of entity, God, real in itself, independently of the human mind?

The question "Does Santa Claus exist?" is about whether Santa Claus is real, not about your belief nor about whether there is such a character in children's stories. Likewise, our question, "Does God exist?" is about whether God is real, *not* about your belief or about whether there is such a character in religious stories. Regardless of what you or I or anybody else believes, (some sort of) God either does or does not exist, in the sense of being real independently of our conceptions and creative imaginations. (We are for the moment leaving it open as to exactly what sort of "God" we are talking about.)

Now, do you *believe* God exists? This question is about you. It asks for the status of your belief regarding the existence of an entity that, quite independently of your or anybody's belief, either does or does not exist, in the sense of existing without being dependent for its existence, as such, in any way on thought and the creative modeling abilities of the mind.

So what do you believe? Do you believe God is real? Some say "Yes." Some say "No." Some say "I don't know." Most who say Yes, and most who say No, claim their answer expresses an opinion or a belief, not knowledge. Some claim their beliefs do express knowledge. Let us call any believers who believe, one way or the other, whether God exists, "Yes-Believers" or "No-Believers," depending on what they believe. No-Believers believe God does not exist. Yes-Believers believe God does exist. In this way, we do not misrepresent the fact that those who commonly call themselves "nonbelievers" are also believers: they believe God does not exist.

What about those who answer, "I don't know"? The answer is ambiguous; do you mean you don't know whether God exists because you don't have enough evidence to be convinced one way or the other, or do you mean you don't know what you believe? If the former, then you are misunderstanding the question. "Do you *believe* God exists?" The question asks what you believe, not what you know or are convinced of nor even what the truth about God is. It is like asking, "Do you believe there is life on other planets?" Without knowing whether there is extraterrestrial life, without being convinced one way or the other, the mind can answer this question simply by reporting to itself its own feeling, hunch, or guess.

On the other hand, if by saying "I don't know" you mean you do not believe one way or the other because you simply have no beliefs regarding the existence of God, then you belong in a category with all those who have no beliefs about the existence of God. Let us call this category "Non-Believers." The Non-Believer, in the sense we are using the term, believes neither that God exists nor that God does not exist. The Non-Believer does not believe one way or the other.

For every belief, these three categories are mutually exhaustive; that is, they cover every possible attitude a person could have on every conceivable topic. For instance, is there a glass of orange juice on my desk right now as I am writing this sentence?

11

Probably with regard to this not very important issue you are a Non-Believer. It's not that you doubt there is orange juice on my desk. You don't have a belief one way or the other. Nor is it a problem of not having enough evidence. People often believe things without having any evidence for their belief. For instance, regarding the orange juice question, suppose that you, an orange juice mogul, are a Yes-Believer; every morning you wake up and, smiling, you say to yourself, "Yes siree . . . everyone in America at this moment is having a glass of orange juice. Praise the orange groves!" Suppose you really believe this. We give you a lie-detector test and you pass; you truly believe everyone is drinking orange juice most of the time. Your confidence level is at 100 percent. On the other hand, if you are a No-Believer with regard to the orange juice issue, you believe that right now there is not a glass of orange juice on my desk. Whereas the Non-Believer has no belief one way or the other.

On the topic of God, then, we have two main categories: Believers and Non-Believers. Believers are divided into Yes and No subcategories. This categorizes everyone on any topic: Yes-Believers, No-Believers, and Non-Believers. On the topic of the existence of God, then, where do *you* stand?

0.4 Evidence, Justification, and Belief: When Is Conviction Warranted?

Yes-Believers and No-Believers have something in common: belief, one way or the other. And they may have something in common with Non-Believers: they might not profess to know whether God exists. Yes-Believers and No-Believers both believe something is the case; they differ in *what* they believe regarding the existence of God, not *whether* they believe. The Non-Believer does not believe one way or the other but may agree with those Yes-Believers and No-Believers who profess to believe whether God exists.

Is there a God? The answer depends on the nature of reality itself, on the way the world is. Do you *believe* God exists? The answer depends on you. If yes, then with regard to the existence of God you are a Yes-Believer. If no, you are a No-Believer. If you do not believe one way or the other, you are a Non-Believer.

Now, you have a *right* to believe anything you want about anything you want. This right, like any other right, is dependent upon, and made possible by, a set of legal rules within a social and political framework. It is an amazing right to have, one which the writers of the United States Constitution created when they turned an idea, a concept, into reality. Without that framework there would be no "rights" in the legal sense, in the same way that nothing can be *against* the law unless there are laws, all of which exist exclusively within the mind's dominion. If everyone tomorrow simultaneously decided that there were no more laws, no more countries, no more political systems, then starting tomorrow all the laws, all the countries, all the political systems would instantaneously cease to exist.

Having a right to believe whatever you want about anything you want means you have a right to think: You have a right to conceive of alternatives. Thus, what you think and what you believe is up to you. Belief is, in that sense, like thinking, a subjective, personal matter. But even here there are some definite limits; some beliefs, if you let them be known in inappropriate contexts, might lead not just to persecution but prosecution, ending in your incarceration.

Now, although you have a right to believe anything you want, not all your beliefs are justified. Whether a belief is justified depends on how you come to have it. A belief is justified to the degree that it is based on reasonable evidence. Suppose you believe the president was murdered. To what degree this belief is justified depends on the quantity, quality, and corroboration of evidence you have that the president is dead. Quantity of evidence is determined by how much of it you have. Quality of evidence is determined by whether your information is

1. firsthand
2. secondhand
3. thirdhand

and so on. Corroboration of evidence is determined by how many independent sources the information comes from:

1. 1 source = 0 corroboration
2. 2 sources = 1 corroboration
3. 3 sources = 2 corroborations

and so on. And of course the evidence must be reasonable. What do I mean by "reasonable"? I mean the same as *thinking* in the sense defined above: the considering of alternatives. In other words, the evidence has been questioned: you've considered how something that appears to be so might not be so (via thinking—mental modeling) and concluded that the likeliest—i.e., most reasonable—possibility is that in this case things are the way they appear to be.

For instance, an event occurs: The president is murdered. John is out walking when a car drives by in the street. The driver yells, "The president has been assassinated!" If that's the first John hears of it and he is now convinced that the president has been murdered, John's belief is unjustified. The quantity of evidence—one piece of information (a man on the street claiming the president is dead)—and the quality of evidence—thirdhand at best—and the corroboration—just one source—does not warrant a conviction. It warrants, at most, a suspicion. John has *some* reason to suspect that the president may be dead but not enough evidence to draw any final conclusions. The problem is John didn't think about it; that is, he didn't reason—he didn't consider what the alternatives might be: the driver might be a prankster, a lunatic, or simply mistaken, and so on.

John goes home and turns on the radio. He hears the announcer say that the president has just been critically wounded. John now has another piece of evidence, this one probably secondhand. Firsthand means you experience the event directly. Secondhand means you get the report from an eyewitness. Thirdhand means you get the report from someone who got it secondhand. And so on. John now has one corroboration. He reasons that while it might be some sort of hoax, perhaps a radio play in the style of Orson Welles's famous broadcast of H. G. Wells's *War of the Worlds*, it would be unlikely—though possible—that the driver was listening to the same station. So John flips to another station—the result of reasoning about the evidence—and hears the same thing. He hears what sounds like a reporter at the scene. This third piece of evidence—this one secondhand—gives John a second corroboration. At this point to believe that the president is dead would be reasonably justified. *How* reasonably justified depends to what extent it is based on reasonable evidence. By "reasonable evidence" I mean someone else could think about it, i.e., consider alternatives, and as a result become convinced by that evidence.

Next, John turns on the TV and sees Connie Chung announcing that the president has been shot and killed by a religious fanatic. By now the quantity, quality, and corroboration of reasonable evidence is justified enough to *warrant a conviction*. When the quantity, quality, and corroboration of reasonable evidence is justified enough to warrant a conviction, I will call that evidence "reasonably convincing." This doesn't necessarily mean you are convinced. Although whether a belief is justified enough to warrant a conviction depends not on you but on the reasonable evidence, whether you are convinced depends on you. That is, "reasonably convincing" refers to the evidence: It is of a reasonably sufficient quantity and quality to warrant a belief. "Reasonably convinced" refers to the relationship between you and that reasonably convincing evidence: The evidence has settled the issue, it has been singled out from the alternative models as the best model. For you, the issue is closed.

Your belief may nevertheless turn out to be false. A mental model, after all, no matter how good, is not the thing. For instance, it might turn out that, unbeknownst to John, the president was not shot at all; it was a hoax, an impostor took his place, and so on. But John's belief was still justified enough to warrant a conviction. It would be like a case in which a suspect is convicted of murder when he has confessed to it and all the evidence says he did do it, but in fact he did not really do it. The conviction would have been false but warranted. It wouldn't be like taking an innocent person off the street and framing him for a murder he did not commit. *Just because it may always turn out that we are wrong does not mean that we can never be right.*

Notice that, given what I mean by "reasonably convinced," you cannot be reasonably convinced of something unless the evidence is reasonably convincing. But you might believe it nonetheless, based not on having been convinced by the evidence but by having been converted through seduction, indoctrination, or brainwashing. I will reserve the word "converted" for such nonevidential beliefs. (We'll discuss this concept again in the next chapter.) Note, too, that you have a right—even when the evidence for the belief is convincing—to choose to *suspend judgment*. For instance, say you believe something is so because you have convincing evidence that it is so but, in spite of that, you choose not to accept it. In other words, the evidence may warrant belief, but for some reason you do not accept the belief. Why? Well, you might do it for scientific reasons. Perhaps you wish to continue inquiring into whether something that apparently is so really is so, searching beyond ordinary levels of justification. And you cannot do this effectively unless you suspend judgment and have an open mind. Or, you might do it just to be different. Everyone says the Earth goes around the sun. You say, "I choose not to believe." They say: "What's your evidence?" You say: "I don't have any, but I choose to exercise my right to suspend judgment." Or, you might do it to be philosophical. For instance, you choose to suspend judgment about whether the Earth goes around the sun or the sun around the Earth because you are curious to see whether this belief matters, what function it has in the overall framework of beliefs, whether it really is known to be true, and so on. Any of these reasons to suspend judgment might be interesting, perhaps even revealing.

On the other hand, suppose in response to the heliocentric view of the solar system, you say, "I'm *convinced* otherwise: The Earth does not go around the sun—the sun goes around the Earth." The heliocentric Yes-Believer asks: "What's your evidence?" You say: "I haven't any." In this case, one of two things is going on. It might just be that you're confused about language. For unless you have convincing evidence, you're wrong in saying that you are "convinced otherwise." You have a right to be wrong. But you're mistaken: you're not really *convinced* that the sun goes around the Earth. Why? Because you don't have any evidence! Suppose, however, you actually do believe that the sun does go around the Earth, even though you have absolutely no evidence for this. You feel as psychologically confident about the Geocentric View as you do, say, about the number of fingers on your right hand. In that case, you're not merely confused about language. Your belief is more than just wrong. It's *unreasonable.* Your right to be unreasonable is much more restricted than your right to be wrong. Though you do still have a right to be unreasonable, up to a point.

Similarly, it would also be unreasonable if, when someone asks John whether he heard the president has been murdered, he says, "Yes, I heard it but I doubt he's really dead; how can you trust the media? He's probably only hiding." It is *possible* that the president is hiding but it is not very probable; based on the evidence presented, it's more probable that the president is dead. John's suspension of judgment in this case, given the evidence, would be unjustified enough to be unreasonable. On the other hand, if John now believed that the president was indeed dead and had been murdered, John's belief would be justified enough to warrant conviction. When the quantity, quality, and corroboration of evidence warrants a conviction, I will thus call that evidence "reasonably *convincing*," or simply "convincing" for short.

Again, keep in mind that even our most reasonable evidence might be all wrong. But you are not justified in believing that the evidence is all wrong unless you have some evidence that the evidence is all wrong! For instance, if John were directly involved in the conspiracy to fake the murder of the president, this would reasonably justify his belief that the president was not really murdered. This belief, too, might turn out to be wrong—John could have been involved in a *double* conspiracy, and the president, unbeknownst to John, really is dead. But John's belief is not justified enough to warrant a conviction unless John has reasonably convincing evidence.

0.5 Evidential Responsibility: When Is Suspended Judgment Warranted?

On the way to work news anchor Connie Chung hears on the radio that the president has been shot and killed. She gets to the CBS studios, turns on the TV and sees Tom Brokaw report the murder, sees Peter Jennings report it, and so on. At this point, Connie Chung is as justified as John is in believing that the president is dead. The quantity, quality, and corroboration of evidence is the same. Probably she now also believes the president is dead, just as John does. In this way beliefs can be a sort of shorthand way of reporting to ourselves how much evidence we have available that something is so. But although John would *not* be warranted in suspending judgment about the death of the president, Connie Chung is justified in suspending judgment. In fact, it would be unjustified for her simply to go on the air and report that the president is dead. Why? Didn't we just consider

John in the same situation, hearing the news on the radio and the TV and being reasonably justified by that evidence to have a warranted conviction?

Connie and John are not in the same situation, however. Connie isn't just reporting the evidence to herself. She is also reporting it to John and to you. She is herself an important evidential link. The same evidence that warrants a conviction for John warrants a suspension of judgment for Connie. In John's mind the issue can justifiably be settled at this point but not in Connie's. She must go on to check with CBS reporters on the scene, the wire services, and so on, because she has a much higher level of *evidential responsibility* toward the event in question than John. The *evidential responsibility* is determined by the believer's own role in the quality level of the evidence. Connie Chung going on the air and announcing, "The president is dead," is itself secondhand information and this may be as close as John, you, and others in the audience can get to the truth. John announcing the news to his neighbor, after hearing Connie Chung report it, is itself thirdhand information. *The closer you are to being a firsthand link, the more warranted you are in suspending judgment,* so that you can raise the corroborative level of the evidence. You cannot do this unless you remain critical. You must continue to check other sources. To do it with an open mind, you must suspend judgment. It is like being a judge in court: You may already have reasonable evidence to warrant belief that the suspect is guilty of murder, but you will suspend judgment until both sides have had their say, until all the available evidence is in.

That is why Connie Chung, unlike John, is warranted in suspending judgment concerning the president's death. John has a right to do so too. But John is not *warranted* in doing so. By suspending judgment, Connie Chung will be much more efficient in bringing forth from the reporters on the scene the best evidence. She might herself believe that the president is dead, but she will demand evidence from her reporters, almost as if she didn't believe. She might do well by playing devil's advocate. She will insist on being in direct contact with the reporters, scrutinizing what they say, questioning them not because she does not believe them but because she wants to make sure the truth gets out, cross-examining reporters whom she personally knows, some of whom may be eyewitnesses, doubting what she hears until it is better confirmed, and so on. In her capacity as news anchor, Connie Chung, unlike John, can't get her news from the other networks! To do so is to weaken the entire evidential framework in which we live as a society. In this situation Connie Chung's suspension of judgment, therefore, unlike John's, is warranted until she has the reports from eyewitnesses about whom she personally has enough reasonable evidence to be convinced.

For John, on the other hand, to suspend judgment about the death of the president on the grounds that he does not have direct personal contact with eyewitnesses, and so on, would be unjustified. Direct personal contact with eyewitnesses is not required to justify John's belief. For John to claim that this is required would be to misunderstand the role John plays in the overall evidential framework concerning the life or death status of the president. It is to inflate his level of evidential responsibility—to make himself more important than he really is.

Consider now the situation from the point of view of the vice president of the United States. He hears from the news and also from eyewitnesses, such as the president's bodyguards, that the president has been murdered. Is the vice president justified, on the basis of hearing these reports, in believing that the president is in fact dead? Yes, of course. However, if you are the vice president, your evidential responsibility toward the life or death status of the president is higher than Connie Chung's. You have to be an eyewitness yourself; you have to personally check everything out for yourself. *Until you do, suspension of judgment is warranted.* For the vice president to allow himself to be persuaded by any reporters, no matter how good and reliable they are, that the president is dead, and not to check this out himself, would be unreasonable. For him to accept as true what he is justified in believing is true, would in this situation be unjustified! Remember, once you allow yourself to be convinced of something, the issue has been settled for you. You're done with it. The question is closed. And you cannot open a question with a closed mind. You have to open your mind first by suspending judgment.

After the vice president sees the president's body and surmises the situation himself, consults with all the best autopsy experts, Secret Service, FBI and CIA authorities, and so on, all of whom corroborate the evidence that the president is dead, for him then *not* to accept that the president is dead on grounds that it might all be a hoax, that maybe there's a secret enemy plot, perhaps aliens kidnapped him, and so on, would be so unjustified as to be unreasonable. He had better go and do his job as the new president!

Is this the highest level of judgmental responsibility? No. One can still go a level higher. Suppose, after the assassination of the president, the vice president appoints you to be the head of something like the Warren Commission on the assassination of President Kennedy. All the evidence is handed over to you. You would then be warranted in suspending judgment so that you can consider all sorts of conspiracy theories. You cannot do this without suspending judgment! You can't say, "All right, let me see what clever plots may have secretly unfolded behind the government's back, maybe a foreign government plot, maybe aliens trying to take over the Earth—though of course I'm completely convinced that there haven't been any such plots." If you're convinced, your mind is closed. You can't look into all the obscure possibilities if you're convinced there aren't any! You must keep an open mind. And, in this case, reports of eyewitnesses—even being an eyewitness yourself—are not enough. Why? Because your level of evidential responsibility is highest of all. You have to pass final judgment. You have to consider all the alternatives, even exotic ones. This of course again means *thinking*. Ironically, *the more you think,* the less you believe—not because you are undercommitted but because you are overcommitted. Your horizons are broadened. You see more because there are more alternatives, more models, to look at. The possibilities are increased. You are more free.

Philosophy is a sort of exotic thinking. The philosopher is to truth what the head of the Warren Commission was to the assassination of President Kennedy. All the angles have to be considered. All points of view become fair game. Everything and everyone is suspect. Imagining exotic, even bizarre, even "really bizarre" alternatives—one of the most important skills in philosophy—becomes absolutely essential when your level of evidential responsibility toward whatever it is you are thinking about is maximal.

Here, at this crossroads, philosophical inquiry veers sharply from religious inquiry, at least by *my* book. In religion, the highest responsibility concerning God and related issues lies in religious authorities. In philosophy, the person in the position of highest responsibility is *you*. This means that while you are engaged in philosophical inquiry into the question of whether God is dead or alive, whether God exists or not, and all related questions, if you have any opinions about God without having yet thought about it in the ways we've described, and you fail to suspend judgment, not only are your beliefs not justified—you are irresponsible.

In general, then, we can state the following relationship between responsibility and the justification of beliefs:

> The amount of·evidence required to justify a belief, b, increases proportionally with a person's evidential responsibility toward b. ·

This means justification is neither all or nothing, nor absolute. Not only can justification be a matter of degree and vary from situation to situation, it is also dependent on your level of evidential responsibility.

0.6 Zones of Justification: Rank-Ordering Our Beliefs

Generally, the more your belief is based on reasonable evidence, the more justified it is. Note, however, that the amount of reasonable evidence on which your belief is actually based is not a subjective, personal matter at all. It is a fact about you. Just as legal rights themselves are predicated upon a legal framework and cannot exist without that framework, quantity, quality, and corroboration of evidence required to justify a belief up to the point at which it becomes a warranted conviction depends on a generally accepted *evidential* framework.

In other words, whether a belief is justified and, if so, to what degree, is not in any sense a private matter but a public one, defined in terms of the evidence you have, specified within a particular "comfort zone." Within this comfort zone, some beliefs are more justified than others. Thus, "The Earth is round," "Tables and chairs exist," "Superman is not a real person," and so on, are typically much more justified than "I am twelve feet tall," "I am the creator of the cosmos," "Chickens are fast plants," and so on, which are unjustified. There is convincing evidence for the first set of beliefs; on the basis of that evidence these beliefs are justified in comparison to the second set, which, in comparison to the first set, is unjustified. Thus, we can say that "The Earth is round" belongs in the "justified zone" compared to "I am twelve feet tall," which belongs in the "unjustified zone." Beliefs regarding the origin of the cosmos, the existence of God, the moral status of abortion, and so on, we can for now place in what we can call the "uncertainty zone."

This means that, using our terminology, if all your beliefs came about not through convincing evidence but through, say, indoctrination, then *none* of your beliefs are reasonably justified. You don't know anything, you're not even justified in any of your beliefs. You haven't been convinced—you've been converted, programmed, like a robot or a machine. In that case, even if what you believe is true, you are not justified in believing it. You're in a complete state of ignorance about everything!

None of our three zones of justification are black-and-white categories. As we shall see in the next section, each justification zone has within it further degrees of justification. Within the justified zone, some of your beliefs are more justified than others. If you are an undergraduate college student, your belief that you exist is far more justified than your belief that you will someday graduate. Your belief that you will graduate is in turn more or less justified, depending on your grades. Suppose you are in your third semester and your GPA is 0.0. You say, "I'm not worried, I know I will graduate." But—unless you have successfully bribed all your teachers—you do not really mean you *know* you will graduate. You mean something like, "I refuse to worry, I still believe in myself, I have not lost my confidence."

Our three zones of justification can be put on a continuous chart, as in the "target" drawn in Figure 1. The numbers correspond to degrees, or levels, of justification within each zone using a rough estimate of probabilities based on the quantity, quality, and corroboration of available evidence. At the bull's eye, zone 1, are those beliefs whose probability of being true, relative to others, is so high as to warrant conviction. Since this is the highest level of justification, we shall demarcate it with the name "warranted conviction."

When we thus inquire into whether there is reasonably convincing evidence for some belief, it means we are asking whether the quantity, quality, and corroborative evidence places the be-

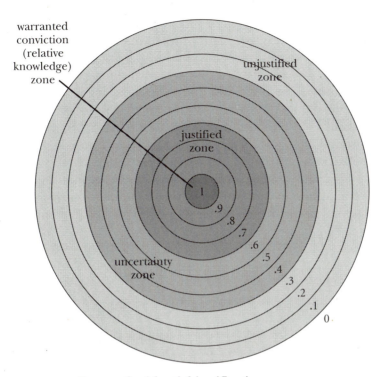

warranted conviction (relative knowledge) zone

unjustified zone

justified zone

1
.9
.8
.7
.6
.5
.4
.3
.2
.1
0.

uncertainty zone

FIGURE 1.   Zones of evidential justification

lief into the warranted conviction zone of justification—zone 1. For instance, that you are presently reading a book can safely be placed right inside the bull's eye, in the warranted conviction zone. At the outer fringe of the target, inside the 0 circle, are beliefs like "I will now jump up and touch the moon," whose probability of being true is so low as to make their falsehood a virtual certainty. At the middle, at .5, are beliefs like "If I flip the coin it will land heads," whose probability is virtually *uncertain*, meaning that according to the reasonable evidence they have roughly an equal chance of being true as of being false. Note that the justified zone, uncertainty zone, and unjustified zone are drawn with a rather wide margin of error: 30 percent. We could choose to make different categories, but this will do for now.

Suppose before you were born your parents wondered whether you would turn out to be a boy or girl. Their belief that, if born, you will be human would be a warranted conviction, in the bull's eye of the justified zone. The probability that humans will give birth to another human rather than, say, an orangutan, is virtually 1. There might be individual cases where the baby is not human, but the probability that it will be human is so much greater that we can safely call it a virtual certainty. Your father's belief that it will be a girl would have fallen smack in the middle of the uncertainty zone, within the .5 circle. Your mother's belief that it will be a boy would also fall there, within the .5 circle. Your grandfather's belief that it will be a demon from hell would of course have fallen nowhere within the justified zone, not even the uncertainty zone, as would Uncle Joe's belief that the child will be a divine creature with supernatural powers, both of which belong well inside the unjustified zone.

0.7 Evident Probability: What Are the Odds?

Do you believe God exists? Some of those who answer "yes" or "no," like some of those who say "I don't know," claim their answer expresses not just belief but knowledge. Typically, this means either that you have so much evidence for or against the existence of God that your belief qualifies as knowledge, or else your belief is so strong, psychologically, that you feel it belongs in the category of knowledge. In the next chapter we shall disambiguate these concepts when we discuss, in detail, the relationship between the psychological feeling of certainty and the evidential basis of certainty. For now, let us merely add the categories "Yes-Knower" and "No-Knower," keeping in mind that by "knowledge" we simply mean beliefs that are in the warranted conviction zone of justification relative to your other beliefs.

This means that, for our purposes, any of your beliefs qualifies as knowledge when it is a *warranted conviction* relative to your other beliefs. If we are realistically going to embark upon a journey in search of God, we cannot begin with unrealistic expectations. We have to remain within the realm of what is possible. Knowledge in some absolute sense may or may not be possible. But this much is certain: absolute knowledge is not possible unless relative knowledge is also possible. Second, as we are about to see, we can precisely define what knowledge is in the relative sense and distinguish various beliefs accordingly. (To require more than this before embarking on our journey is a bit like deciding not to go to the moon until you've got a propulsion system that can get you to the stars. That's a formula for avoiding space exploration. And, if you're going to make it to the stars, getting to the moon first is probably a good way to begin.)

Suppose you believe the Earth is round and, relative to your other beliefs, the amount of evidence you have for this belief puts the proposition "The Earth is round" in the bull's eye of the justified zone: the warranted conviction zone. You then (relatively) know that the Earth is round. Yes-Knowers and No-Knowers are people who classify their beliefs regarding the existence of God into the warranted conviction zone. This doesn't mean, necessarily, that they can offer absolute proof that their belief is true. Absolute proof is not our concern. Rather, it means merely that they can offer as much reasonable evidence for the existence of God as they can for the existence of, say, George Washington (if they are Yes-Knowers) or as much reasonable evidence for the nonexistence of God as they can, say for the nonexistence of Santa Claus (if they are No-Knowers). After all, it may be impossible to *prove*, absolutely, that there is no Santa, just as it may be impossible to *prove*, absolutely, that George Washington existed. But this does not prevent us from distinguishing between beliefs that, within a generally accepted comfort zone, can be placed in the very bull's eye of the zones of justification, in comparison with some others, from those that cannot. Again: Just because we might always be wrong does not mean we can never be right.

To be convinced of something in this relative rather than absolute sense means your belief is justified with reasonable evidence. How much, of what type, and so on can vary from situation to situation. But keep in mind that what matters is how you came to your belief, not whether after having been indoctrinated you can come up with reasonable evidence for your belief. That's not reasoning but *rationalizing*. If you've been indoctrinated into believing something by an authority and you later in life rationalize that belief, your intelligence and reasoning ability is conditioned by the way that authority thinks, not by the way the world is. We will fine-tune these concepts in the next chapter. For now, we can simply categorize some beliefs as falling into the warranted conviction zone using our concentric circles within the zones of justification.

Say you categorize yourself as a Yes-Knower with regard to the existence of God. This means the amount of evidence you have for the existence of God places the proposition "God exists" at the very bull's eye of the justified zone—the warranted conviction zone. You have as much evidence for your belief that God exists as you do, say, for your belief that the Earth is round, that Indians exist, that corn flakes are more nutritious than pebbles, and so on. On the other hand, say you categorize yourself as a No-Knower. This means that the amount of evidence you have against the existence of God places the proposition "God does not exist" in the very center of the justified zone, inside the bull's eye, while the proposition, "God exists" is in the 0 circle; that God exists is as unjustified, according to the evidence you have, as the belief that there are cows that can jump over the moon, that the Earth is flat, and so on.

By "warranted conviction," then, I mean a specific type of belief: beliefs that, *relative to all your other beliefs,* are most centered within your justified zone; that is, they have *evident probability* 1. What do I mean by *evident probability?* Consider the following example.

There are ten black boxes on a table, indistinguishable from the outside, each containing ten marbles. You get to look inside only five of them. Here is what you see:

Box 1:	9 white,	1 black
Box 2:	4 white,	6 black
Box 3:	9 white,	1 black
Box 4:	10 white,	0 black
Box 5:	8 white,	2 black
Total:	40 white,	10 black

You have no idea what colors the marbles are in the other five boxes. The boxes you peeked in are closed and then shuffled with the other boxes until you don't know which is which. You are then told that you will be allowed to draw one marble from one box. You are given $100, which you must bet only on white or black. If your color comes up, you get another $1,000. If not, you get just the $100 for playing. You'd like to win the $1,000. How should you bet?

You're free to do as you want. You have a right to bet on black or on white. If black is your favorite color and you feel lucky when you bet on black, you are free to bet on black if that is how you wish to play. But you are not *justified* in doing so. You saw 40 white marbles and only 10 black marbles. The *evident probability* of your drawing a white marble is four times higher than your drawing a black one.

Now, looking at the zones of justification, where should you place the proposition "I will pick a white marble"? Suppose, after thinking about it, you decide the answer is "0.1." But that's wrong. The belief that you will pick a white marble is justified to a much higher degree than you had realized: 0.4. You can be wrong, even about yourself, even about your own opinions about yourself.

You would calculate the evident probability as follows. You looked into half the boxes and thus there is a 0.5 chance of getting to pick from that set, which contains 40 white and 10 black marbles. *If* you do get to pick from that set, the actual probability for which is 0.5, *then* the actual probability of picking a white marble is 40/50, or 0.8; that of picking a black marble is 10/50, or 0.2. But you have no way of justifying a belief concerning what the actual probabilities are. You don't have enough information. You don't know if you are picking from one of the boxes in the set you looked at, nor what color the marbles are in the other five boxes that you didn't get to see. But nor are you in a complete state of uncertainty. You can calculate the *evident* probability. The total *evident* probability of picking white—given your particular information base—is $.5 \times .8 = .4$; the total evident probability of picking black is $.5 \times .2 = .1$.

All you have to go on is the "evident" probability because you don't actually know what all the parameters are. The other five boxes might contain all white marbles, in which case the actual probability of your picking a white marble would be 90/100, or 0.9. But since the ten boxes are indistinguishable and you do not know whether the box you will pick from is one of the five boxes you peeked into, you cannot base your bet on the actual probabilities (you do not know what they are) but only on the evident probabilities: The *evident* probability of your drawing white is 0.4, that of drawing black is 0.1. If the other five boxes contain all white marbles, the actual probability of your drawing white (unbeknownst to you) is 0.9, that of drawing black is 0.1. In that case, the evident and actual probabilities of drawing black would happen to coincide (though you would have no way of knowing this).

Jeff now comes in and gets to play the same game. He too gets to pick any five boxes. Here are the results:

Box 1:	0 white,	10 black
Box 2:	2 white,	8 black
Box 3:	2 white,	8 black
Box 4:	1 white,	9 black
Box 5:	5 white,	5 black
Total:	10 white,	40 black

Jeff, too, would like the $1,000. How should Jeff bet? He would be justified in betting on black. Indeed, the evident probability for Jeff that he will draw black is 0.4, that he will draw white is 0.1. Again, keep in mind that this is only the *evident* probability, that is, the probability from Jeff's perspective. The actual probability is unknown to Jeff (but not to the people running the game).

Now it is Amy's turn to play. She gets to look inside *all* the boxes. Here is what she counts:

Box 1:	9 white,	1 black
Box 2:	4 white,	6 black
Box 3:	9 white,	1 black
Box 4:	10 white,	0 black
Box 5:	8 white,	2 black
Box 6:	0 white,	10 black
Box 7:	2 white,	8 black
Box 8:	2 white,	8 black
Box 9:	1 white,	9 black
Box 10:	5 white,	5 black
Total:	50 white,	50 black

What is the evident probability in Amy's case? If she thinks it is anything but a fifty-fifty proposition, that is, 0.5 for drawing black and 0.5 for drawing white, she is wrong. Notice that, in her case, the evident probability and the actual probability are the same

28

because she got to look inside all the boxes before picking a marble.

Evident probability can vary from person to person relative to the information each person has available when making a decision.[1] In the three cases above it was (1) 0.4 white, 0.1 black, (2) 0.1 white, 0.4 black, and (3) 0.5 white, 0.5 black. The actual probability does *not* vary; in each case it was 0.5 for either color. But—and this is very important—evident probability is neither subjective nor arbitrary. It is what it is, in each case, absolutely. There is a definite right and a wrong *for each person*. You can be wrong—dead wrong—about your own position.

0.8 Relative Knowledge

Regarding the question "Is there life on other planets?" Nick classifies himself as a Yes-Knower. This means, automatically, that on this question Nick is a Yes-Believer. It would be very strange to profess to know something that you did not believe to be so. We do sometimes say things like, "I know I won the lottery, but I don't believe it," to mean something like, "I am so incredibly surprised that I won!" This does not really mean you don't believe you won; it means you believe you won but you find this event incredulous. You might be surprised, you might not be able to accept the event calmly, and so on. But that's very different from hearing your winning number announced and then never cashing in your ticket because you believe this is just a hoax cooked up by your enemies to make a fool out of you, in which case it would be more proper for you to say, "They tell me I won but I don't believe this; I do not *know* I won; I believe I didn't win; it is all just a trick."

So if on the question of the existence of extraterrestrial life Nick classifies himself as a Yes-Knower, this means that according to our scheme above, the amount of evidence Nick has for the belief that there is life on other planets puts that belief inside the center of the justified zone; it is a warranted conviction. Nick claims to know that Martians exist. But remember: Though Nick has a right to believe whatever Nick wants about the existence of Martians, or anything else, whether his belief that Martians exist is justified depends on how much reasonable evidence—the quantity, quality, and corroboration—Nick actually has that this belief is true. And in saying that he is a Yes-Knower with regard to the existence of Martians, Nick is committing himself to claiming that he has as much evidence for this belief as he does for his belief, say, that there is life in India. This means the evident probability in both cases, according to Nick, is the same. *And whether or not this is true is not up to Nick.* Rather, it is up to the quantity, quality, and corroboration of evidence Nick has for the existence of Martians. Nick has to have more evidence for this belief—it has to be more evidently probable—than for beliefs that are in his uncertainty zone and your unjustified zone. The amount of evidence Nick has for the existence of Martians—the evident probability that there are Martians from Nick's perspective—is an objective fact about Nick. If Nick doesn't have the amount of evidence he thinks he has relative to his other beliefs, then he is mistaken in thinking he knows that Martians exist, even in a relative sense. Nick does not really know it, according to his own criteria.

People often exaggerate, sometimes without even realizing it, how much evidence they have for some belief. They may classify a belief as knowledge by thinking they have more evidence than they actually do—that their belief is more evidently probable than it actually is—just because they would like their belief to be true. Part of the problem is that our language encourages us to do this; we say things like, "Did you know that . . ." when what we really mean is, "Did you hear that. . . ." Paying very close attention to the quantity, quality, and corroboration of evidence for various beliefs we hold to be true and then comparing them using the zones of justification chart can help us avoid being duped by our own wish to be right even when we are not. This can be done simply by remembering that if you have less evidence for belief B than you do for belief A and A is not in the warranted conviction zone, then neither is B.

In other words, suppose Nick claims to know that Martians exist. We ask, what is your evidence? Nick tells us he once saw a flying saucer. He was on the beach at night and saw a bright light hovering over the ocean. Well, if this is Nick's best evidence, then in saying that he *knows* Martians exist, *Nick is clearly mistaken.* His belief that Martians exist is not reasonably justified enough to warrant a conviction! Nick *believes* there is life on Mars, yes. But, clearly, this is not in the same justification zone as his belief that there is life in India. He saw pictures of India, many people have been to India, he actually met Indians, he's eaten Indian food, and so on. *In claiming he is convinced that Martians exist, Nick is making a category mistake.* He is misusing language. "But it's enough evidence for me," he might say. But that's wrong. Nobody is doubting that Nick saw a light over the ocean, nor his right to believe, on the basis of that experience, that there are Martians. But in calling this belief knowledge, Nick is misfiling his experience. He is putting it on the wrong shelf: He is placing his belief regarding the existence of Martians in the same category as experiences of eating at Indian restaurants, on the basis of which he can rightly say he knows what Indian food tastes like. Nick has a *right* to put his belief about Martians into the same category as his belief about Indians. But he is not *justified* in doing so; it is plainly a mistake. He saw a light over the ocean, which does justify his belief that he saw a light over the ocean; but that this light was a Martian spaceship is unjustified. The evident probability that these were Martians is too low to be knowledge even in the relative sense in which we are using the term. It could just as easily have been a Venusian spaceship as a Martian one, or a plane, or a balloon, or ball lightning, and so on. The more things it could have been, the lower the evident probability that it was the one thing Nick thinks it was. If this is the experience on which Nick's belief in Martians is based, he definitely does not know that Martians exist.

Of course, *anything* we think we see—such as the light on the ceiling—could be an infinity of possible things; a Martian in disguise, a god, a spy device, a dream, and so on. The truth might be that we *never* know what anything is. But, again, it would be a mistake to conclude, on the basis of this possibility, that we cannot distinguish our beliefs according to the zones of justification, that we can't tell which beliefs are relative knowledge and which are not. Though absolute certainty may forever be beyond our reach, some of our beliefs are more justified than others using the concept of evident probability.

Having the concept of evident probability is very important for our purposes. The reason is that it would be unfair to require higher or lower standards of evidence to justify our beliefs about God than the standards we use for our other beliefs. Often, when people don't want to think about certain important issues—

either because they are afraid, or stubborn, or just lazy—they evoke a double standard: one standard for the things they ordinarily think about, another standard—usually an impossibly high one or a ridiculously low one—for the "big" questions. Now, *all* our standards might be completely wrong; ultimately, it may turn out that *none* of our beliefs about anything are ever really justified. But, as we shall see in even more detail in the next chapter, we do have enough standards already in place to get well underway in our journey.

One of the most important ingredients to good philosophy is having an open mind. This is not an abstract thing but a specific thing. It means that, like an impartial judge, you are fair to all positions. And what does being fair to all positions mean? *It does not mean never make up your mind about anything.* You couldn't eat, you couldn't walk, you couldn't do anything! *It also doesn't mean accept all positions regardless of whether they are right or wrong, dumb or intelligent.* You would become an idiot. *Nor does it mean not having any beliefs, having a "blank mind."* How would even thinking be possible? *Rather, good philosophy requires suspending judgment concerning the beliefs you do have so that you can be fair to all positions. This means using critical thinking to scrutinize them with equal force.* Philosophy is suspended judgment, not lack of judgment; it means fair play, not charity.

So we have two subclassifications within our overall Yes-Believer, No-Believer, and Non-Believer categories: Knowers and Non-Knowers. Knowers claim to have enough reasonable evidence to warrant conviction about the existence of God; they claim to have relative knowledge, one way or the other. Such claims can be tested according to the standards outlined above, which we will further fine-tune in the next chapter. These two categories are subcategories at the extreme ends of the Yes-Believer and No-Believer categories. Yes-Knowers claim to have a warranted conviction that God exists. No-Knowers claim to have a warranted conviction that God does not exist. All those in the category of Non-Knowers are either Yes-Believers (who believe God exists), No-Believers (who believe God does not exist), or Non-Believers (who do not believe one way or the other).

In Figure 2, the dotted lines on the left side of the Yes-Believer category and on the right of the No-Believer category, as well as the long double arrows above each of them, signify that

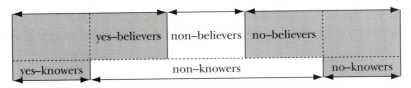

FIGURE 2. Categories of belief

the Yes-Knowers category is within the Yes-Believer category, while the No-Knowers category is within the No-Believer category (since you can't know something unless you also believe it).

Each and every human being, including you, is represented somewhere in these categories. Where do you stand?

Note

1. For a more detailed exposition of the relation between mathematical concepts like probability and thinking, see David Goloff and Daniel Kolak, *Mathematical Thought*, Macmillan, 1995.

CHAPTER 1

What Do You Believe?

1.0 Propositional Relativity

THERE ARE AT LEAST AS MANY CONCEPTIONS OF GOD AS THERE ARE religions in the world. Fortunately, our three categories of belief regarding the existence of God (Yes-Belief, No-Belief, and Non-Belief, along with the subcategories Yes-Knower and No-Knower) are not limited to any particular conception. This is because whether you conceive of God in Christian, Jewish, Buddhist, Hindu, Muslim, or even your own terms, the question is not so much about the *content* of your belief as it is about the *extent* of your belief on this topic in either the Yes or No direction. That is why for the time being we can be rather ambiguous about what exactly we are talking about when we use the word "God."

34

What about the word "belief"? Here we cannot be as tolerant of ambiguity and vagueness. We must, if we are to proceed with our journey, make sure we pin down precisely what we are talking about and stick to just that one meaning. Generally, "I believe the Earth revolves around the sun," means I hold a particular proposition to be true, in this case, the proposition "The Earth revolves around the sun." Propositions are sentences that can be either true or false, like "The Earth is the sixth planet from the sun," "God exists," etc.

Some propositions are true, some are false. Some true propositions are held to be true and some false propositions are held to be true. Some false propositions are held to be false and some true propositions are held to be false. Whether a proposition *is* true is independent of whether it is *held* to be true. Even if everyone believed the Earth was flat, the Earth would not be flat. But since whether a proposition is true is independent of whether you or anybody else holds it to be so, what, then, makes a proposition true or false?

Some proposition, *p*, can be true in one of two ways: either *p* accurately says something about itself (is true "by definition," in virtue of its own meaning) or *p* accurately says something about the world (is true in virtue of the way the world is). "Bachelors are unmarried males," "A triangle has three sides," and "Unicorns have one horn" are examples of the former; "Texas is bigger than California," "A diamond can cut glass," and "Mt. Everest is the tallest mountain" are examples of the latter. "Shut the door!" and "What time is it?" are sentences but not propositions, since they cannot be true or false. Only those sentences that can be true or false are propositions.

Most of us would agree that "The Earth is round" is a true proposition and "The Earth is flat" is a false one. It might turn out that we are wrong. Someone—say, a powerful alien—could have been cleverly deceiving us about this. In that case, the true shape of the Earth is not what we thought it was. This only means we were wrong about the actual shape of the Earth, not that its shape varies according to what we believe. The Earth's shape does not change according to our attitudes; the Earth does not require our avowal to have the shape that it has. What makes the proposition "The Earth is round" true is the shape of the Earth itself, not our avowal that it is so.

But wait. What about the proposition "The Earth is an oblong spheroid?" Now "The Earth is round" does not look so true! Likewise, it seems grossly misleading to call my three-month-old male nephew a bachelor. So, perhaps, when defining "bachelors" as "unmarried males," we should replace "males" with "males of a marriageable age," and when talking about the shape of the Earth we should replace "round" with "oblong spheroid." As we shall see, however, we can avoid these sorts of complications by adding the following important qualification, which I call "the principle of propositional relativity":

> A proposition is *relatively true*, or just "true" for short, if, within the family of available propositions on the subject, it best represents the facts according to the reasonable evidence.

Given a family of just two propositions about the shape of the Earth, "The Earth is round" and "The Earth is flat," I should call the first true and the second false. If a third proposition is added to this family, namely, "The Earth is an oblong spheroid," I should then call the first two false and the third one true.

Propositional relativity means that we are taking a rather modest approach to truth: We are choosing to ascribe to the word "truth" a narrow meaning allowing us to sort out which propositions are relatively true and which are relatively false. Such relative ranking does not ascribe to any proposition the status of absolute truth or absolute certainty. Given the topic of this book, however, it behooves us to take this modest approach! After all, we should be perfectly happy if, at the end of our journey, our beliefs regarding the existence of God can be justified to the same degree as propositions like

a. Trees come from seeds.
b. The Earth revolves around the sun.
c. There is no Santa Claus.
d. The sun will rise tomorrow.
e. George Washington was the first president of the United States.
f. Winters in the northern hemisphere are colder than summers.
g. The universe is older than 1 billion years.
h. Other people (besides myself) are conscious.

and so on. In this way, we can for now get around without knowing the truth in some absolute sense. We need but notice that, as a matter of fact, using evident probability we do rank some propositions, such as (a)–(h), as more likely to be true than the following:

i.   Apes will evolve to fully human levels of intelligence.
j.   The universe is older than 18 billion years.
k.   The sun will rise 100 million years from today.
l.   The Redskins will win the Superbowl next year.
m. The project to map the human gene will be completed by 2001.
n.   Some day there will be no more trees.

and so on. Similarly, we weigh (a)–(n) as more likely to be true than the following:

o.   A cow once jumped over the moon.
p.   Martians have invaded the Earth.
q.   The Earth is being held up by Atlas standing on a turtle.
r.   The sun is made of cheese.

and so on.

In terms of their evident probability, relative to each other, some propositions such as (a)–(h) are regarded by you as being very probably true, (i)–(n) as possibly true, (o)–(r) as very likely false. You can thus use the principle of propositional relativity to demarcate your zones of justification.

In other words, we are getting around various traditional epistemological difficulties concerning the question of *how* we can know the truth. Traditionally, there have been thought to be at least three basic conditions necessary for you to *know* that some proposition, *p*, is true:

1. you believe that *p*
2. *p* is true
3. your belief is justified

"Justified" usually was taken to mean that you have sufficient evidence for *p*—that normally, in similar contexts, the evidence would prove that *p* is true.

These three conditions contain many well-known problems and paradoxes, leading some philosophers to conclude that, ultimately, nobody knows anything. Such "universal skepticism" may ultimately be correct. But this does not prevent us from using doors rather than windows when exiting tall buildings, eating corn flakes rather than pebbles, or reading rather than eating books when we want to digest them. You *might* be better off eating rather than reading this book—after all, you never tried this—but you are more likely to learn the book the "old" way. By jumping out a window you might only break a leg and avoid the axe murderer who, unbeknownst to you, was waiting for you in the elevator. But usually the elevator is safer. You might find that eating pebbles gives you all the vitamins and minerals you need and for free; but probably it won't. And so on.

The problems of epistemology are profound, deeply interesting, and central to philosophy. But by being extremely careful with our language we can formulate a method of inquiry that avoids various pitfalls. Thus, although it is very difficult, perhaps impossible, for us to say at this point what knowledge of the truth in some absolute sense is and how we might get it, we can embark upon our search for God using distinctions we already have. God might have, or even in some sense *be*, ultimate and absolute truth; but we can't get there with absolute certainty because, right now, we don't have it! We each have but a storehouse of propositions, some of which we would all regard, on the basis of *evident* probability, as more probably true than others and therefore as relatively justified. We shall thus use this as our yardstick to sort out our beliefs within the zones of justification. It allows us to map out within the zones of justification a *comfort zone* in which to operate.

For our purposes, then, it will be enough to note that our beliefs already come ranked relative to each other *in ways that are not purely subjective.* Our justification for any belief may turn out to be completely wrong; but how much evidential justification there is for any belief is not a matter of opinion. It is a fact about that proposition and about the amount of evidence you have for it. On our relative map, a warranted conviction may turn out to be false. But the justification level *is* what it is, regardless of its ultimate status. This sort of yardstick—using evident probability and evidential justification—provides us with a wide comfort zone within which we can compare how, relative to our other beliefs, the belief that God exists is ranked as our journey progresses.

So we are choosing to give up all pretense to absolute knowledge by relying, instead, on the fact that we each have a comfort zone within which beliefs are ranked relative to each other according to reasonable evidence. Using this comfort zone of rank-ordered beliefs, we can compare our own beliefs with each other, even compare each other's beliefs. This is all we need to proceed in our search.

Clearly, whether some proposition, p, is true is independent of our attitude toward p (if everyone believed that the Earth was flat, the Earth would not suddenly flatten itself out). But then what does it mean to have a particular attitude toward p? That is, what does "holding p to be true" mean? In other words, what does it mean to have a belief? (To say it means you believe that p would be circular.)

Some philosophers have claimed beliefs are active states of mind in which you rationally accept p to be the case. Others have claimed beliefs are passive states of mind predisposing you to accept or reject propositions when they are presented. Still other philosophers have thought beliefs are not mental states at all; "holding p to be true" simply means you are likely to act some particular way with regard to p. (Believing that God exists, for instance, would in that case mean you are disposed to worship God, etc.)

Thus, in claiming my belief that something described by a proposition, p, is the case, do we mean

I consciously accept that p is true
I have the psychological feeling that p is true
My instincts tell me p is true

or some combination thereof, or something altogether different? If I say I believe God exists, am I reporting that I have come to regard this proposition to be rationally true and so I choose to assent to it? Or am I reporting the state of my emotive response toward the proposition that God exists? Or am I saying something about my behavioral dispositions? In other words, by "belief" do I mean a conscious choice based on educated judgment, an unchosen psychological feeling, a behavioral pattern predisposing me to act in a particular way, or what?

Though we have only just embarked upon our philosophical quest, it should already be clear that, unlike scientific explorations, ours is a journey paved not so much with discovery as it is with decision. We're in the jungle. Our getting somewhere depends, essentially, on deciding at each step of the way what it is that we are looking for and then remaining steadfastly committed to those decisions until we see where a particular set of choices leads. We might not like where we end up. But we are always free to go back and follow a different course.

1.1 Certainty, Psychological Confidence, and Evidential Justification

A belief, then, consists in two parts. There is the proposition—a sentence asserting that some state of affairs is true—and the attitude you have toward it—either affirmative or negative. Propositions come in two varieties: True or False. Attitudes come in two flavors: Yes and No. Thus, beliefs are "propositional attitudes"— that is, beliefs are True or False propositions wrapped in either a Yes or No attitude.

Propositions are about facts. Given the principle of propositional relativity, no proposition is absolutely true or absolutely false. The reason is that, as in the round Earth/oblong spheroid Earth example, what can be counted as true concerning some topic changes over time as the family of propositions of that topic increases. The evident probability of a proposition being true or false depends on what other propositions are available in its family.

Attitudes are about us, about our psychological feelings toward some proposition. They come in two flavors: Yes (acceptance) or No (rejection). The barometer of the degree to which some proposition is true or false, relative to the family of propositions available on that subject, we shall call "the degree of justification that p," as illustrated in our zones of justification chart. The barometer of the degree to which you feel, psychologically, that some proposition is true or false, regardless of where that belief stands in the zones of justification, we shall call "the degree of psychological confidence in p," and we can chart this in the zones of psychological confidence (see Figure 3).

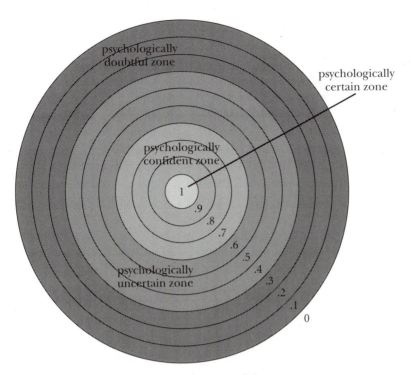

FIGURE 3.   Zones of psychological confidence

This time, the numbers 0–1 signify your level of confidence, a psychological feeling that the proposition is true. Suppose, for instance, that you feel very strongly that you will live long and prosper. You may or may not actually live long and prosper, depending on many factors that are more or less out of your control. But for you, at this point in your life your *psychological feeling of confidence* in the proposition "I will live long and prosper" is so strong that you cannot even bring yourself to imagine how it might be possible that you will die sooner than you think. You rate the proposition "I will live long and prosper" as a 1.0 on the chart. Suppose, however, that after your yearly physical your doctor says you have only six months to live. Suddenly the feeling of confidence that you will live long and prosper takes a nose dive and you rate your confidence level as 0.1 on the chart. You quit your job and school and live a wild and crazy life for six months, at the end of which you are still alive. You go back to the doctor and she says sorry, it was only a mistake and by all indications you will live to a ripe old age. You go back to your life as

41

usual (with no money and no job), only now you no longer rate the proposition "I will live long and prosper" as a 1.0 but a 0.9— still high, but your faith has been somewhat shaken.

Why make the distinction between levels of evidential justification and levels of psychological confidence? Because, unfortunately, our level of confidence in p (the degree to which we feel, psychologically, that p is the case) does not always correspond with the degree to which p is evidentially justified to be the case. If this unfortunate state of affairs weren't so, credit card companies would not make nearly the profit they do. It is well known to credit card companies that given the opportunity to do so, many, perhaps most, people tend to spend more money than they have, and so credit card companies give people that opportunity! It isn't that people don't have plenty of evidence available to tell them how much money they make. They do. Nor, if they are in debt, are they missing the information that would tell them how much they owe and how much they should save to get out of debt. Indeed, not only can a good accountant or financial advisor go over your records and very quickly tell you if you are in the black or in the red and by exactly how much, the prognosis for what is likely to happen to your situation next year and the year after will be fairly clear, including what would happen instead if you make certain changes. The problem is that people tend to have a higher degree of confidence in their earning power and financial status than the justification in terms of the actual amount of money they have to spend warrants. The reason? Just as we want to be right even when we are not, we want to be rich even when we are not. Our desires blind us; our imaginations fill in the blind spot.

In other words, our psychological attitudes are often out of sync with the evidential justification available. Sometimes the two are in sync. When the two are balanced—that is, when *confidence in p* and *justification that p* are equal—we can call the belief that p is the case "relatively rational." Calling a belief in this sense "*relatively rational*" is merely to say that there is an equal ratio between the *evidential justification that p* and the psychological feeling of *confidence in p*. We are not passing judgment on whether relatively rational beliefs are a good thing to have, whether they are always the best thing to have, and so on. There could be lots of cases in which it might be bad to hold relatively rational beliefs. For instance, some propositions (particularly ones about you)

42

might be of a special type such that if your psychological attitude toward them is inflated and not relatively rational but, rather, "relatively irrational," you are more likely to do better in life.

For now, however, we need not raise any normative issues— questions about what we *ought* to believe. We are merely trying to get hold of what we *do* believe, to define our terms, and to get a sense of how our minds work in order to embark upon a search for God.

So when there is a balance between our attitudes toward a proposition, *p*, and the probability that *p* is justified as relatively true among its family of propositions, that is the limited sense in which we shall use the word "rational"—meaning, for now, that there is an equal ratio between degree of Yes or No attitude toward *p* and degree of evidence for or against *p* in your eviden-tial framework. Note, too, that the way we are choosing to use our words, any belief about anything consists in some amount of psychological confidence. There is no such thing as having a belief in anything without some psychological confidence in it! The amount of psychological confidence might exceed the amount of evidential justification or vice versa, or the two might be in equal proportion. We are not making any evaluative judg-ments about which of these is best (which might even vary for different topics and different situations). We are merely making a chart to provide a common map so that we can journey to-gether on what is, surely, one of the great human quests: the search for God.

Some may think this is too analytical, too clinical, on a topic that eludes cold-blooded precision. Typically, such critics are per-fectly analytical and clinical when it comes to issues they seriously wish to explore. There may indeed be mystery beyond our com-prehension, beyond our grasp, where myths and fictional meta-phors are our only hope; but we shall never find it, not even glimpse it, nor be moved by it, or have any other relationship with it, unless we can separate what is truly mysterious and un-known from what the logical analysis of our language (or method of thinking about such things) reveals to be clearly and distinctly within our grasp.

We have thus distinguished between the amount of psycho-logical feeling—confidence in *p*—from the level of evidential justification that *p*; when the two are of equal proportion we shall call the belief "relatively rational." So in asking whether you believe that God exists, we are asking not one thing but two things:

1. What is the amount of your psychological confidence in the existence of God, one way or the other?
2. What is the amount of your evidential justification that God exists, one way or the other?

1.2 Charting Beliefs: Faith, Skepticism, and Rationality

We can now make our Belief Chart, as shown in Figure 4. Starting at point (0,0), the right half of the horizontal axis, labeled "E," represents the amount of evidential justification that God exists in terms of evident probability, on a scale of 0 to 1. To the left of (0,0), also on a scale of 0 to 1, the left half of the horizontal axis, labeled "~E," represents the amount of evidential justification that God does not exist. The upper half of the vertical axis, labeled "C," represents the amount of psychological confidence in the proposition that God exists, again on a scale of 0 to 1. The lower half of the vertical axis, labeled "~C," represents the amount of psychological confidence in the proposition that God does not exist, also on a scale from 0 to 1. Lines r, $\sim r$, f, and $\sim f$ are defined in terms of the e and c coordinates; "$r = \{(e,c) | e = c\}$," for instance, means "r is the line determined by the points (e, c), such that e = c."

Suppose Ann's justification for the belief that God exists weighs in, relative to her other beliefs, as 0.5e. She would mark the point on the horizontal axis, between 0 and E, at 0.5. Her confidence in the existence of God weighs in, relative to her other beliefs, at 0.5c. She would mark the point on the vertical axis, between 0 and C, at 0.5. To find where Ann stands in the Belief Chart, we see where the points meet on the graph: at (0.5e, 0.5c), right in the middle of line r (see Figure 5). Regarding the existence of God, Ann is a Yes-Believer and her belief is "relatively rational."

Suppose Bob's justification weighs in at 0.5~e: He has that amount of evidence against the existence of God. He would mark the point on the horizontal axis, between 0 and ~E, at .5.

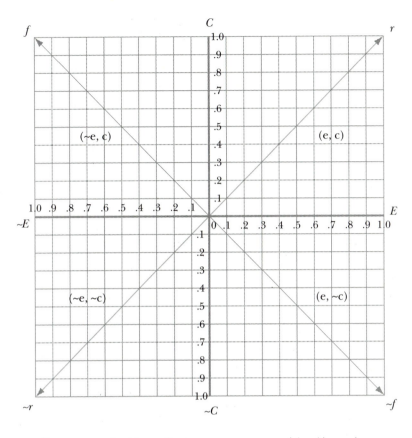

E = amount of evidence for p $r = \{ (e, c) | e = c \}$
~E = amount of evidence for $\sim p$ $\sim r = \{ (\sim e, \sim c) | \sim e = \sim c \}$
C = amount of confidence in p $f = \{ (\sim e, c) | \sim e = c \}$
~C = amount of confidence in $\sim p$ $\sim f = \{ (e, \sim c) | e = \sim c \}$

FIGURE 4.   Belief chart

His confidence weighs in at 0.5~c: he believes that God does not exist. Where does Bob stand on the Belief Chart? At (0.5~e, 0.5~c), in the middle of line ~r. Bob's belief, too, is "relatively rational" but he is a No-Believer.

Carol, on the other hand, finds she is at (0.7~e, 0.5c), close to the *f* line. She is a Yes-Believer whose belief is "relatively skeptical," in the sense that her psychological confidence goes against the amount of evidential justification. She is somewhat like Dave, who weighs in at (0.5e, 0.9~c), near but below the ~*f* line. Dave is a No-Believer whose belief, like Carol's, is "relatively skeptical."

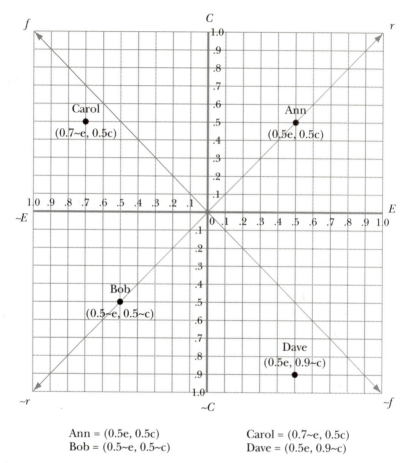

Ann = (0.5e, 0.5c)   Carol = (0.7~e, 0.5c)
Bob = (0.5~e, 0.5~c)   Dave = (0.5e, 0.9~c)

FIGURE 5.   Sample chart

Dave has enough evidence for the existence of God to place the proposition into the 0.5 zone of justification, but his psychological feeling of confidence in the nonexistence of God is so strong it overwhelms the evidential justification. Thus, both Dave and Carol are "skeptics," in the sense that their psychological confidence goes against the evidential justification; the only difference between them is what they are being skeptical *about*, not the act of being skeptical. The difference is one of propositional content, not states of mind! *On our chart, surprisingly, the "faithful" and the "skeptical," though far apart linearly, are much closer than one might ordinarily suppose.*

Note, too, that at this point Carol and Dave are no more at fault for where they stand than are Amy and Bob. Everyone is just reporting the amount of evidential justification for and the amount of psychological confidence in the existence of God. You have the confidence you have, in the direction you have; you can't *choose* how much confidence you have, any more than you can *choose* how much evidence you have. You're merely reporting what the facts about you are.

Suppose, for instance, that Amy, Bob, Carol, and Dave are four students plotting their beliefs regarding the proposition "I will graduate at the top of my class," and their relative weightings come out exactly as they did, numerically, regarding the proposition "God exists." The amount of their evidential justification that they will graduate at the top of their class consists of their grades. The amount of their psychological confidence in graduating at the top of their class consists in their psychological feeling that they will. Now, Carol has plenty of evidence that she will not graduate at the top of her class: 0.7~e. But she also has some confidence that she nonetheless will: 0.5c. She is a Yes-Believer with regard to "I will graduate at the top of my class," and her Yes-Belief is of a type that according to our classification system is "relatively skeptical." What she is skeptical about is *her academic record*. She says, "What do grades show? Not how smart you are but how obedient you are," and so on. That's how she feels! Likewise, Dave's lack of confidence (0.9~c) in his graduating at the top of his class is not in equal proportion to the amount of justification he has that he will graduate at the top of his class, and so he is a No-Believer whose belief is also classified, according to the way we are choosing to use our language, as "relatively skeptical." In fact, in this case Dave is skeptical about exactly the same thing that Carol is—*the academic establishment!* That's how he feels! They tell him he is pretty good and he says, "Don't try to manipulate me with your stupid little grading system!"

What should we say about Carol and Dave? Well, with regard to academic performance, Carol has faith in herself, whereas Dave lacks faith in himself. That is the sense in which we sometimes use the word "faith"—*to refer to levels of psychological confidence that are disproportionate to levels of evidential justification.* It is important to note that faith, in this sense, is very different from psychological confidence. Ann has *exactly* as much psychological confidence in the existence of God as does Carol, no more, no less. But it would be misleading to call both Ann's confidence and Carol's confidence "faith." Ann's confidence in God is apparently driven by, and tied to, the evidential justification that God exists. In that sense, *Ann's belief has nothing to do with Ann.* Whereas Carol's confidence in God is apparently driven by, and tied to, something else that exists within Carol (such as desire, hope, fear). In that sense, *Carol's belief has a lot to do with Carol.*

We would be missing a lot by not using the distinctions we are here making. Faith in the sense that we are distinguishing it may be something of special and unique importance not just to Carol but to all human beings. Potentially, this may be very revealing. It may reveal something about the nature of God, the nature of the relationship between humanity and the divine. Or, it may reveal something about the nature of ourselves, the mind, the self or ego involved in *any* belief. Or both. In any case, the revelation may be deeply profound.

Thus let us take special note and care regarding the two diagonal lines that crisscross at (0,0). The lines r and $\sim r$ consist in an equal *evidential justification* to *psychological confidence* ratio: e = c, $\sim$e = $\sim$c. Thus, r and $\sim r$ are the two halves of the "relatively rational" line of belief. The lines f and $\sim f$, on the other hand, consist in an *inverted evidential justification* to *psychological confidence* ratio. Thus, f and $\sim f$ are the two halves of the "relatively skeptical" line of belief. But, noting the commonly accepted distinction between people who have "faith" and people who are "skeptics," we shall call this line either the *relatively faithful* or the *relatively skeptical* line of belief, depending if it is in the +f or $\sim f$ direction. But you should note carefully that "relatively faithful" and "relatively skeptical" are but the two names of one line, just as are "(relatively) rational Yes-Belief" and "(relatively) rational No-Belief."

In other words, the two halves of the *relatively faithful/skeptical* line of belief have an interesting difference in their polarities. To note this interesting difference, we are reserving "relatively faithful" for the f-line, and reserving "relatively skeptical" for the $\sim f$-line. The word "skeptical," like the word "faith," has a plurality of meanings. Given our distinctions, we see that just as it would be misleading to equate "faith in p" with "confidence in p," so too it would be misleading to equate "skeptical that p" with "lack of confidence in p." Why? Well, as before, Bob's lack of confidence in the existence of God (0.5$\sim$e, 0.5$\sim$c), has apparently nothing to do with Bob but, rather, the relative evidential justification Bob has for p. Whereas Dave's lack of confidence (0.5e, 0.9~c), has apparently a lot to do with Dave. Calling Dave a "skeptic," like calling Carol "faithful," distinguishes the special nature of their respective beliefs.

1.3 Rank-Ordering Propositions

Now, a word about what the numbers mean. Absolutely—nothing. Relatively—everything! Why, for instance, did I make the scale go up to 1 in all directions? Well, we're taking the maximum amount of justification you actually have for whatever it is that you do have justification for and giving it a value of 1. The "1" merely reflects this totality. Likewise, we're taking the maximum amount of psychological confidence you actually have in whatever it is you are most confident in and giving it a value of 1. The reason is the same: Whatever the amount of your maximum confidence, that's how much confidence you have, no more and no less. Hence, 1 in each case represents "100 percent." It's like taking the maximum speed of your car, whatever that actually translates to when it is running at 100 percent, tuned up, foot to the floor, on a straightaway, and calling that "1." Different cars will have different maximums. Yours might be 90 miles an hour. Someone else's might be 160 miles an hour. But in each case we can refer to either maximum as "1," and to the degree of that maximum achieved, say, on any particular drive, using the 0 to 1 scale. We will thus use our "1" to refer to whatever that maximum is regarding the beliefs you drive around in.

Take some proposition for which you have as much justification as possible. For instance, here is a list of propositions, listed from highest to lowest amount of justification, from your present point of view:

1. You exist.
2. Experience is going on.
3. You are reading a book.
4. This book is called *In Search of God*.
5. The author of this book is a philosopher.
6. The author of this book is Daniel Kolak.
7. The author is a male.

8. The author is thirty-seven years old.
9. The author has taken a trip around the world.
10. The author has been to the North Pole.
11. The author swam the English Channel.
12. The author is an alien from outer space.
13. The author is three years old.
14. The author is an alien who has visited every planet in the universe.
15. The author is three days old.

Relative to the other propositions, clearly, for you, (1) has the highest level of justification in that the grounds for believing it are based directly on your immediate experience. It is slightly more evidently probable that you exist than that you are reading a book because, conceivably, you might merely be dreaming that you are reading. That the experience, whether dreamed or real, is going on is of equal rank with (1). Proposition (3) runs close behind; barring the possibility that you are right now dreaming, your belief that you are reading a book is based directly on your immediate experience. Proposition (4) runs closely behind (3). Although you can check the title using your immediate experience, you must flip to the cover to make sure you haven't misremembered it. The book might really be called *The Search for God* but the typesetter made a mistake. And so on. (Note that, in such a situation, we would have to *decide* what the real title is—is the real title what it says on the cover, or what the author says?) But it is not as easy to conceive of how you could be mistaken about it being the case that you are right now reading a book.

Likewise, I might be a theologian instead of a philosopher, but the latter is far more likely given that this is a philosophy book. It is certainly more likely than that the name Daniel is a woman's name. And so on down the list. The age "37" is a reasonable thing for you to believe (much more so than "3 months"), but it is merely an educated guess on your part.

Whether I've been on a trip around the world is, for you, a long shot. But it is less of a long shot than the possibility that I've been to the North Pole. More than likely, I am not one of those few individuals who have swum across the English Channel. And though in elementary school they did call me "Martian," that I am an alien from outer space is so unlikely that clearly it belongs near the bottom of the list. But it belongs above (14), since even if I were an alien it would be very unlikely that I've been to all the planets in the universe, which, in turn, would be less likely than that I've been, say, to all the planets in the Milky Way. At the same time, it seems reasonable to suppose that if you had to weigh (13) and (15) against each other, (14) should be put slightly higher. A three-day-old human who could write this book would be utterly unbelievable, but less so than (13) since a three-year-old genius would be but an extension of what we already have reasonable evidence for accepting as true; whereas (15) seems the most incredulous of all the given propositions. And although obviously there is room to quibble, such that we might disagree about some of the numberings, clearly our disagreement will not vary by more than one number, or at most two.

Now, there are lots of propositions like those above that you can rank order in this way. If on the horizontal axis we put (1) at point 1e, and (14) and (15) at point 1~e, this can serve as our extreme points. (We could have made our scale go from 0.9 to 0.1, as a way of reminding ourselves that nothing is absolutely certain and nothing is absolutely uncertain. But even if that is the case, this is not important; all we are doing is making a relative taxonomy of our levels of relative evidential justification based on ranking propositions according to the scheme we already have. The 0 to 1 scale still allows for this. The 1 does not mean that the belief is absolutely certain; it reflects just that we are referring to whatever maximum we do in fact have.)

Your evidential framework of propositions—the actual sets of beliefs and the relative evidential justification and psychological confidence you have for them, what I will henceforth refer to as your "propositional framework"—might be all wrong. You might be completely wrong about everything. But, be that as it may, you do have a relative scale that may or may not ultimately be correct and, for our purposes, all you have to do is rank the proposition "God exists" relative to such a scale within your propositional framework. Its ranking will change according to reasonable evidence presented and what other propositions are available. In other words, if you believe that God exists, where do you rank this proposition on the Belief Chart, relative to other propositions that you have evidence for and confidence in, in varying degrees? And then we can proceed.

Note, too, that from my point of view—within my evidential framework of propositions, that is, within my propositional framework—on the horizontal axis, which measures evident probability of the truth of that proposition relative to the evidence, propositions (1)–(15) will not all be accorded the same numerical value. Propositions (1), (2), and (3) should remain at the top with the same value (replacing "you" with "I" of course, and "reading" with "writing"). But (4)–(9) from my point of view would each have a higher numerical value.

Notice, however, that the relative order of these propositions should be more or less the same from both your and my point of view. That is, their rank is virtually independent of point of view. The rest of them, from my point of view, are of virtually equal justification; my justification that I have been around the world several times is of the same justification level as my justification that I have in fact not swum the English Channel, nor have I been to the North Pole. The *degree* of justification of these propositions (the quantity, quality, and corroboration of evidence—a lot, a little bit, etc.—weighed using evident probability) would thus differ on my list, while their relative order to each other (which ranking they have on the basis of the relative evidential justification—first place, second place, etc.) remain virtually the same. The bad news is that our propositional frameworks are different and not directly open to the world. The good news is that they overlap and they are open to each other; if we stick together, we may be able to get somewhere.

With regard to my age, however, I would have to put the justification of this proposition up with my name and sex. These would be the only cases, among all those propositions, where my rank ordering would differ from yours. We thus see that there is an imperfect but high degree of correlation among the justification levels of various propositions presented to us. If we apply our Belief Chart one at a time to various propositions, in many—perhaps most—cases, both degrees of justification and rank ordering will be about the same. In some cases the rank ordering will be the same, the degrees different. In others, the degrees of justification will be the same, the rank ordering different. Propositions that do not correspond, even closely, either in degree or rank ordering will, it seems, be in a minority.

You should now have a fuller sense of what I meant before by the "comfort zone" within which we can operate together, with comfort, without having to settle rather difficult epistemological issues. Although there are some propositions to which you and I would accord different degrees of justification, there is more than enough overlap and openness to make a philosophical journey possible.

Let us now turn to plotting degrees of psychological confidence in whether something is the case. This is measured on our Belief Chart above along the vertical axis, from 0 to 1 in the C direction (the affirmative thesis) and from 0 to 1 in the ~C direction (the negative thesis).

Say, for instance, you are a No-Believer. Your justification for the proposition "God exists," relative to the other propositions within your propositional framework, is ranked, according to the scheme above, as 1~e. That means you think the justification against the existence of God is on par with, say, the justification against the existence of unicorns, Santa Claus, leprechauns, and so forth within your propositional framework. Giving the value of 1~e to the proposition "God exists" does not mean you have absolute proof that God does not exist. It means you rank its evidential justification as being equal with propositions that have the lowest level of justification within your propositional framework. What about your psychological conviction with regard to this proposition? Suppose that, at the same time, you feel so confident in God's nonexistence that you rank the proposition "God exists" at 1~c. In that case, on the chart you would mark the point (1~e, 1~c), which puts you right at the tip of ~r, the No-Believer half of what we have named the "relatively rational" line.

Suppose, on the other hand, that while you feel the evidence against the existence of God is overwhelming (still at 1~e), nevertheless you feel very confident in God's existence. Suppose, with all your heart, you feel more psychologically certain about God's existence than you do about your own. In that case, you would plot yourself as (~1e, 1c), right on the f line, which we have named the "Relatively Faithful" line.

Repeating now what was said above, keep in mind that "faithful" is sometimes equated with "confident," but I have been careful to avoid this conflation. By "faith" I mean confidence that exists disproportionately to the amount of your relative evidential justification. Likewise, I am using "skepticism" to mean not just that you are a No-Believer but, rather, that your confidence in the negative thesis is disproportionate to the amount of relative evidential justification. Thus, in our Belief Chart, both the f and ~f diagonals represent varying degrees of *faith*, that is, levels of confidence that are in disproportion to the levels of justification. Using these distinctions, you are "faithful" or "skeptical" depending on how you look at it and what it is that you are faithful about or skeptical about. The Faithful Yes-Believer, typically, is skeptical about disconfirming evidence and has faith (a surplus of confidence) in the Yes view, while the Skeptical No-Believer, typically, is skeptical about confirming evidence and has faith in the No view. Both positions, though the beliefs differ in content, are similar in that they involve levels of confidence in marked disproportion to the levels of justification. I shall call one position "faith," the other "skepticism," meaning that if you fall somewhere on this line your psychology is such that—all else being equal—you have a tendency to resist either confirming or disconfirming evidence, depending on your point of view. So the Faithful Yes-Believer and the Skeptical No-Believer, though they probably consider themselves opposites, are much closer than they may realize; first, they both are believers (they differ in *what* they believe, not *that* they believe) and they are both as far away from the "relatively rational" line as they can get.

Thus, say your relative evidential justification for the proposition "God exists" is all the way to 1e: The evidence you have for the existence of God is on a par with the evidence you have for your own existence. However, for some reason you simply cannot accept this evidence, and you feel with all your heart that God does not exist. Somehow—you don't know how or why—the evidence must be wrong, something is deceiving us, self-deception is involved, not that you have evidence for this, you just feel in your gut that it is so, and you are so repulsed by the idea of God that you cannot possibly get yourself to accept what the evidence says. You then plot yourself as (1e, 1~c), at the extreme end of the bottom half of ~f, the Skeptical No-Believer line. Looking at our Belief Chart, you may find yourself closer in understanding to your polar opposite. Likewise with all the other positions. In understanding these sorts of polar opposites when it comes to beliefs, you may find yourself on the verge of discovering a new closeness to yourself.

Which Way Shall We Go?

2.0 Unreasonable Belief

ONE THING YOU CANNOT DO ON A JOURNEY IS STAND STILL. NOW THAT WE have charted our initial territory, the time has come to move about a bit. Here's why.

Consider, first, a courtroom example. Suppose Jones is on trial for the murder of Smith. We are the jury. The most incriminating evidence offered by the prosecution is the testimony of Mr. Esterhazy, who works in the same building with Jones and Smith. Esterhazy says that on the day of the murder he saw Jones arguing vehemently with Smith in the elevator. He plays his minirecorder, which just happened to be on, and we hear what other witnesses have corroborated as the voices of Jones and Smith arguing about who will win the Superbowl.

We, the jury, must now decide the verdict. Lou is the only one who thinks Jones is guilty. We ask him why. "Because we have proof he was in the building on the day of the murder." We point out to Lou that, on the day of the murder, we also have proof that Esterhazy was in the building! Grudgingly, Lou concedes the point but still thinks Jones is guilty. We ask him why. "Because look at his deranged eyes—is that the face of a murderer, or what?" Another juror, Bob, responds: "What are you talking about? I've never seen such a saintly composure. That guy is completely innocent—can't you see the aura around him?"

At this point, we should all wish both Lou and Bob off the jury. Not because we are convinced Jones is innocent. Not because we are convinced Lou couldn't be a psychic who can tell whether someone is a murderer just by looking into his eyes. Not because we are convinced Bob couldn't be a psychic who can tell by a person's "aura" whether the person is guilty. Rather, we are convinced, within our comfort zone, that under the given laws the evidence does not warrant a conviction. Jones might well be the murderer. But the level of justification—the quantity, quality, and corroboration of evidence presented, ranked according to evident probability—is not enough for us to reasonably conclude that Jones did it. Lou's conclusion is unjustified and unreasonable.

What about Bob's conclusion? It too is unjustified and unreasonable—not because of what his conclusion is but because of how he got to it. In philosophy, as in legal situations such as the one above, what matters is not so much *what* you think but *why* you think it.

Thus, ideally, when we give our verdict, "Not Guilty," we are not saying that we know, with absolute certainty, that Jones did not commit murder. He might well have. What we are saying is that, given the evidence, his guilt has not been sufficiently established to warrant a guilty verdict. Our conclusion is not absolutely certain but it is reasonably enough justified to be relatively rational. Lou's and Bob's conclusions are not. Even if it turns out that Lou or Bob is right, their beliefs are so unreasonable as to be *relatively irrational.*

2.1 Pride and Prejudice

To have a fair trial, what is the most important criterion in selecting a jury? It is this: that no juror has made up his or her mind in advance of being presented with all the evidence, reasons, and arguments. If your mind is already made up, you are *prejudiced,* which means, literally, "to prejudge," to judge in advance. You cannot go inquiring into something if you have already made up your mind about it. When it comes to inquiry, a made-up mind is a closed mind.

That is why, for the purposes of our journey, it is so important that we suspend, as best we can, our judgments about the topic of God. This is not meant in some abstract terms. It means we must proceed without prejudice. That is essential to doing philosophy. Here, then, are explicit and detailed instructions for proceeding without prejudice. (Indeed, you might wonder: if your mind is already "made up," *who made it up*—you or peer pressure, or TV, or those who were in charge of your upbringing, indoctrination, and conditioning?)

If, according to the Belief Chart, you are a Relatively Rational No-Believer at (0.5~e, 0.5~c), you must use the evidence presented in the following pages to move your justification to 0 so that, hopefully, your psychological conviction will follow until you are as close as you can be to the ideal starting point, (0,0). I say "hopefully" because of course you cannot change your feelings the way you can change your clothes.

Say you are a Faithful No-Believer at (0.3~e, 0.3c); it is then up to you to use the material presented in this book to try to move your levels of justification so as to bring yourself as close to (0,0) as you can. And so on for whatever your position is. If you are halfway between the horizontal axis and the Relatively Rational Yes-Belief line, *r*, say at (0.4e, 0.2c), you must try to balance the numbers out to bring yourself to (0,0).

In other words, since this is a book in which we are not reading about philosophy but trying to *do* philosophy, we must engage in philosophical activity. Our first philosophical activity will be to find how to move ourselves into different points of view from the one we now have so that we do not prejudge the issues. Being able to shift points of view is one of the main skills philosophy has to offer, not so much for the purposes of changing our views, but for the purpose of freeing ourselves from attachment to our own points of view so that we can really see and understand other points of view. Remember, this "seeing" is not with your eyes but your mind's eye: The mental modeling of alternatives requires suspension of belief in the alternative view, which you call not "an alternative view" but "*my* view." If you don't remove your point of view before trying to see a different point of view, then you're looking at another point of view through your own. The other point of view will then seem less in focus, less true, less "correct," than yours. It's like trying out different lenses without first taking off your own.

Suppose you are an atheist who thinks people who believe in God are just "crazy." You meet a fundamentalist Christian who tries to "convert" you into believing that the fundamentalist Christian point of view on God is correct. You listen, you ask questions, and you listen some more. After hearing what the Christian has to say, you walk away shrugging your shoulders because now the Christian position sounds even more preposterous to you. You say, "I really tried to see things from the Christian's point of view but there's just no way anybody in his or her right mind could see things that way. What a bunch of loonies." Meanwhile, the Christian is walking away, having heard your atheistic views, still wondering how anyone in his or her right mind could be so crazy as to believe that God does not exist! How can such varying differences be possible? Well, in this case, both of you are forgetting that the key ingredient to having a particular point of view *is that the point of view feels true.* To each of you your own point of view feels true even when you are listening to the other point of view perhaps because you forgot—or were too afraid, too stubborn, or too unwilling—to suspend judgment, to remove your prejudices, to step out of your own view to see the other's point of view. Or perhaps you just didn't know how. This book will teach you enough about the complexities of the language and logic of belief to learn how. But if you are afraid, stubborn, or unwilling to change, your own brain will give you plenty of excuses not to learn. Our purpose is not to change but to learn how to change. If this is dangerous, then so be it.

Not being able to see things from other points of view makes it possible for us to live in our singular models of the world without ever realizing that our world is but one model among many possible worlds. To realize that our view is but one among many is as upsetting as it is liberating. On the other hand, if we don't know how to see this about ourselves, we are not to blame! Innocence may not be bliss, but it does get us off the hook psychologically and lets us avoid a lot of responsibility.

In other words, one problem is, as we've already seen, that evidential justification is not the only issue. A high level of justification might allow you to accept a point of view intellectually, *but unless there is also some degree of psychological conviction to go with it, the view will not feel like your own.* As long as the conviction isn't there, the view feels foreign. But how do you really suspend your own point of view when you are already in it, bound up to it, emotionally and intellectually attached? After all, your conviction is not under your conscious control! You can't just say to yourself, "All right, I will now have a completely strong sense of psychological confidence about X," any more than you can order yourself to be sad or order yourself to stop being angry. *What then is in control?* We shall address such interesting questions later. But here we should notice that it is precisely this aspect of a belief—that it is not under your conscious control—that makes it feel *real.* This is also why people are afraid to see things from other people's point of view. They're afraid, often, of losing control. The true philosopher is not afraid, not because the philosopher is so firmly entrenched in a particular view but precisely for the reason that the philosopher is not attached. This does not mean that the philosopher just accepts any particular view. Rather, the philosopher's fearlessness in engaging conflicting points of view comes from three things: (1) knowing the unknown, (2) knowing a method, and (3) willing to feel psychologically insecure. The first means you can identify the gaps and inconsistencies—the blind spots, what is unknown—in any view; a good philosopher is hard to trap. The second means not just going on in a particular way but being consciously aware of what that way is. A good philosopher is not just thinking about where to go but about the road that gets you there. The third means the philosopher dares to be afraid.

It is because of all the sorts of considerations we've discussed thus far that developing the skill of being able to move about in the Belief Chart is essential to doing philosophy. It's not a good idea to do this if your goal is, say, forming a group of religious converts. If what you want to do is manipulate people into accepting your own point of view, trying to move them to (0,0) on the Belief Chart will not serve you nearly as well as trying to move them to (e1,c1). You are much more likely to succeed in manipulating them by making yourself and them completely committed to your point of view. But of course it is then very unlikely that you will ever succeed in discovering what may be manipulating *you.*

Indeed, one of the biggest mistakes people make with philosophy in general and philosophy of religion in particular is that they turn to it looking for reinforcement for what they already believe. It is like watching a football game. They root for their team regardless of how they are doing. *Philosophy is not a spectator sport.*

2.2 Charting a Course

Within the comfort zone that we have charted out there are some definite constraints. For instance, there are some definite rights and wrongs *relative to your own rank ordering.* The following example illustrates this.

Suppose Nicole's position on the chart identifies her as a relatively rational Yes-Believer at (0.8e, 0.8c). To begin her philosophical inquiry she must return to (0,0) but can't see how to do it. She should start by making a list of the strongest evidence she has, at this point in her life, for the existence of God. Suppose Nicole's key evidence is the Bible. In the section on the arguments from holy books in Chapter 4, she should pay careful attention and study all the reasons presented there as to why holy books are bad evidence. There are several arguments and lots of reasons given. Now, while it is true that, say, a Catholic Yes-Believer theologian might be able to counter these arguments against holy books with very clever responses, to which a rational No-Believer theologian (such as one of the "God is dead" theologians at Harvard divinity school) could present further counterarguments, and so on, *Nicole probably does not at this point have such arguments available with which to defend her position.* Nor should she look for them. Not yet. Wait until after she is at (0,0).

Similarly, suppose Kim is a relatively rational No-Believer at (0.8–e, 0.8–c). She should list the strongest reasons she has, at this stage of intellectual and emotional development, against the existence of God. Suppose the key evidence is that the scientific world view can explain things without reference to God. Kim must then focus on the sections in Chapter 11 criticizing science's ability to answer ultimate questions and study these criticisms diligently until she has a sufficient grasp of them and can no longer defend her view. Again, while it is true that, say, a clever, relatively rational No-Believer scientist could no doubt counter Kim with additional arguments, which no doubt could be further countered by a clever relatively rational Yes-Believer, *Kim probably does not at this point have such arguments available with which to defend her position.* Nor should she look for them! Not yet. She should wait until after she is at (0,0).

The same holds for wherever you are on the Belief Chart. It also holds for whatever higher level of sophistication you may have regarding the topic of God. It means you have to do more research. The method presented here works, in principle, for any field. It is a step-by-step philosophical technique for getting to a neutral vantage point from which any inquiry, into any topic, should proceed if it is to achieve original insight. That we can do this with rigor and precision regarding our grandest, most "metaphysical" beliefs about God, about which there has been disagreement and debate for centuries without resolution, should help convince us that it is possible to do this with beliefs where the metaphysics is less apparent.

In this book, then, pay especially close attention to the parts that will get you as close to (0,0) as possible. Go to the following chapters with that goal in mind. When you are finished, we shall meet again at the end of the book. Our journey together will then end. Yours may then begin.

The rules are simple. Find yourself first. Put aside all your intellectual accumulations and emotional attachments. Then go in search of God.

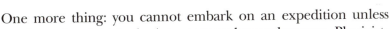

One more thing: you cannot embark on an expedition unless you have the right tools. Astronomers have telescopes. Physicists have microscopes. Archeologists have shovels. Surgeons have scalpels. What are the most important tools of the philosopher? Questions.

What Does Believing Involve?

3.0 Belief *In* vs. Belief *That*[1]

WE MUST DISTINGUISH MORE PRECISELY TWO VERY DIFFERENT TYPES OF belief along the lines already carved out. To see the difference in meaning, consider the following.

Your friend Tobe has been a terrible drunkard for over ten years. At least once every year Tobe becomes destitute and comes to you for help, swearing to go off the booze forever. This year, once again, Tobe has come to you for help. And, as you have done a dozen times before, you choose to help your friend. Not because you believe this time Tobe has finally seen the light and will, once and for all, sober up. Indeed, all your evidence suggests Tobe's sobriety will once again be short lived. After all, Tobe has more than a decade-long track record. The reason you help Tobe is that you love Tobe as a friend. You have chosen to believe in Tobe in spite of the evidence that, this time next year, Tobe will be hitting the bottle yet again and will come to you for help.

To believe *that* Tobe will stay off the booze is in this case clearly to go way beyond the bounds of reasonable justification: evidentially, it would be unreasonable. Believing *in* Tobe, in the sense that in spite of the evidence to the contrary you refuse to give up faith in Tobe, is altogether a different matter. It may even be a noble thing to do. It would be like continuing to believe *in* humanity in spite of evidence that in this century alone over eighty million people have been killed in wars, more than in any other century, often in the most gruesome way, and so on. To believe *that* we are finally out of danger is to be ignorant. To believe *in* ourselves is to not lose hope.

So with regard to the question of the existence of God, we must distinguish these two types of Yes-Believers: those who believe *that* God exists vs. those who believe *in* God. To believe *that* God exists means you have *some* evidence. *What is driving your belief is the level of evidential justification.* Your belief may be like an educated guess or a hunch, or you may have so much evidence that it warrants a conviction. In that case, you would have relative knowledge that God exists. To believe *in* God means you are supporting a set of beliefs unsupported by evidence, perhaps even contrary to the evidence. *What is driving your belief is you, your own psychology, your ego.*

Finklestein is chairman of a huge corporation. For six years in a row the company has lost money, each year more than in the previous year. Things are getting worse. At the board meeting we ask Finklestein what the prognosis is for next year. Finklestein says, "I think it looks very good. I see the end of our troubles in sight."

Suppose Finklestein is not lying. Finklestein does believe this. What we would want to know is whether Finklestein believes *that* the company will improve or believes *in* the company. It makes a big difference. Do we want to stay on our present course? Do we want to replace the chairperson? Do we want to look for another job? And so on. It is good to have confidence. But it is also good to have a sober view of where we stand.

Finklestein claims not merely to believe *in* the company but to believe *that* the company will improve. Now, what does this mean? It cannot mean that Finklestein just very, very strongly believes *in* the company. That's still belief *in.* Belief *that* requires at least *some* evidential justification. Perhaps not enough to warrant a conviction—the strongest possible level of justification—but at least 0.7 or above in our zones of evidential justification chart (i.e., at least above the uncertainty zone). We cross-examine Finklestein for the evidence—not whether Finklestein knows the company really will improve next year; no one could justifiably claim to *know* this (not even relatively)—only that, at best, there is enough relative evidential justification to make it a good bet. Finklestein gives the following evidence: "I went to a fortune teller who told me things would improve dramatically."

At this point we would take issue with the status of Finklestein's belief. Not whether Finklestein believes, but whether the belief really is of the sort Finklestein says it is. Sure, hearing a fortune teller say something you would like to hear is likely to make you feel better than hearing what you don't want to hear or just pretending. But this is not really *evidential justification.* It is just a tricky way to reinforce your *faith*—your level of psychological confidence over and above your level of evidential justification. You have a right to do this. It might even be a good thing under certain circumstances, in terms of being in your self-interest. But presently we are trying to ascertain whether the professed Yes-Believer regarding the existence of God believes *that* God exists, in the sense of having some, but incomplete evidence, or whether this is merely belief *in* God, in the sense of not having any evidence (or even evidence to the contrary) and having *faith* in the existence of God. Both of these are called "belief" but they are very different states of mind. As just mentioned, in the former case what is driving your belief is the evidence. In the latter, what is driving your belief is something else. That something else is your own psychology—your ego, your desire to be right, your desire for things to go well, your fear, or whatever, and typically it cannot be touched by any amount of confirming or disconfirming evidence.

People often confuse these two very different types of belief. As the example of Finklestein shows, you can be wrong about what you believe. So, once again we need to do some serious disambiguating. One of the things we want to do is find out what we actually believe and the status of that belief. "Maneuvering about" through the conceptual landscape is impossible unless we ascertain, first, exactly where we are. People often misunderstand what they take to be their own beliefs. They *think* they know where they stand and why but often they are mistaken: their mental model of themselves—of their own mind—is flawed. Sometimes, we may even deceive ourselves into thinking we believe something when we believe just the opposite.

So: Does the Yes-Believer believe *that* God exists, or does the Yes-Believer believe *in* God? Keep in mind what our purpose is. We want to move close to the unprejudiced starting position, (0,0), on our Belief Chart. Our purpose is not to change our beliefs, destroy our beliefs, or anything of that sort. Rather, we wish to learn how to dislodge ourselves from attachment to our particular point of view in order to start a philosophical journey afresh, innocent, like children. We can always *choose* to go back to where we started. Indeed, often a philosophical journey will lead us back to where we started so that we can, for the first time, be in a position to *choose that path for ourselves.*

3.1 Psychologically Yours vs. Philosophically Yours: What Makes a Belief *Mine*?

Presently, we are concerned with whether the Yes-Believer, like Finklestein in our story above, is mistaken about the nature of his or her own belief about God. The key question is not *what* you believe but *how* you came to believe it. Just as whether you have (relative) knowledge about something is not up to the strength of your psychological conviction but up to the strength of your evidential justification, so too whether you have belief *that* or belief *in* depends not on the psychological state of mind you are in but on the nature and amount of evidential justification and how you came to have it. Is your belief the result of having become convinced of a conclusion on the basis of extrapolating from the available evidence using reason, making an educated guess, and so on, or is it the result of having been indoctrinated, the result of conditioning by authority?

This is an important question. After all, what are beliefs *for*? Ideally, being aware of what we believe, the nature of our beliefs, and why we believe what we believe, serves two sorts of important functions. Either our beliefs help direct us toward the truth or else they are indicators of our deep commitments about what we think we most care about. Realizing you believe *that p* tells you that, all else being equal, the proposition *p* functions within your propositional framework as being more likely to be true (more evidently probable) than false. For instance, if you believe cigarette smoking is not bad for you, this may lead you to keep smoking; if you believe smoking is bad for you, this may lead you to quit. You might not know for certain whether it is good or bad but we do not have knowledge about all the things that concern us.

Beliefs *that p* play a vital role in determining how we live our lives. These beliefs can and do change over time based on changes in evidential justification provided we have the wisdom to take some kind of charge over our own psychological states. Religious *beliefs that*, on the other hand, can have especially profound effects over the duration of our lives: they may determine not just how we live and what we live for, but how we might be influenced in our thinking about the overall meaning of our lives and even of all life, even the afterlife, not only in terms of what our lives are for and what they mean, but what we should be striving for in terms of our personal development, in this life especially but possibly also the next. After all, religions often speak in terms of our lives on Earth being significant indicators of how we are likely to spend eternity. Think of how careful we are when it comes, for instance, to planning our financial futures. Our financial futures will last, at most, only a few years; what about all of eternity? Should we not place extra care in our beliefs regarding such matters?

Similarly, *beliefs in* play an equally vital role. Our deepest values—the things we most believe in—structure nearly everything we do. If you believe in the Republican Party, you may become a Republican; if you believe in the Democratic Party, you may become a Democrat. If you believe in art for art's sake, you may become an artist; if you believe in money above all things, you may become an investor, a banker, accountant, and so on. And again when it comes to religious belief *in*, what may be at stake is not just our eternal soul, if we have one, but how we view our lives now. How should we live? What should we commit ourselves to? What are our deepest personal, religious, and moral values? These are not just the interests of a self—*such beliefs help form the very psychologi-*

cal contours that are the self.[2] Beliefs *in* are not just beliefs we have; to a certain extent, these are the beliefs that we *are*.[3]

So the first key question in examining our beliefs is to find out how you came to believe what you believe. Does the Yes-Believer, after having thought about it, gathered some evidence, and reasoned about what God might be and whether God exists, now believe *in* God or *that* God exists? Or both? Or, is the belief merely the result of persuasive indoctrination, persuasive conditioning by authority, and so on? If the latter, then it could be argued—as I am about to do—that the persuaded Yes-Believer is not truly a Yes-Believer: The persuaded Yes-Believer neither believes *in* God nor *that* God exists! My argument might not be a good one. It might be the case not only that you disagree; you may have a much better argument showing that what I am about to say is not the case. Here's the argument. You decide.

Suppose we go out for ice cream. You take me to a place that has 148 different flavors. You order your favorite: Tutti-Frutti-Macadamia-Nut-Lima-Bean. I order vanilla.

Somewhat surprised, you ask me why, with all these fantastic choices, I have ordered plain old vanilla. I explain that my favorite ice cream just happens to be vanilla. "What about French Vanilla?" you ask. "Never tried it." "Vanilla Bean?" "Nope." "Raspberry?" "Never had any." Now you are even more surprised. You ask me what flavors I have had. "Vanilla," I answer. Now you should not just be surprised, you should suspect that when I reported that my favorite ice cream is vanilla, though indeed it is my favorite of all the flavors I tried (I tried only vanilla), it is, at best, misleading to call vanilla my *favorite*. What I should say, instead, especially if I wish to use my own language properly, is that I don't really know what my favorite ice cream is, since I have only tasted vanilla.

Our story does not end there. Incredulous, you inquire into how I came to be a vanilla eater. It turns out I come from a long line of vanilla eaters. My parents raised me to eat only vanilla. They told me that other flavors exist but that I should, if I know what's good for me, never sway from vanilla. But now, after discussing it and thinking about it, suddenly I remember that once—just to show me how the other flavors were not for me—after my father and I had a few beers together he gave me some chocolate ice cream to try. It made me sick.

Now, in a sense, of course, I do like vanilla best. But the truth might be that I only *think* I like vanilla best and that, in reality, what I like best (though I don't know it) is Macadamia Nut! Likes and dislikes are a completely subjective matter, a value judgment. But *what* your likes or dislikes actually are is an objective matter, a factual judgment. Your personal tastes are a question of value but what they are is a question of fact.[4] What you actually believe *in*, too, is a question of value. But what you actually value and what you think you value may be quite different.

What I am claiming with regard to belief *in* God, then, is that this is a much more deeply personal thing than what flavor of ice cream you like. But just as it would be incorrect for me to say that I like vanilla best if I've been conditioned by authority (my vanilla-eating father, who comes from a long line of vanilla eaters) to eat only vanilla, so too it would be incorrect for me to say that I believe *in* God if I've been conditioned to have that belief. Properly speaking, I can only believe *in* God if I came to this on my own—say, after having sampled lots of different views, including atheism, or perhaps after seeing the impossibility of justifying belief *that*. Which means that people who have been persuaded, indoctrinated, or conditioned to think they believe *in* God, don't really believe! They only think they do. Thinking means seeing alternatives. They are in that category, already mentioned before, of people who live in their fantasies, not their realities.

3.2 The Illusion of Belief

What is a conditioned belief? A belief, you will recall, is a propositional attitude. A proposition is the statement about some such-and-such being a so-and-so. An attitude is the psychological response toward that proposition, how you feel about it. But if this attitude is but the result of conditioning by some authority, such as parents, teachers, priests, rabbis, and so on, then this attitude is not really *your* attitude. It is a conditioned response, a reflex psychological reaction that you have been trained to have. In a purely psychological sense, the belief is yours. In a more important philosophical sense, the belief is not yours but someone else's, which now is "yours" only in the sense that you have been conditioned into having it.

This leaves us, perhaps, with the possibility of having a belief *that p* on the basis of conditioning. But even that will not do. Remember, believing that *p* is the case means you have some evidential justification for *p;* perhaps not enough to make it a warranted conviction (relative knowledge), but some; perhaps enough to make it a good hunch or, better yet, an educated guess. But if you know that the belief came about as the result of conditioning by some authority, then you also know that you would believe whatever you would have been conditioned to believe, independently of whatever evidence there may exist for it.

For instance, suppose you are a Hindu because your parents are Hindus. Is your belief a good hunch or an educated guess? Hardly. You know that had you been born to Christian parents, you would probably be a Christian; had you been born to Muslim parents you would probably be Muslim, and so on. Your belief is, at best, belief *in.* (But probably, given what was said in the previous section, not even that.) But is this commitment really a personal commitment, or is it just a conditioned reflex? We are not asking whether your belief *feels* like a personal commitment but whether it actually is. Commitment means you have committed yourself to something. But if your attitudes towards some propositions are but conditioned responses, this is, at best, commitment in the sense that ants are committed to building anthills and bees are committed to building beehives. It should hardly be considered, even, to be personal faith, in the sense of being an internal, *personal* thing; it is an external thing you have thrust upon yourself from the outside, perhaps without even realizing it. It is self-deception.

Notice that I am not making any value judgments about whether belief of either sort—belief *that* or belief *in*—is good or bad. Rather, I am saying that unless you came to (what you think is) your belief in the proper sort of way, *you do not even have any real belief.* Just as it is possible to have the illusion of knowledge, it is possible to have the illusion of belief.

We are now beginning to see why being able to move to point (0,0) on our chart is not just some esoteric exercise in which we learn how to pretend not to believe what we believe for the purpose of embarking on a philosophical journey. The neutral zone may turn out to be the doorway to *real* belief: even, perhaps, to real knowledge—maybe about God but definitely about ourselves.

69

Notes

1. I follow Alvin Plantinga's initial distinction in "Rationality and Religious Belief," in Kolak & Martin, eds., *The Experience of Philosophy*, 2nd ed., Wadsworth, 1993, though I think it is an egregious error for Plantinga to make the distinction and then, "for purposes of economy," to "use the phrase 'belief in God' as a synonym for 'belief that God exists.' " There is nothing synonymous about them, as this chapter should make clear.
2. See my "Finding Our Selves: Individuation, Identification and MPD," forthcoming, *Philosophical Psychology*.
3. For a detailed argument, see my "Metaphysics and Metapsychology of Personal Identity," *American Philosophical Quarterly*, 30 (1993), No. 1, pp. 39–50.
4. For a more complete analysis of the relation between factual judgments and value judgments, see our "Values," in Kolak and Martin, *Wisdom Without Answers*, 2nd ed., Wadsworth, 1991, pp. 106–120.

Are Scriptures
Convincing Evidence?

4.0 Persuasion, Conviction,
and Belief by Conversion

CONVINCING EVIDENCE FOR THE EXISTENCE OF GOD, ACCORDING TO MANY
Yes-Believers, is found in scripture: ancient texts proclaiming to
be the official word of God, offering descriptions of God, instructions from God, testimonies of people who claim to have directly
witnessed God's acts, and so on. These so-called "holy books"
have exerted an enormous influence on large numbers of people
over many centuries. They move and they inspire. But are they
convincing evidence?

We cannot determine that scriptures offer convincing evidence for the existence of God simply by the fact that scriptures
do succeed in persuading many people to believe that God exists.
It all depends on *how* they do it. After all, if an evil psychiatrist

used a special paranoia-inducing drug to persuade you that your friends are conspiring to destroy you, that drug would not be evidence that your friends are conspiring to destroy you. Nor would it be proper to say "it's evidence to me." It isn't. You don't even realize the drug was used. You just have the feeling—the attitude—that your friends are trying to do you in, disconnected from any real evidence.

So just because something succeeds in persuading you does not mean it is convincing evidence. By "convincing" I don't mean just having the power to create or alter attitudes. You might read a tabloid report about aliens from outer space, visitations from Elvis, or messages from heaven and be persuaded by the evidence offered that aliens exist, that Elvis still lives, that there is a heaven, and so on. But such tabloids succeed at persuading, not convincing. They may trick you with fake evidence, bad arguments, and so on. That so many readers are so easily deceived in this way does not make those tabloids convincing evidence. It shows, rather, how very easy it is to persuade large numbers of people of something without offering them any convincing evidence that it is so. Similarly, lots of flim-flam artists are very good at using their skills of fabrication, persuasion, and deception to persuade people. The way I am using the terms, being persuaded is not the same as being convinced; those trying to convince rather than persuade offer evidence, not trickery.

Scriptures might thus succeed in persuading people that God exists without offering any convincing evidence for the existence of God. The fact that they move and inspire people to believe that God exists, by itself, does not make scriptures evidence for God, any more than a novel or movie that persuades you to believe X is evidence for X. A powerful emotional drama may be so inspiring and so persuasive that it creates a psychological confidence level of 1.0; but, by itself, it *may carry evidential justification of 0*. It succeeds by *converting*, not by *convincing*.

Often, "being convinced" and "being converted" are used synonymously; I am carefully distinguishing the two. You've been convinced that some proposition, p, is true when your attitude toward p is the result of having been given evidence that causes the Yes attitude. If your attitude is caused not by evidence but by persuasion through emotional drama, you've been *converted* into believing that p is true.

So, do scriptures produce conversion or conviction, and what exactly is the difference and how can we tell? For if scriptures merely convert rather than convince their Yes-Believers, then Yes-Believers who believe that God exists based on scriptures have no evidence whatsoever for the existence of God. Their beliefs are, literally, make-believe.

4.1 Psychological Attitudes vs. Cognitive Attitudes: Conversion vs. Conviction

A belief is a propositional attitude. I can try to influence what you believe—your Yes or No attitude concerning some proposition, p—in one of two ways: influencing your attitude with evidence (trying to convince you) or influencing your attitude with emotion (trying to convert you). It is very important to notice that, ultimately, both the evidential way and the emotional way require either creating an attitude where there is none or shifting your attitude one way or the other.

Propositions are about the world: They are (linguistic) representations of purported facts and they come in two varieties, (relatively) true and (relatively) false, according to the principle of propositional relativity and as measured by our zones of evidential justification chart. Attitudes are about you: They are feelings of psychological confidence toward each of those propositions and they come in degrees, as measured on our zones of psychological confidence chart. Usually we think of those attitudes purely in terms of how we experience them, that is, as *psychological* phenomena—an evaluative Yes or No feeling toward some proposition p. But often, perhaps always, these *psychological* Yes or No attitudes are the effects of what I call an underlying *cognitive attitude*. By "cognitive attitude" I mean not p's psychological standing in your emotions—whether p feels true or false—but p's logical standing in your propositional framework—whether p functions in your thinking as either true or as false.

For example, my psychological attitude toward the proposition "Doors are safer exits from tall buildings than windows," is Yes, and that proposition's cognitive attitude is True; in other words, it is well within the center of the justification zone. But when I use doors rather than windows to exit tall buildings, it is not because I then have a high level of psychological confidence toward the proposition "Doors are safer exits from tall buildings than windows." I am not aware of having any psychological attitude whatsoever toward that proposition. I just go out the door. But how did I know to go out the door rather than jump out the window? Well, the cognitive attitude of the proposition is True, with a very high degree of evidential justification; it stands in the very center of the justification zone in my propositional framework (as described by the zones of justification chart).

The cognitive attitude of a proposition is its logical setting, a sort of logical glue that holds the proposition in the True or False position within the propositional framework, allowing it to function as such. The psychological attitude toward it—the feeling of psychological confidence—is the psychological glue that holds you to the proposition, allowing you to function in accordance with that proposition being true. What this means in terms of the difference between trying to sway you toward some proposition p with an evidential appeal (trying to convince you) versus trying to sway you toward p with an emotional appeal (trying to convert you) should now be clear. The emotional appeal is an attempt to short-circuit your cognitive process. The evidential appeal is an attempt to revise it.

Say you believe *that p* such that p's cognitive attitude—how it stands in the propositional framework—is True and your psychological attitude toward p is Yes. The psychological attitude is a way of announcing to yourself, using a sort of psychological shorthand, p's cognitive attitude. But if your psychological attitude toward p comes from p's cognitive attitude within the propositional framework, where does p's cognitive attitude itself (its functioning as True within the framework) come from? Your Yes psychological attitude toward p—how it feels (true)—is conditioned by p's cognitive attitude (true). Now we're asking: What conditioned the cognitive attitude?

One thing is for sure: *You* didn't do it. You can't just tell yourself that something is so and then believe it; you cannot *convert* yourself into believing that p by saying, "I will now believe that p," "Come on now, I really want to believe that p, p is good, p is great," and so on. Try it! Say to yourself, "I will now believe, for the next twenty-four hours, that the Earth is flat." There may be ways around this, through some sort of self-hypnosis, but it would be very difficult and ordinarily you cannot do it. (Self-deception would occur when the psychological attitude is Yes and the cognitive attitude is False.) You can, however, *convince* yourself that something is so. For instance, try to convince yourself that this book has 237 pages. Go ahead, try it! What did you do? You turned to the last page and found some evidence. That number might be a misprint. It might be a clever trick. Perhaps I had the compositor put the wrong numbers somewhere along the way just to make a tricky point. But you can find more evidence, say, by counting all the pages. You could still make a mistake. But in the end you can convince yourself of the number of pages. You will then believe it to be so. You will have a Yes psychological attitude toward the proposition, "*In Search of God* has 237 pages," because its cognitive attitude is True. And you just did that. You set the cognitive attitude of a proposition by using evidence. Your cognitive attitudes are open to conditioning—alteration— by evidence. This is how you are able to learn.

So some of the cognitive attitudes of the propositions about which you have a Yes psychological attitude come from evidence, which either you gathered yourself or someone presented to you. Cognitive attitudes of propositions based on conversions, however, cannot ordinarily come from you, nor are they based on evidence. How do they get there? What short-circuited your cognitive process, creating Yes psychological attitudes without giving you any evidence, without a corresponding True cognitive attitude? How is this possible?

Well, your psychological attitude toward some proposition, p, is a psychological phenomenon consisting in an evaluative Yes or No feeling toward p. Emotional appeals, say through drama, can directly affect those evaluative feelings by setting up a situation in which your emotions are literally being moved about until a Yes attitude toward p is achieved via dramatic devices designed to have this effect. You are then left with a belief—a propositional attitude—for which there is no underlying cognitive attitude. In other words, you believe that p even though p has no cognitive attitude, within your propositional framework, of True. Your cognitive process has been short-circuited. Instead of the Yes psychological attitude being generated as a result of an underlying cognitive attitude, there is just the psychological attitude and the proposition, as it were, hanging from the psychological attitude, the feeling. And for some reason the human brain seems unable or unwilling to discriminate between (1) evidentially unsupported propositions hanging from psychological attitudes that make the proposition feel true and (2) evidentially supported propositions erected upon cognitive attitudes that make the proposition function as true within the propositional framework. By failing to discriminate, the brain is prone to fabrication: not by making up the evidence to fill in what is missing—which, after all, unless its psychology is divided, as in multiple personality disorder, would consciously be noticed[1]— but by using psychological bridges to leap across the gaps in its logic. As a result, we are vulnerable to deceptive manipulation by our own psychologies.

4.2 A Question of Evidence

How can we learn to discriminate between whether we are being convinced by evidence—informed—or whether we are being converted by emotional persuasion—deceived? Unless we can understand this, we cannot answer the question of whether scripture or anything else, for that matter, is evidence.

What then is the difference between conviction and conversion? Is it that the emotional persuasion is a fiction, an elaborate lie, whereas the evidence is true? Not necessarily. A theatrical drama might depict a true situation exactly as it happened, while the evidential presentation might turn out to be mistaken or a hoax. So the difference between attitudes caused by evidence and attitudes caused by emotional persuasion toward some proposition p has nothing to do with how the attitudes feel (they can be phenomenologically indistinguishable) nor whether the propositions are true (they can both be false). Rather, what distinguishes the evidential conviction from the emotional conversion are two conditions:

1. independent accessibility
2. relevance

Suppose you read a book that asserts some proposition, p, to be true and you now believe that p. Were you convinced or converted? Did the book produce an evidential conviction or an emotional conversion? The Independent Accessibility Condition

76

says the book is not evidence for p unless it gives you access to the facts represented by p *independently of the author's say-so, that is, independently of the author's authority.* The Relevance Condition says that what caused your shift of attitude concerning p *must be relevant to the facts represented by p.*

Say p is "George Washington was a British spy." You read the book and you believe this. Is it conviction by evidence or emotional conversion? The answer does not depend on whether the author believes he is telling the truth, whether he himself was convinced or converted to this belief, nor even on whether Washington really was a British spy. Rather, the book is evidence for p only if it (1) provides independent access to p and (2) swayed you using only relevant information. There are several ways to tell. Suppose the author has a high level of evidential justification for p. Do you, after reading the book, have the same level of evidential justification as the author? Or is the author merely reporting his conclusions and seducing you by substituting emotional persuasion and getting you to accept his conclusion by emotional conversion? Unless the book provides you with some evidence that raises the evident probability of p being true *independently of the author's say-so,* the amount of evidence provided by the book for p is absolutely zero. It is merely conversion through emotional persuasion.

Likewise, if the information in the book causing the shift in your attitude toward p is irrelevant to whether p is true, then again the book is using not evidence but emotional persuasion. For instance, say Washington is depicted as a cheater at cards and a swindler (he may have been but it's irrelevant), as having many lovers (what does that have to do with whether he was a spy), as an alcoholic, and so on, depictions that lower your confidence in him as being a great American patriot. It works because the mind is subject to logical fallacies, which in many ways are like the viruses that corrupt a computer's logic. The fallacy, no doubt much simplified, goes roughly something like this:

Spies are bad and dishonest people.
George Washington was bad and dishonest.

Therefore,

George Washington was a spy.

Washington may have been any one of those things but to try to convert you into accepting the truth of p by converting your attitudes with dramatic devices that work, in part, because of such underlying logical fallacies (in this case, that of affirming the consequent) means you are being converted through the manipulation of your emotions for the purpose of persuading you that something is so without showing you that it is so. It is belief by conversion—even if all the dramatic depictions in the book are true.

On the other hand, suppose the book reprints certain hard-to-find documents along with their locations, interviews historians whom you can go talk to, quotes lengthy passages from Washington's diary, reveals secret British records, offers detailed arguments, etc. All of these things may or may not be forgeries, hoaxes, logical mistakes, and so on. That's not the point. Rather, the point is that the author has tried to convince you by providing you with all the materials that convinced the author in the first place. And remember: When your cognitive attitudes are conditioned by evidence you are in a sense being manipulated, but by the way the world is; the person ultimately in control is you. When your cognitive attitudes are conditioned by dramatic substitution of evidence through emotional drama, you are being manipulated by someone else's view of how the world is and you are out of your own control; you are subjugating your mind to someone else's control. In other words, for the author to become convinced that p is true and then not to give you the evidence but, instead, to offer you drama in place of that evidence, keeps the cognitive attitude—whether p functions as true or false within your belief framework—under the control of the author.

Satisfying the Independent Access and Relevance conditions, on the other hand, makes the cognitive attitude of p independent of the book and the author. That is why books sometimes do not satisfy these two conditions *on purpose*. This is something that popular science books and popular philosophy books have in common with scriptures. It's very different with college textbooks and journal articles that, if they are good ones, give you not just information (that may or may not ultimately be true) but also a method for verifying and testing that information and other information, hopefully teaching you how to go about making such discoveries independently of the book or article. You can disagree with calculus all you want, you can doubt it, but it works. You can hate logic but it works. You can disagree with conceptual analysis but it works. The fact that most students don't *like* college textbooks and research articles has to do with the fact that, typically, these authors do not try to seduce you by emotional persuasion. Rather, they try to convince you with evidence, reason, argument, and method of analysis. This is much harder and less "fun." It doesn't feel as exciting. Conviction by evidence has no powerful drama to amuse you but it makes you far more powerful. Why, then, are you more predisposed to persuasion by drama? Isn't it conditioning? Whoever conditioned you in this way, were they looking out for you or causing you harm, trying to make you less powerful?

Generally, when you have evidence for something you have a possible link to it. For instance, suppose you have evidence that Smith killed Jones. You found something that might link Smith to Jones's murder: fingerprints, an eyewitness, the murder weapon hidden in Smith's garage, and so on. These things lead you back to the source. If you present these things to a jury in an attempt to affect their attitudes about who murdered Smith, you're trying to convince them using evidence. You're trying to lead them back to the source. If instead you tell them a moving story designed to make Smith look bad and to turn the jury against him, to seduce them into hating Smith and being converted in this way to believe that Smith killed Jones, and so on, then you're using emotional persuasion through drama. You're not leading them to the source but away from the source toward yourself, using their emotions to sway them. They are connecting to the power of your dramatic presentation, not to the quality of the evidence. This is a formula for making leaders and followers; it makes followers less powerful and leaders more powerful. If the manipulator succeeds, then the follower will have to come to the leader and listen. The leader will have become an "authority."

We should now understand what it means to ask whether scriptures (or any books on anything) are evidence. As always in philosophy, it is important to understand the question before trying to answer it. The fact that scriptures have led many people to believe that God exists does not, by itself, establish that scriptures are evidence for the existence of God. It depends on whether they convince or convert. Both processes can have the same effect. To determine whether scriptures are evidence for the existence of God, then, it is not enough that they cause people to believe. They must do so without relying, for the shifting of attitudes, upon emotional persuasion. This, in turn, means that to be evidence, the scriptures, like anything else, must satisfy the Independence Condition and the Relevance Condition. Do they?

4.3 Truth, Propositions, and Descriptions

Many, perhaps most, people who believe God exists base their views on scriptures regarded by their church, synagogue, or temple as being divinely inspired. The first problem with the idea that scriptures are divinely inspired has nothing to do with whether the particular scriptures themselves are, in fact, divinely inspired. They may well be. You might believe it to be so. All your friends and family might believe it to be so. But remember, first, that whether some scripture *is* divinely inspired has nothing to do with your or anybody else's belief. It has only to do with whether God really did inspire the authors: God either did or did not inspire the writing. Whether God did in fact inspire the writing depends not on what anybody believes but on whether God really exists and whether God really did, in fact, inspire the writing of those scriptures.

Second, *if* the scripture indeed is divinely inspired, which does not depend on you, then certainly it is true that what you have there is the word of God. But unless you yourself have *some* way of connecting those words to God, the existence of the words themselves, regardless of whether divinely inspired or not, doesn't give you *any* evidence whatsoever for the existence of God.

To see why, suppose that, as it turns out, God directly inspired your friend to write a book. You're wondering whether God exists. Your friend gives you his book and says, "Look no more. Your search is over. Here's the evidence!"

But of course your friend has not really offered you any evidence for the existence of God. The problem isn't that the book is not divinely inspired; we're assuming it is. The problem, rather, is that unless you have some way of connecting those inkblots on the page with God, then the amount of evidence that those divinely inspired words are in fact divinely inspired is absolutely zero. What is missing? After all, didn't your friend *tell* you that they were divinely inspired? Doesn't that count for something?

Not necessarily. What we would have to ask your friend is *why* he thinks his book is divinely inspired. If he says, "It just is," and can offer no evidence as justification (and it's not just that he's withholding it), then he is mistaken in calling his book *evidence* for the existence of God. Suppose, on the other hand, that he says, "God told me so." God *may* indeed have told him so. But unless your friend has evidence that it was God who told him so, his claiming—*whether your friend says it to you or to himself, whether verbally or in writing*—that God told him so is no evidence whatsoever for it being God that told him so.

In other words, whether God inspired something to be written has nothing to do with us but with whether God in fact actually did inspire the writing. But whether we have evidence that some written word is the word of God *does* depend on us; it depends on the evidence we have and our ability to interpret and understand it as such. And unless you have convincing evidence that some scripture is, in fact, divinely inspired, and you believe *that* it is divinely inspired, then your belief is the result of emotional persuasion. You are not really convinced. You are merely converted.

In other words, I am claiming that unless along with your psychological attitude toward the proposition "These scriptures are divinely inspired"—the psychological feeling of confidence— you also have justification that the scripture is, in fact, divinely inspired, its being so—the truth—*is out of your reach, even if you believe it to be so!* All you are in contact with is that psychological feeling of confidence. You are not connected to the truth. It is like your feeling hurt that friend A betrayed you, based on what friend B told you, when B made it up but A did, unbeknownst both to you and to B, betray you. Your feeling is unjustified, even if that is the feeling you would have had had you convincing evidence that A did betray you. To believe without convincing evidence is a lot like guessing with your feelings. Your hurt based on A's betrayal stems not from the source of the hurt—A's betrayal—but from a lie, B's lie that (unbeknownst to B) A betrayed you; your feelings connect you not to the source of the hurt—A—but to the source of the lie, B. The actual source is out of your reach—*even though what you believe is true.*

To understand why this subtle difference is so important, suppose you are a detective in search of a murder weapon and you find a gun in the house. Suppose the gun was, in fact, the murder weapon. You present the weapon to the court. First question: Is this the murder weapon? You answer, "Yes, I believe with all my heart that this gun is the murder weapon." The next question is: *Why* do you believe this?

Suppose you answer, "I believe the gun is the murder weapon because the first police officer on the scene told me so." Now, in this scenario we are assuming that it is in fact true that the gun is the murder weapon. Furthermore, you and the police officer both believe the gun is the murder weapon. You both hold the same proposition to be true. And the proposition is, in fact, true. Now let's look at *your* belief. How did you come to have it? Did the first officer convince you with evidence or convert you? Well, suppose he just said to you, "Here, this is the murder weapon." Suppose you now believe this. How could you, based only on his say-so? The way you could is the same way that people are often able to believe something without any convincing evidence just because someone whom they accept as an authority told them so. Sometimes people use external authorities to short-circuit their own cognitive process; it is as if the brain, lacking the evidence for something it wants to believe, and being able to convince itself with evidence but not convert itself without evidence, subjugates itself to an external authority as a way of getting around its own cognitive apparatus. The image of the authority is the brain's way of getting around its inability to seduce itself directly; it has to do it indirectly, through the image of that authority.

The whole process is an elaborate self-deception. In some ways (though I shouldn't wish to push this analogy too far) it is a bit like the brain giving itself an orgasm through a fantasy. Why doesn't the brain just give itself the pleasant sensation without the need to seduce itself through manipulation of its own psychology by its own images? The fact that it doesn't suggests that, perhaps for evolutionary reasons, it can't. But it can trick itself. Likewise with getting itself to believe something that it would like to believe. The brain can't just directly reset, i.e., rewire itself. But it can, indirectly, using its own psychology, trick itself.

So in the simple case of the murder weapon, the Yes attitude toward the proposition "The gun is the murder weapon," instead of being caused by a cognitive attitude conditioned by the evidence, is itself the cause of the cognitive attitude: The psychology conditions the logical setting within the propositional framework. The process is backward but the effect still feels, psychologically, the same. The psychological Yes attitude results from emotional persuasion by an authority, which then makes it possible to hang the proposition from this attitude, instead of the psychological Yes attitude resulting from a cognitive attitude of True.

Your belief that the gun is the murder weapon is thus belief by conversion. Believing *that* the officer believes something to be the case and believing that what the police officer believes *is* the case is not enough: To have a belief by conviction you must also have evidential justification that what the officer believes to be true is true. Otherwise, your belief is belief by conversion, regardless of the faith you have in the officer. It does not qualify even as a good hunch. You could say, "I have a hunch he's telling the truth," or "I have a hunch he's lying," but now you're just reporting a psychological feeling that, unless you have some justification that it's a good barometer of the truth, is the same as guessing. It's like saying "I guess so" with your feelings. It's arbitrary, but the arbitrariness is hidden by a real psychological feeling. And because that feeling is not under your conscious control, it feels not arbitrary, not make-believe, but *real.*

Suppose, then, that we ask the police officer why he believes that the gun was the murder weapon. He says, "Because the gun is black and there are black curtains in the room where the victim was found." Now, again, the gun is the murder weapon. You both believe that the gun is the murder weapon and you both happen to hold a proposition true that is, in fact, true. But the officer's belief happens to be true because he happens to have stumbled upon the gun by chance and he made a terrible inference (black curtains, therefore black murder weapon) that, by luck, happens to lead to the right conclusion. The jury would rightly conclude that although the gun *might* be the murder weapon, certainly neither you nor the officer has convincing evidence that the murder weapon is the gun.

Notice now that you and the police officer both may have done terrible damage to the case. By presenting the real murder weapon as evidence in an incorrect and erroneous way, you may have cast doubt in the minds of the jury about the gun; in that way, you may cause great harm for the very cause in which you yourself most believe. Blind faith, like a bad argument, is dangerous; it can blind not just you but others as well. (This would be similar, for instance, to when criminals go free because the police did not follow the correct procedure in arresting them.)

Suppose, however, that another detective comes forth with a fingerprint analysis and ballistic results. These confirm the gun was in the hand of the accused murderer, that it was fired at about the time of the murder, and that the bullets in the gun are of the same sort as the bullet in the victim. The second detective, too, believes that the gun is the murder weapon. He, too, holds a proposition to be true that is, in fact, true. Unlike you and the first officer on the scene, however, the second detective doesn't just hold that particular proposition to be true; he doesn't have only the psychological attitude "Yes" and the cognitive attitude "True." In a very important sense, as we shall see, because his psychological attitude is based on the cognitive attitude, *he has even more: He holds the very thing that makes that proposition true,* namely, the cognitive attitude based on evidence that makes that proposition function, within the propositional framework, as True.

This should strike you as rather remarkable, if not preposterous. After all, haven't we already established that what makes a proposition true has nothing to do with you but, rather, is based on the way the world is? Yes; what makes the proposition "The Earth goes around the sun" true is the orbit of the Earth. But according to our Principle of Propositional Relativity, a proposition is true or false relative to what other propositions are available *in our descriptions of the world.* And we don't have direct access to the world but only indirect access, through our descriptions.

There was a time when the proposition "The Earth goes around the sun" was not available. But was not the true orbit of the Earth, even then, available? Well, available to *whom?* To someone whose perceptual and conceptual apparatus has no moving Earth in it, *that* description of the solar system is *not* available. To someone with the concept of a moving earth, that description is available. *But what about the real description?*

Two things must be kept in mind. First, *descriptions are propositional models.* Second, *descriptions require describers.* When you're thinking about a "real" description of the solar system, what are you doing? You're trying to picture the solar system being some

84

particular way independently of anyone's picture of it, that is, independently of any model. But *you're* picturing the solar system that way rather than some other, and *you're* holding *that* picture—that model—rather than some other! That description's being *evidently so*—the evidential justification for it—is specifically tied to somebody's description, someone having some such picture—a model—of it as "really being so." Descriptions, after all, which consist in propositions, are also part of the world through which we interact with each other and with ourselves. A sentence is meaningless unless there is some textual scheme of interpretation, some propositional framework, a description, or model, into which it fits as a true or false proposition, that is, a propositional framework within which that proposition's cognitive attitude functions as True. You could say that space, time, and matter themselves describe the true motions of the solar system independently of any observer. But, first, these too are descriptions within a propositional framework. Second, even if you conceive of space, time, and matter in the abstract, as having some such-and-such but unspecified mind-independent attributes that make some such-and-such but unspecified motions, this picture too is a description, a model within a propositional framework. There is no way out: We are limited to talking about our descriptions of the world.

This goes against the conventional wisdom, which in its naive realism says that the "true picture" of the solar system, with either the sun moving around the Earth or the Earth moving around the sun, exists prior to, and independently of, the propositional framework through which our picturing of it, our model, is constructed. According to the naive realism view, truth exists in some absolute sense, independently of any propositional framework. According to the view we are here developing, the only truth we can talk about is truth in terms of cognitive attitudes as they exist within a propositional framework, that is, within a model of the world.

In our courtroom analogy, this would mean that it is a mistake to call the gun "the murder weapon" unless there is a propositional framework in which it can be held to be so with some level of justification. This sounds preposterous until you remember that when you're picturing the scenario, you have a way of keeping track in your head of the gun from the murder to the trial, such as saying to yourself, "All right, now this gun *is* the gun that, unbeknownst to the first officer, was the gun used in the murder." *That's* a propositional framework, a model. Or you make some actual pictures in your head and assign to them some specific significance and meaning. That too is a model, a propositional framework. In the world you imagine there is some such objective, third-person point of view on all things—perhaps God's?—keeping track of everything. But that too is a picture, a model, painted in a propositional framework.

Thus in saying that the second detective holds not just a true proposition but also that which makes the proposition true, I am saying that he holds that upon which the proposition's cognitive attitude—whether it functions as True or False—is based and, furthermore, that this is all we have to go on! Which means that, in the case of scriptures, it is a mistake to say that what we have before us is the word of God unless someone can provide a propositional framework that reasonably and justifiably *makes* it so.

4.4 Derivative Evidence

Let us suppose some particular scripture that Tom believes to be the word of God *is* the word of God. That is, God actually wrote the words or directly inspired someone to write them. Again we must ask: How did Tom come to believe that his particular holy book is the word of God?

Probably Tom came to his belief via his parents, who told him that a particular book was the word of God, or some religious authority told him this. Or, Tom just came across it himself and decided that this was the word of God. We are now supposing that the book in question is, in fact, the word of God. The question is: How did Tom's authorities—and how did Tom—reach this conclusion? Probably Tom's parents were told this by the religious authority, who in turn was told this by some other religious authority, and so on. With each step, the link between Tom and God becomes weaker and weaker. Why? Because even if the belief being passed down from one authority to another is true, at each step of the way, one authority accepting the word of another authority *is but the passing of a proposition without any propo-*

sitional framework. It makes the proposition, as such, meaningless in the sense that it is just a sentence, neither true nor false because it has been taken out of any possible context that could possibly make it true. It is like the first officer telling a second officer that the gun is the murder weapon, who tells a third officer, who tells a fourth, and so on, until finally the word gets to you. *The amount of evidential justification being passed down the line is absolutely zero.*

Lest you think that I've loaded the example by making the first officer's inference ("black curtains, black gun, therefore . . .") a bad one, notice that in the case of scriptures whether or not God actually did write them is completely irrelevant. To see why, suppose the first officer was in fact the murderer. Suppose he tells the second officer, "I killed Jones with this gun." He is confessing to the murder of Jones. If on the basis of this you believe that the gun is the murder weapon and that the first officer was the murderer, you actually do have some evidence. The confession is evidence. The fellow might be lying or covering up, but you are hearing that officer confessing to you, which certainly gives you some evidence.

Suppose now that, armed with this strong evidence, you report the confession to Officer C. On the basis of your report, C now believes what you believe. Does C have a belief by conviction or belief by conversion? *Your* belief is belief by conviction. C's belief is belief by conversion! Why? *Because confessions cannot be passed down by word of mouth.* In an important sense, cognitive attitudes are like the brain's own confessions about what it experienced, in that they cannot be passed down by word of mouth. Only if a proposition is passed down along with the evidence so that the proper relationship between the cognitive attitude and the psychological attitude is preserved can the psychological attitude, which is based on that cognitive attitude, be belief by conviction rather than belief by conversion.

In other words, the strongest chain is only as strong as the weakest link. As in the story above, any number of people in this long chain of believers may have come to believe what is, in fact, a true proposition not because they were convinced by evidence but simply because they were persuaded, either by an emotional conversion or through indoctrination, or conditioning by authority; whomever the belief was accepted from may in turn have been converted instead of convinced, and so on, thereby breaking the link between Tom and what that proposition represents.

Thus, once again, with regard to the question of whether scriptures are convincing evidence, unless Tom has been convinced through evidence that indeed this is the word of God, Tom's belief is merely an emotional persuasion by conversion and for Tom *those scriptures are not evidence.* In other words, what makes it possible for us as philosophers to determine whether scriptures are evidence for the existence of God is that—as if by magic, literally without having to leave our armchairs—the most important work to be done on this question has to do with *us.* We don't have direct access to the authors of the scriptures. We do, however, have direct access to the authors of our propositional frameworks: ourselves. How the proposition stands within us is about us. It requires self-examination. Which is difficult but "doable."

And so what is ultimately at issue here is precisely this: Does the Yes-Believer, on the basis of scripture, have convincing evidence that God exists? The answer depends not on how strongly you believe in the scripture—in the amount of psychological confidence you have—but, rather, on how you came to believe in the scripture, whether you came to believe it was the word of God because of evidence presented in a proper manner. If not, the scriptures give the Yes-Believer no evidence whatsoever for the existence of God. None.

Suppose, for instance, that religious authority A, who told Tom, or Tom's parents, that the particular holy book which Tom takes to be the word of God *is* the word of God, came to believe this through conversion. People often do this; no human is infallible. The probability that the religious authority's belief came about through conversion rather than conviction may be high or it may be low, but it is not 0. Likewise for authority B, from whom authority A's belief is derived. The same is true for authority C, who taught B, and likewise for D who taught C, and so on across the centuries. The more authorities there are between Tom and the original author of the scripture, the probability of there being no weak link gets weaker and weaker.

Again, keep in mind that what is here in question is not whether the belief that a particular holy book is the word of God is true but, rather, whether the belief is based on conviction by evidence or on conversion through emotional persuasion. Emotional persuasion, which carries no evidential justification, can be passed down without evidence. Evidential conviction cannot.

4.5 Conflicting Evidence and Divine Inspiration

The problems raised thus far for the Yes-Believer who believes that God exists based on scripture are compounded by the fact that there is not just one holy book but many. If there were just one book that all the authorities over the ages agreed was the word of God, the difficulties thus far raised would still be there but they would be somewhat diminished. Of course there would then be the problem of lack of corroboration, since having just one source gives you a corroboration of 0. However, the Yes-Believer does not have that problem but the opposite problem. The problem is this. Suppose Tom is a Christian. Tom believes the New Testament is the word of God. Furthermore, Tom believes that scriptures are exempt from the various difficulties raised thus far in this chapter. According to Tom, the New Testament is thus evidence that Jesus Christ existed, that he was no ordinary mortal, that he was the one and only true God (or part of the one true Holy Trinity) and that therefore God exists. Is Tom's belief then not belief by conversion but belief by conviction?

Hardly. By this reasoning, Tom would have to conclude just the opposite: Jesus Christ was *not* God. Why? *Because a dozen other holy books claim that someone else, not Jesus, is God.* To see why, let us go back to the courtroom case. Suppose we get a police report that says "Jones is the murderer." A police report is quite a document. It is not just the testimony of eyewitnesses; it is the testimony of police officers who have sworn to uphold the law. It looks bad for Jones. But then the defense attorney presents a surprise: ten more police reports, from other precincts, that name ten other people as each being the sole culprit! On the grounds that police reports are convincing evidence, what are we to conclude on the basis of these reports? Well, eleven people are accused. There is one police report per suspect, each of which weighs heavily in favor of a guilty verdict. But, for each suspect, there are *ten* police reports, which together weigh twelve times more heavily in favor of the suspect being innocent.

In the case of holy books, we are in a somewhat similar situation. The God of the Bhagavad Gita claims to be the one true God. The God of the Koran claims to be the one true God. The God of the Old Testament claims to be the one true God. The God of the New Testament claims to be one true God (or one of the three true Gods who together are the one true God). The God of the Theravada Buddhist Canons claims there is no God! And so on. Would the real God please stand up?

But now it gets even worse. Suppose it turned out, in the courtroom example, that an officer presents a police report from his precinct and, at the same time, suppresses the conflicting police reports from other precincts. What would we conclude? Wouldn't we conclude that somebody is being set up, that it is a clever conspiracy? Then we must ask the Yes-Believer: Did the religious authorities who indoctrinated you with a particular set of religious beliefs while you were young and most deeply impressionable present, say, the Bhagavad Gita in the same light they presented, say, the Old Testament? Did you study the Koran? Were you given the Pali canons? If not, why not? Are they not as good as the ones you were given? Less accurate? Would the leaders of those other religions agree? And so on.

Note, too, that there is a grave similarity between "world view" acquisition and language acquisition. While you are young you can learn a foreign language by immersion in a few months. To teach you a foreign language when you are older, with or without immersion, takes many years and sometimes is impossible; even when it succeeds, the new language always will seem foreign. So we must ask whether presenting a particular religious view to children is really fair to them. We say we have "freedom of religion" in the United States. But what this means, in effect, is that you have the freedom to indoctrinate your children with whatever beliefs, superstitious or otherwise, you want, forever binding them (probably in the way you were bound) to those particular views. The brain of a Catholic, for instance, may remain bound to the Catholic world view even if the Catholic at some point rebels.

You might say that it was not your religious authorities' intent to teach you religious views other than the ones they believed in. Perhaps that is the whole of it. But, in that case, clearly you are not getting evidence but, at best, emotional persuasion through belief indoctrination.

Thus, if someone's belief that God exists is based on acceptance of a particular holy book as the word of God, this individual has been converted into that belief, not convinced of it. Other, conflicting holy books exist. Unless the Yes-Believer has evidence that the other holy books are not true, and so on for the other difficulties, the belief is, at best, merely the result of emotional persuasion; it is belief by conversion. The proposition held to be true might even be true: God might exist. Or, even if God does not exist, the belief might be of great value (or not). And so on. But the evidential justification is *absolutely zero:* it carries no evidence whatsoever for the existence of God.

In other words, belief by conversion through scripture may be beneficial, it may make you feel good (or not), and so on. *The very scriptures might even be evidence for the existence of God.* But if you came to believe them on the basis of emotional persuasion, then *even if every word written in them is true, they are not evidence for you.* The possibility of their being evidence for you has been destroyed by those who indoctrinated you with them. To indoctrinate you with the truth—to persuade you of the truth rather than convince you—is to sever you from the truth forever.

Well, maybe not forever. There is a way to turn belief by conversion into belief by conviction. All you have to do is start afresh and begin looking at the evidence. And that is precisely what this book is designed to do. We are trying to get to a neutral starting point from which such a journey can begin afresh, so that you can finally, perhaps for the first time, really ask the question "Does God exist?" with an open mind, without any prejudice, without having your head severed from your heart by imposed answers.

4.6 Intrinsic Difficulties: The Problem of Inconsistency

Are scriptures convincing evidence for God? We have thus far focused on extrinsic difficulties, that is, problems that arise not with anything that the scriptures actually say but that are external to those scriptures. We now turn to the merits of the individual testimony itself presented in a particular holy book. Can it provide you with convincing evidence for God? In a courtroom, the testimony of witness A can be discredited by the testimony of witness B, if B contradicts A. They can't both be right. That would be an extrinsic difficulty with a particular witness's testimony. But what if the witness contradicts himself, or somehow contradicts other propositions that have a high level of relative evidential justification?

In the case of most holy books, there are certain passages that do not square with the purported facts. Such discrepancies raise doubts about whether this could truly be the word of God. Each blemish may not be so potentially devastating with regard to claims of belief by conversion; but if the question is one of belief by conviction, such difficulties become much more important.

Another sort of intrinsic difficulty, of even grander proportions, concerns the question of how to interpret some particular holy book. Consider, for instance, the sheer variety of Christian religions each of which claims to be based on the same book. Catholics and Protestants, to name but two, differ so widely in their interpretations that church leaders and followers alike sometimes consider it a matter of life and death. Why is this such a problem for the evidential status of holy books? Well, it is one thing to claim that you have evidence that your particular holy book is true when it is clear what the book says and what it means. But given the latitude of interpretation, the burden is upon the Yes-Believer to provide not only evidence that this book is the word of God, but that the correct interpretation of the holy book is such-and-such. This means, in effect, that the Catholic Yes-Believer must have evidence that the Protestant interpretation is false, that the Quaker interpretation is false, the Seventh Day Adventist interpretation is false, and so on. Given the numerous alternative interpretations, grave doubts can easily be raised about anyone's claim to belief by conviction, rather than by conversion, regarding any of them.

This type of problem, in a nutshell, is that for some particular set of beliefs to be beliefs by conviction (based on evidence) rather than beliefs by conversion (based on emotional persuasion), the propositions constituting that family of beliefs must bear some minimally resilient linguistic structure with regard to the truths they represent: If there is too much ambiguity, if the propositions are open to too many conflicting interpretations, they cannot sustain the truth, which itself is not ambiguous. This would be analogous to saying that at some point a photograph, if it is too blurry, cannot properly be called a true picture of you.

In other words, suppose you have a police rendering of a suspect. Could it possibly be a "true" rendering if person A looks at it and sees a black woman while person B looks at it and sees a white man? If this wide latitude of interpretation is common with regard to this particular drawing, then this latitude of interpretation itself can be a significant factor in deciding that the drawing is not a reliable rendition of the truth.

Similarly, since beliefs are propositional attitudes and propositions are sentences that are either true or false, if the latitude of interpretation is too wide, then this casts doubt on whether the sentence is even a *possible* rendition of the truth. Consider, for instance, the following sentence:

"God is love."

Is this sentence true? *Is it even a proposition?* Well, perhaps. But, given the latitude of possible interpretation of these words, it seems that, as it stands, this sentence is just too ambiguous for us to say whether it is true or false. Furthermore, given the nature of the language in which this sentence lives, the words as they stand are just not precise enough for us to tell whether they even *possibly* represent the truth or not. Therefore (barring some disambiguating explanations), the sentence "God is love" has a tough time making it even to the propositional level, much less the propositional *attitude* (belief) level. This means that, under the scenario just described, someone who professes to believe that God is love *is probably mistaken.* Not because God is *not* love. Because beliefs are propositional attitudes and "God is love" is, by the looks of it, not even a proposition. If it isn't a proposition, it cannot be a belief. There may be a psychological attitude toward some proposition, and this may be the closest the person can come to saying what it is, but unless the person can do some explicative self-searching, that sentence is not it. No conviction is warranted.

4.7 The Big Bang: A Smoking Gun?

As evidence for the existence of God, what most holy books have to offer are various miracle stories. Supposedly, these miraculous events occurred as reported in the particular scripture, have no naturalistic explanation, and thereby present us today with convincing evidence for the existence of God on the basis of events that happened in the past.

As evidence, these miracle stories are only as convincing as the scriptures themselves are good documents, historically accurate, and so on. We have already seen some reasons why the scriptures are not even evidence, much less convincing evidence. We now turn to a difficulty that raises grave doubts about whether the scriptures can even *possibly* be evidence.

Clearly, the miracle stories described supposedly happened a long time ago in a land far, far away. It is difficult at best to authenticate the stories. But this is not the issue I am presently about to raise. The question now will be: *Is it possible that holy books are an attempt to bury the path to evidence?* Are they cover-ups of the best evidence for the existence of God? This may sound preposterous. But, given the argument I am about to present, it may have to be weighed as a real possibility. Consider, then, the following.

Many people who believe God exists also happen to believe, as a matter of fact, that the best evidence for the existence of God comes from the particular scriptures that comprise the official holy book of their religion. It is also true that, as a matter of fact, many people who go to church, synagogue, temple, or shrine, and who profess to believe that God exists, are merely pretending. Not all believe as they say they do. Some act only as if they do believe; they say they believe, but they do not really believe. There are many such so-called "Sunday believers." While they sit in church or temple they believe, sort of, and then the rest of the week they do many of the things forbidden them by their holy books under threat of eternal damnation. Perhaps it is only weakness of will. But they misbehave according to the tenets of their own religions in so many ways that one wonders: What makes such pretense possible? Is it not that, deep down, they do not really believe what they profess to believe? In other words, using our terminology, their cognitive attitudes do not correspond with their psychological attitudes; it is a case of self-deception.

Suppose Jones says, "I truly believe in a Tree God, yes I do, a Tree God who sentences anyone who cuts down a tree to eternity in hell. I praise the Tree God forever." Jones then cuts down a tree to make a bench in his backyard! Surely this would be some evidence that Jones does not really believe what he professes! And surely if Jones says, "Oh, my will was weak," we should doubt him!

Or, suppose Smith says, "I truly believe that if you lie and cheat you will go to hell," and then Smith lies to his friend and cheats her *out of ten dollars*. This, too, would be some evidence that Smith does not truly believe what he professes to truly believe.

One does not have to be a scriptural expert on the various holy books and an all-knowing psychologist to realize that most people who belong to some of the major religions do not take their professed beliefs seriously. I am now suggesting that what makes this possible is that, in many cases, the scriptures are recognized by these people to be rather shoddy evidence. After all, people are not dumb. Once they think about it a little, they know perfectly well what counts as evidence and what does not. Even the most uneducated people in our society do a superb job when required to serve on juries. Their brains and minds function extremely well when it comes to serious matters. So it stands to reason that there must be some way they have of getting themselves off the hook when it comes to their own religious views.

My argument, then, is this. There is better evidence for the existence of God than scriptures. If people were really convinced, they would become deeply religious beings. Deeply religious beings, such as the ones described in the holy books—Jesus, Buddha, Mohammed, Krishna—do not make it their top priority to gather worldly goods. Jesus, Buddha, Mohammed, and Krishna do not wage military or economic war on other people. Indeed, if the spiritual beings described in the various holy books have anything in common, it is that they preach *against* worldly possessions! Various cultures seeking strong economies and world dominance must find a way to get their people off the track from the best evidence so that they will *not* become deeply religious, so that while on the surface they can be religiously reverent, deep down they will in fact view the spiritual founders of their own religions with doubt. Thereby, they would avoid the spiritual life that their natures, left to their own devices, might lead them to.

Hence the existence of popular religions *may be to keep people from being truly religious!*

This seems as preposterous as, if true, it is insidious. But it is possible that what I have just described is true. *How* possible it is depends on the quantity, quality, and corroboration of the other available evidence for the existence of God. What is the other available evidence?

Well, the strongest evidence from scriptures concerns miraculous events that have no other explanation except a supernatural one, leading us to posit, by elimination, the presence of divine intervention. These reports describe events that happened a long time ago in lands far away and therefore subsume the evidential justification of the reported events under the category of the validity and authenticity of historical documents. Here all sorts of new difficulties arise, leaving lots of room for interpretation, argument, dissent, and so on. The scriptural evidence is no better than the best means that religious and philosophical scholars, historians, and scientists have for reaching the past. It is well known by these scholars and historians that even the best means available do not provide a direct viewing of the past.[2]

All documents exist in the present. They must be interpreted from the vantage point of the present. For instance, suppose you have a book that says it is the official story of David Crockett. Whether or not it is does not depend on what it says but, rather, on what the historical evidence surrounding it says. Who was Crockett? What was he really like? What were his views? If there are several different and conflicting accounts, this will make it that much more difficult for the historian to decide on the degree to which the events reported in the book are true. And so on.

Once you place the question of the nature and existence of God into a historical setting, the evidential status of your beliefs becomes subsumed by the best available historical methods. These are not infallible. They are often unreliable. Usually they are proprietary to some orthodoxy in charge of the "official" interpretation.

Consider the following. Suppose it turned out that there was better evidence than any scripture for the existence of God *right here and now*. Suppose this better evidence was all around you, all the time. Not that this evidence, necessarily, absolutely *proves* the existence of God, nor even necessarily warrants a conviction.

Rather, it is just that the present evidence here and now is more convincing than the evidence from scripture. What if there is such evidence? What would we make of anyone who tried to divert attention from this better evidence, which is here and now and available to all who wish to look at it, to evidence that is based on reports of people no longer alive, whose authenticity and strength is predicated on what the present religious authorities assert to be so?

In other words, what if there turned out to be a smoking gun, but the prosecutor, who knew about the smoking gun, had instead presented documents of dubious origin in lieu of the smoking gun? "The smoking gun" is often used in legal jargon as some telling evidence that makes for an open and shut case. Suppose a videotape of Smith brutally killing Jones exists. The prosecutor's leading witness is a self-professed psychic who claims that Smith did it. Why put a psychic on the stand if the videotape exists? To do so would be to sabotage the proceedings. The videotape, on the other hand, would be the smoking gun. And so on.

What I am claiming, then, is that in the case of God, there is indeed *better* evidence than scripture: the universe. It exists. It is here. It is well ordered. The point isn't that we might not be able to account for the existence not just of us but of everything. It's not that we can prove the universe and everything in it is a miraculous, unaccounted-for phenomenon of the first rank. There *may* be some natural explanation for the existence of the universe. But compared to the evidence presented in scriptures, the universe is a smoking gun, a miracle of cosmic proportion. Shouldn't we therefore turn our attention to the universe?

Again, the point is not that the existence of the universe proves that God exists, nor even that it warrants a conviction—not even that it is convincing evidence. We shall consider these questions in the next chapter. Rather, the point is that relative to the existence of the universe, the existence of scriptures pales by comparison. If the Yes-Believer thinks the most convincing evidence for the existence of God is found in scripture taken to be the word of God, then regardless of whether the scripture is the word of God, *the Yes-Believer is wrong.* The scripture may indeed be the word of God such that everything in it may indeed be perfectly true. But weighed against the existence of the universe, inkblots on a page, regardless of their content, must, at best, come in second. And, given the difficulties raised thus far with regard to the inability of scriptures to provide us with evidentially convincing beliefs about God, how did the Yes-Believer come to the mistaken belief that scripture makes for better evidence than the universe? Who deceived the Yes-Believer? How? Why? *

Scriptures may or may not be written by the hand of God. Even if the scriptures are correct, you do not *have evidence* that they are the work of God. But, if they are correct, the universe itself *is* the work of God, and even if the scriptures are incorrect, the universe still, by the looks of it, is not man-made but may be the result of some cosmic miracle of the most unbelievable, incomprehensible kind. So why would anyone, or any scripture, direct us to attend to what is, at best, a possible work of God, rather than attending to what, if that very scripture is correct, is definitely and unmistakenly the direct work of God?

Few religions and few holy books say forget these inkblots you are looking at (though some do) and look, instead, directly at the world or at yourself to find God. Most scriptures say look at these words, at me, me, me, not at the actualities surrounding you on all sides. Is this not the mind's own self-deception of the most unholy kind?

Notes

1. See the sections on dissociation and multiple personality in my "Finding Our Selves: Individuation, Identification, and MPD," forthcoming, *Philosophical Psychology,* and also Kolak & Martin, eds., *Self & Identity,* Macmillan, 1991.
2. For a detailed account, see the "The Historical Challenge" section of *Self, Cosmos, God,* Kolak & Martin, eds., Harcourt Brace Jovanovich, 1993.

Did God Create the Universe?

5.0 The Origin of the Universe

WHERE DID THE UNIVERSE COME FROM? WHAT IS ITS ORIGIN—THE ORIGIN of *everything:* space, time, energy, matter? Many regard the existence of the universe to be convincing evidence for the existence of God. They think the universe is so convincing as evidence that the proposition "God exists" has as high a degree of evidential justification as, say, "There was a Roman Empire," "I had great-grandparents," "Atoms exist," "Dinosaurs once roamed the Earth," "Australians exist," and so on; it is, they claim, a warranted conviction. The Roman Empire might be a historical fiction, you might have been immaculately conceived, the evidence for dinosaurs might have been faked, and so on. But the amount of evidence is overwhelming that unless some such extraordinarily unlikely state of affairs is the case, we have reasonable evidence to have a warranted conviction about the existence of Rome, great-grandparents, atoms, dinosaurs, Australians, etc.; indeed, these beliefs belong at the very center of our zones of evidential justification. Likewise, there may be some other explanation for the existence of the universe, such as it coming about spontaneously and randomly by accident, but this is so extraordinarily unlikely that the existence of the universe justifies the belief that God exists to a very high degree.

Does the universe provide evidential justification for the existence of God to the degree that we have evidential justification for the existence of Rome, great-grandparents, atoms, Australians and so on? We must remember to be fair; we should not require more of God than of Rome. The same standards apply. And here the Yes-Believer points to what even the most hard-nosed skeptic would have to admit is one awesome object by any standards: the universe.

Suppose Carl is a Yes-Believer. One night, staring up at the cosmos, amazed by the wonder of it all, suddenly it just felt true: God created all this! The Yes-attitude toward the proposition "God created the universe" occurred spontaneously to Carl while he was contemplating the cosmos. Carl claims to be convinced that God exists. We ask what convinced him. The answer: "The universe convinced me!" Given what we said in the previous chapter about belief by evidential conviction vs. belief by emotional conversion, however, Carl is clearly mistaken. Not because God didn't create the universe. God may well have. Carl's response is wrong because he was converted, not convinced. In a sense, he was converted into believing that God exists by his own emotional response to the universe. This is no more evidence for the existence of God than, say, if one night, staring up at the cosmos, you're emotionally moved by the absurdity of existence to believe that what we call the universe is but an experiment in some giant alien's petri dish. This would be no evidence whatsoever that the universe was created by a giant alien. It would be, at best, self-persuasion through (your own) emotion.

In the last chapter we saw that it is not usually possible to persuade yourself that some proposition is true. If you want to affect your beliefs, you have to do it by convincing yourself with evidence. The case we've just considered suggests that sometimes, when we are in a heightened emotional state, such as the feeling of awe produced by staring up at the cosmos on a starry night, we can at that moment convert ourselves to something which we would like to be true, or think may be true. It is as if the brain uses such special moments of extraordinarily heightened sensation to implant into its propositional framework some proposition for which it lacks sufficient evidence required for belief by conviction. To be evidence for the existence of God it is not enough that the universe inspires us. It will not do simply to point and declare: "Look! There! God!" It is not like saying, "Look! There! The Universe!" There is no denying that the proposition "the universe exists" is justified. But what reason do we have to go from "the universe exists" to "God exists"?

At this point Carl might respond with the following: You would have to be really apathetic and uninquisitive, or a really hardened skeptic, not to feel amazement and wonder at how all this could be here. Plants, people, and planets don't just appear out of nothing. They come into existence as the result of some prior cause. Thus, just as we can infer the existence of your great-grandmother from the fact that you exist, so too we can infer the existence of God from the fact that the universe exists.

5.1 Homo-Magicus: Creation of Something from Nothing

It is difficult to imagine how it could be possible that you had no great-grandmother. But we can imagine it. You might be the first of a new species of "spontaneous homo-magicus," beings who appear on the scene suddenly and from nowhere, magically altering historical records and brainwashing everyone, including themselves, with an entire, faked history. This of course is hardly a likely story; certainly, it does not justify denying that, in spite of the fact that neither you nor anyone else can *prove* that you are not a homo-magicus, nevertheless, you do have enough evidence to justify your belief that you had great-grandparents. It belongs well in the center of the zones of evidential justification.

It is difficult to imagine that you really could have suddenly and spontaneously popped into existence from nothing. But it is not impossible. We just did it, using the concept of homo-magicus. Where did this concept come from? I invented it using one of those "exotic thinking" scenarios that are so important to philosophy. Like the concept of an invulnerable Superman who flies and has X-ray vision, the concept of homo-magicus may be a conglomerate derived from various experiences and ideas. Superman is an imaginative and exaggerated combination of various things, like a strongman, a bird, X-ray machines, and so on. Homo-magicus is an imaginative and exaggerated combination of things like conspiracies, seeing rabbits pulled out of hats, magic tricks in which people disappear, and so on. All concepts are inventions of the human mind. Some, like the concept of a waterfall, the concept called number, the concept of gravity, and so on, we have good reason to believe apply to the real world. Other concepts, such as Zeus, the Fountain of Youth, the ether (a substance that pervades the entire universe), and phlogiston (a material substance that causes combustion and inflammability), were once thought to apply to reality but are no longer considered as such. Others, like the tooth fairy, Santa Claus, and the Wicked Witch of the West, were never invented for the purpose of trying to apply new concepts to the real world but, rather, to amuse children (or perhaps convert them into believing certain things).

What about the concept of homo-magicus? It does not, as far as we know, apply to the real world. We might, though, all be of the species homo-magicus, presently self-deceiving ourselves into thinking we are the result of a long history, each of us having spontaneously popped into existence out of nothing. But if it is difficult to accept that we are such beings, how much more difficult is it to accept that the whole universe had such a spontaneous and unaccounted for origin, uncaused, from *absolutely nothing!* If the concept of homo-magicus is hard to swallow, the concept of Cosmo-Magicus is that much harder still.

So perhaps the universe is convincing evidence for God. The Yes-Believer would in that case be justified in believing that, on the basis of the existence of the universe, God exists. We might not know the precise nature of the originating source of the universe, just as we might not know *who* your great-grandparents were. But even if you are an orphan, we are justified in believing that you had a great-grandmother; we just don't know who she was. Similarly, we might not know who or what created the universe, but that there was a creator—that the universe did not just spontaneously appear from nothing without any cause—seems to have even more convincing evidence than that you had great-grandparents. If your belief that everyone who exists has a great-grandmother is reasonably justified, the belief that the universe has a God may also be reasonably justified to a very high degree, perhaps even at or near the center of the zones of evidential justification. Perhaps the existence of the universe makes the belief that God exists a warranted conviction.

We do not know all the details in either case. But just as we do not need to know what your great-grandmother was like to be justified in believing that you had a great-grandmother, so too we might not need to know what God is like to be justified in believing that the universe had a creator. But we *do* know what it is like to create something. It takes skill, intelligence, energy. Movies, art, books, societies, technology, and so on all require a great amount of creativity and dedication. How much more awesome is the universe than any of the things we humans have created. How much more awesome than us must be the creator of the entire universe!

5.2 Finding the Right Cause: What Is the Role of Argument?

A strong case for the existence of God—or so it seems. As is often the case in courtroom dramas, what at first glance presents itself as obvious and incontrovertible evidence ends up falling apart under cross-examination. It is not necessarily that the piece of evidence—a murder weapon, fingerprints, eyewitness testimony, or whatever—entirely disappears or ceases to exist. Rather, the *argument*, which uses that piece of evidence to finger the accused, turns out to be a *bad argument*.

There is no such thing as "evidence without argument." Presenting evidence for something consists in two things: the evidential object (i.e., the gun, the eyewitness testimony, the police report, the fingerprints, etc.) and the evidential argument (the reasoning involved in using that evidential object to finger the accused). *As evidence, the object is only as good as the argument.* And the problem with presenting the existence of the universe as evidence for the existence of God is that the evidential object—in this case, the universe—is a wondrous centerpiece of a bad argument.

Keep in mind: Presently at issue is whether a Yes-Believer could be convinced (not just persuaded) that God exists on the basis of the existence of the universe. Granted, the universe exists. We have our evidential object. But what is the status of the argument linking that evidential object to the suspect it supposedly fingers, namely, God?

If Carl thinks the universe is evidence for God independently of any argument linking the universe to God, then clearly Carl does not have an evidential basis for his belief. He believes it; he believes the existence of the universe provides evidence for God. This belief may turn out to be true. But if Carl calls his belief justified, or if he thinks he is convinced that God exists, *then Carl is wrong.* His belief is unjustified. He has, at best, been persuaded that God exists.

In fact, Carl's belief is as unjustified and unreasonable as the prosecutor tossing a gun to the jury and saying, "There, see? Jones is the murderer." The jury sees a gun. By itself, what does that show? That a gun exists! You have to make the case that this gun is the murder weapon and that indeed it was Jones who used it on the victim. This requires making an argument. Even if you have a videotape, you can't just show it and point to the screen and say, "See? Jones is killing Smith." You are pointing, after all, not at the event but at electrons on a screen; you have to link the videotape to the actual murder, link the images on the screen to Jones, make the case that it isn't an actor, and so on, *all of which require making arguments.*

So what is the *argument* linking the universe to God? Carl has his evidence: the existence of the universe. This evidence is presented in the form of a proposition that is the first premise of an argument, call it A1, that might go something like this:

A1
1. The universe exists.
2. "Q exists" implies "P exists," where P is the cause of Q.

Therefore,

3. The cause of the universe exists.

Propositions (1) and (2) are the premises, (3) is the conclusion. Proposition (1) we know is true (in the relative sense, of course, with a very high degree of evidential justification, placing it at

1.0 in our zones of evidential justification chart). Is (2) also true? Well, let's think about it. Can we be justified, on the basis that a tree exists, in believing that the cause of the tree exists? Depends on how precisely we wish to use words. Trees come from seeds. No seed, no tree. Tree, therefore seed. But the seed is no longer there. Or is it? Is that the seed there, grown up into an oak? At what point does the seed cease to exist and the seedling begin? When does a tree begin to exist as a tree rather than as a seedling?

Notice what happens. Ordinary language quickly turns wobbly and we have to proceed slowly and carefully. Words and sentences don't have absolute, clear-cut meanings independently of any context or usage. We must carefully choose the borders we wish to highlight using our words, to be sure of what we are thinking about. Thought, after all, consists in the manipulation of sentences to construct models, and alternative models, of reality. If our sentences are not clear, our thoughts will not be clear. We will make a bad model; our conceptual maps will only get us more lost. We must therefore pay very close attention to the medium in which we think: language. Our language must become a precise tool. Ordinarily, when we are just chatting, this may be desirable but it is by no means essential. When going on a philosophical journey, *it is absolutely mandatory*. Else we sink quickly into quicksand.

So: What shall we *decide* to agree to mean by "P is the cause of Q"? Here we have to keep in mind where we are trying to get to. We are trying to find convincing evidence for the existence of God. Our most convincing evidence at the moment is the existence of the universe. The universe is our "Q," the thing, the object, the puzzle whose existence needs to be explained as the result of some cause, and we would like to make God our "P," the cause that explains the Q and thereby solves the puzzle. So what sense shall we give to the word "cause"? Does a seed cause a tree? Does water? Does sunlight?

There are at least two different important senses of "cause." There is what Aristotle[1] called the *material cause*, "that from which, as its constitutive material, something comes," and what he called the *efficient* cause, "the source of the first beginning of change . . . [such as] the father is the cause of the child." If we are to say that God is the cause of the universe, do we mean the material cause or the efficient cause, or both, or cause in some other sense? (Aristotle identified two others: *formal* cause, that which makes the tree a tree rather than something else, like a rock, and the *final* cause, the purpose and function that the tree serves.) It depends on your concept of God. Do you conceive of God as something separate from the universe, made of different "stuff," existing outside it and independently of it, or do you conceive of God as being identical to the universe, in the sense that the tables and chairs around you, all the atoms making up everything, your thoughts, the stars, the murderers and the murdered, the homeless, the rich, are all God? When a tiger devours a gazelle, is that God devouring God? When a man kills a man, is that God killing God? When a bridge collapses and crushes someone, is that God collapsing on top of God? When Jones decides to murder Smith, is that God deciding to murder God?

There are such pantheistic concepts of God, especially in some Eastern religions. The question is, if by "God" you mean the universe itself, not something separate from it, will this allow us to apply (2) above to a proposition where "P" = "God" and "Q" = "the universe"? That is, does it make sense to say that X is the cause of X?

Many, perhaps most, Yes-Believers conceive of God as distinct from the universe. God the creator, God the Father, God the prime mover, God the first cause, and so on, suggest an entity whose existence is not limited to the spatial and temporal borders of the universe nor the things in the universe but, rather, extends beyond the universe. The universe derives its reality and its existence from God, not the other way around.

Second, at face value at least, it does not make a lot of sense to say that the universe caused itself to exist. The universe has to exist before it can cause anything else to exist, including itself. The idea of bringing about one's own existence seems, at best, paradoxical. Any claim to knowledge, or warranted conviction, or justified belief, that presupposes some paradoxical proposition to be true is going to be suspicious and, at best, deeply problematic. Why?

Well, perhaps we can imagine how someone might *suppose* that a paradoxical sentence, like "It is the case that Jones did it and it is not the case that Jones did it," or "This sentence is false," *might* somehow be true; but it is difficult, at best, to imagine how anyone could ever be *convinced* that some such sentence is true. Such a belief would involve not just a Yes psychological attitude toward a self-contradictory sentence or paradoxical proposition, but also a cognitive attitude on which that psychological attitude is based. Such a cognitive attitude might of course be hanging from the psychological attitude without support from the rest of your propositional framework, in which case it would be belief by emotional conversion. For you to have belief by evidential conviction, the cognitive attitude must come first, the psychological attitude second. And your cognitive attitudes, unlike your psychological attitudes, do not come in degrees. Like the propositions themselves which they hold in place within the propositional framework, cognitive attitudes come in two all-or-nothing varieties: True or False. Paradoxical propositions would therefore seem to be impossible to hold, except through emotional persuasion. The evidential basis of your belief would thus, at best, be deeply suspect. Not on the grounds that we know everything and we know that what you believe isn't true but because paradoxical propositions are not the sort of propositions that have a high degree of relative evidential justification, with an evident probability around or near 1. Rather, if p is paradoxical, or self-contradictory, its evidential justification is virtually 0.

5.3 The Cosmological Argument: The Quantum Superforce, Nothing, and God

Presently we are examining whether the Yes-Believer really is convinced that God exists on the basis of the evidentially justified belief that the universe exists. Once again, notice that to answer these sorts of questions we do not need to go back in time to see who or what made the universe, etc. Without leaving our armchairs, we need but think philosophically. Whether or not you are convinced, on the basis of the universe as evidence, that God exists, does not depend on how strongly you believe but, rather, on (1) how strong your evidence is and (2) how good the argument linking the evidence to your belief is. (And remember that strength of evidence is measured in terms of quantity, quality, and corroboration.) These are not subjective judgments but can be determined objectively, within a wide comfort zone, as we've already discussed. Thus, if Carl, a Yes-Believer who professes to be convinced that God exists, has not yet started thinking in terms of evidence and arguments, *then his belief that he is convinced that God exists has all along been false.* Carl therefore should already, at this point, move his position on the chart a little closer to (0,0).

Notice, too, that if Carl is suddenly scuttling about, looking for evidence and arguments to reinforce his belief, then Carl must surely realize that—while he may at some point be able to become convinced about the existence of God—presently he is not really convinced. Let us thus construct the best argument we can for the evidence at hand.

Here again is argument A1:

1. The universe exists.
2. "Q exists" implies "P exists," where P is the cause of Q.
3. Therefore, the cause of the universe exists.

We know where we want to get to: God. The conclusion does not get us to God but, at best, to a cause of the universe. To suppose that the universe caused the universe seems, at least for right now, contradictory. Moreover, it would not lead us to a concept of God as something separate from the universe, in the sense of the existence of a divine creator, which would raise the question of why add the word "God" to the word "Universe." If the two are one, it seems redundant to use either the word "God" or the word "Universe."

Thus, not only is it quite natural to assume that the letters "Q" and "P" do not refer to the same thing—that Q P—but this will be the only way that we will be able to have some *meaningful* concept of God as something over and above, different from, the things around us. If I ask you, "Do you believe Zwabongo exists?" and you ask, "What do you mean by Zwabongo?" and I say, "The universe," you would rightly want to know why I didn't just ask whether you believed that the universe exists! I must have something else in mind or else my words are just redundant.

We thus need to amend premise (2) of our argument, as follows, or else it will not be possible for the argument to lead us to God:

1. The universe exists.
2. "Q exists" implies "P exists," where P is the cause of Q and P Q.

108

3. Therefore, the cause of the universe exists with an identity separate from the identity of the universe.

Suppose we now believe, on the basis of this argument, call it A2, that (3) is true. We then accept that the cause of the universe exists *whose identity is wholly other.* I say "wholly other" because if by "universe" we mean the totality of all things, as understood in some naturalistic sense, then the identity of God would be somehow separate from everything around you that you can see, hear, touch, and feel; God is, in that sense, "wholly other."

This is not to say that God could not somehow become one with something in the universe, such as an individual person or even a rock, but merely that presently we are conceiving of God as a "something beyond everything," which, regardless of how difficult or even contradictory an idea this is, might at the very least evoke a sense of deep and mysterious awe.

But this still does not get us to God. Argument A2, if we accept it, allows us to be convinced, on the basis of being convinced that the universe exists and that all things have a cause other than themselves, that the universe had a cause other than itself. It does not convince us of what that cause is (it only, at best, converts), nor that this cause qualifies as being God in any important sense of the word. (Again, if we then accept the argument, we are not convinced but persuaded. Which means we don't have evidence for God.)

Another problem is that many physicists today believe that the universe is ultimately the effect of a unitary *superforce*, which causes space, time, and matter. This quantum superforce caused the big bang; at the moment of creation, the quantum superforce created space, time, and matter from nothing and then itself split into gravity, electromagnetic force, and the strong and weak nuclear forces that now govern the whole universe and everything in it. The physicist Paul Davies writes:

> The most important scientific discovery of our age is that the physical universe did not always exist. Science faces no greater challenge than to explain how the universe came to exist and why it is structured in the way it is. . . . in the last few years that challenge has been met. For the first time in history we have a rational scientific theory of all existence. This revolutionary breakthrough represents an advance of

unparalleled magnitude in our understanding. . . . Together these investigations point towards a compelling idea, that all nature is ultimately controlled by the activities of a single *superforce.* The superforce would have the power to bring the universe into being and to furnish it with light, energy, matter, and structure. . . . The world, it seems, can be built more or less out of structured nothingness.[2]

The physicists may be right or wrong. They too may ultimately be involved in contradiction. But that is not the issue. Someone might say, "But who can understand a complicated concept like quantum superforce?" Well, who can understand a complicated concept like God? Certainly one is not simpler than the other. You might not know how the quantum superforce works, but you can learn how it works by studying quantum physics. You can study theology forever and you will never learn how God works! *How* did God create the universe? By saying "Let there be light"? How did this work? God's wish actualizes it? How does God's wish actualize something? It just happens? That's not much of an explanation. Quantum physics can do a *lot* better than that.

The question, then, is: if the *superforce,* which is just a natural, "blind" force, without consciousness or personality, caused the universe, is the superforce God? Well, it is a blind, natural force. Is it smarter than us? Hardly. Can it outthink us? Well, as a force it is very powerful—according to theory, it is the most powerful force in existence. Gravity is powerful—no human can overcome it (except briefly)—but there is no reason to think that gravity is conscious in the way that we are nor, for that matter, that it is wiser or more intelligent than us. Monkeys and plants are more intelligent than the brute force of gravity. Thinking along these lines, it seems, would lead us to being convinced not that the superforce is God but, rather, that there is no God. Not because there is no cause of the universe. Because the cause of the universe is just a natural phenomenon. The superforce is not God. So unless we can show that God, not the superforce, caused the universe, we are not reasonably justified in believing that God exists. Our belief is not even a conviction but, at best, the result of emotional conversion. Which again leaves us with no evidence whatsoever.

But it does more. Remember the point about the round Earth/oblong spheroid Earth example. According to our Principle of Propositional Relativity, a proposition is true only if it is the best representation of the purported facts from its family of available propositions. If you have only two propositions, "The Earth is flat" and "The Earth is round," the latter is true, the former false; add a new proposition, "The Earth is an oblong spheroid," and the first two are both false, the third is true. What contemporary quantum cosmology has done is analogous to adding a new proposition to the family of propositions addressing the mystery of the origin of the cosmos. "God is the cause of the universe" *might* have been justifiably true before twentieth-century science. Today, it has been dislodged from its former position; just as Copernicus and Galileo dislodged the Earth from its privileged position in the center of the solar system, dealing a mortal blow to the religious orthodoxy, so quantum mechanics dislodges the proposition, "God is the cause of the universe" as the centerpiece of the great mystery. The quantum physicist has brought new propositions into the family, among them "The superforce is the cause of the universe."

Thus, as is so often the case with any miracle stories, the problem is that different causes have like effects. If the whole universe is regarded as a miracle (meaning an event that can have no natural explanation) then we cannot become convinced that God did it unless we first become convinced that we have excluded all other causes. Until recently there were no other contenders, no alternative causes. This is no longer true.

To understand the alternative cause problem, suppose that, for instance, my dog Snoopy is sick and dying. I take him to a vet who says Snoopy's days are numbered. Deeply upset at the idea of losing my beloved dog, I go to another vet, then another, and they all say there is nothing anyone can do. As a final gesture I take Snoopy to a faith healer. The healer puts her hand on Snoopy and says, "Praise the Lord." Lo and behold, suddenly, miraculously, Snoopy is healed!

Am I, on the basis of this "miracle," convinced that God exists? Only if I am convinced that this is the *best explanation* among various alternative explanations. What are the alternatives from which I must *decide* what caused Snoopy's sudden recovery? Here are a few:

1. God did it.
2. Snoopy's own body spontaneously and accidentally fixed itself.
3. My brain, suffering at the idea of losing Snoopy, tapped into some hidden healing power within itself.
4. The healer is an extraordinarily powerful human being, whose pineal gland, unbeknownst even to her, has miraculous powers.
5. Snoopy is a Martian.

And so on. How many such alternative explanations are there? Many, to say the least. They must be rank-ordered according to our Principle of Propositional Relativity and our zones of evidential justification. It is hardly obvious that possibility (1) is the likeliest explanation. In any case, to be convinced that (1) is the correct explanation would require being convinced that the other alternatives are not as good.

The problem, in other words, is that God is conceived as an ultimate being in every way and the universe, remarkable as though its existence is, does not *necessarily* point to such an ultimate entity. For centuries, the fact that it did not necessarily point the way was blunted by the fact that there was no serious alternative to God. Until recent developments in quantum physics, there was no serious alternative explanation for the origin of the cosmos besides God except, possibly, "no cause." But just as once there was no naturalistic explanation of the mystery of the sun, rain, "what was holding up the Earth," and so on, and people used to *perhaps* be evidentially justified in believing in the Sun God, the Rain God, Atlas, and so on, science has provided alternatives. And although before this century science had no naturalistic explanation for the origin and cause of the universe, this is no longer true.

Thus, we cannot simply assume that the cause of the universe is an ultimately greater sort of entity, in the sense implied by the concept of God, than the universe or the physicist's explanation using quantum tunneling events, virtual vacuums, the spontaneous creation of something from nothing, and so on. Such scientific explanations might not be true, but they are alternatives; unless the Yes-Believer is convinced that quantum mechanics is wrong (not just emotionally persuaded) about the spontaneous creation of universes from nothing,[3] then the Yes-

Believer is not really convinced, on the basis of the existence of the universe that God exists. And, again, if you say that this evidence is too complicated for you, then you are simply ignoring the alternative evidence. You would then, at most, be entitled to suspend judgment.

At best, another argument besides A2 would be needed, such as one showing that we cannot conceive of a lesser thing giving rise to a greater thing. But that, too, would deny altogether the concept of evolution. The plants and animals that are alive today are much more advanced than their ancestors of 200 million years ago.

So the problem is that God is conceived as a being greater than ourselves in every way, a supreme being. And, neither argument A1 nor A2 lead to such an ultimate entity. They don't exclude that some such entity might be the cause of the universe, but neither do they make a convincing case for such an entity. To make the case in court that Jones *might* be the murderer is not enough for the jury to conclude, on the basis of such an argument, that Jones is guilty. A1 and A2 only convince, at best, that the universe had a cause, not that the cause of the universe is God. People who think they are on this basis convinced that God exists, are mistaken. Given the latest science, according to which that first cause might have been non-God, i.e., quantum superforce or perhaps some other sort of as yet unconceived natural phenomenon, the Universe as evidence for the existence of God cannot in this way be convincing.

5.4 The Double Standard Fallacy and the Infinite Regress

The difficulties do not end here. Let us for the moment suppose that the Yes-Believer comes up with some additional evidence that makes it more reasonable to suppose that the ultimate cause of the universe is not superforce but a being that, indeed, would rightly be called God. We then come to a second difficulty. What caused God?

Now, why would we ask this? Well, look at premise (2): "Q exists" implies "P exists," where P is the cause of Q and P Q. Premise (1) establishes the given evidence: The universe exists.

Premise (2) tries to build a logical bridge to the conclusion that the universe is the result of some external cause. But premise (2) says that anything that exists has a cause other than itself. So, if we accept the above argument, and if the Yes-Believer succeeds with an additional argument to show that this external cause of the universe is God, we can ask: What caused God?

If God was created by something else, then what we call "God" is not God, in the sense of an ultimate creator, but merely a link in a long chain of causes. Let us call whatever caused God, "SuperGod." By premise (2), if SuperGod exists, then there must be a cause of SuperGod—SuperDuperGod? And then . . . SuperDuperGooperGod? And then . . .

To avoid such an infinite regress, the Yes-Believer could say that God did not come about as the result of some external cause. This might well be the case. But, in that case, the argument above has just defeated itself because the argument asks us to accept that nothing can exist without having come about as the result of some external cause. We are then asked to accept the idea of God, who did not come about as the result of some external cause. Well, in that case, if these argument(s) succeed, they fail. They show that we can conceive of something existing without having come about as the result of some cause other than itself.

At this point, the Yes-Believer might wish to claim that God is special. The universe is not the sort of thing that can exist without having come about as the result of some cause other than itself; God, unlike the universe, is that sort of self-caused, or uncaused, entity. This might be correct. But presently the issue is whether the Yes-Believer really is convinced that God exists. And at this point, the Yes-Believer would have to justify the conviction using such a double-standard: one standard for God, one standard for the universe. The universe cannot exist uncaused or as its own cause; God can. If the Yes-Believer is convinced of, rather than merely converted to, the proposition that God exists, then the Yes-Believer must be convinced that the universe cannot exist as its own cause or be uncaused. But how could anyone possibly be convinced of such a thing? Can you look around, wave your hands through the air, and just say, "See, look at all this—not the sort of thing that can just come about by itself, from nothing!" You can believe this to be so, but how could you be convinced that this is so about the whole universe, what it can do and what it cannot do? On what grounds could you be *convinced* of this?

Indeed, again many experts on the topic of what the universe can and cannot do—physicists and cosmologists—would disagree. They might be wrong and the Yes-Believer might be right, in the sense that the Yes-Belief might turn out to be true. But what is here at issue is whether the evidential justification of Yes-Belief is sufficient to warrant conviction or even reasonably justify belief. The Yes-Believer certainly has a right to evoke a double standard in the argument for the existence of God. But unless the Yes-Believer knows something the physicist doesn't, it is simply presumptuous on the Yes-Believer's part or anyone else's simply to decree what the universe can or cannot do. To do so is to remove the claim that God exists from the realm of conviction to the realm of belief by emotional conversion. Evidentially, "God exists" is for the Yes-Believer at best a fifty-fifty proposition.

Notes

1. Aristotle, *Metaphysics.*
2. Paul Davies, *Superforce,* New York: Simon & Schuster, pp. 5–7.
3. See, for example, E. P. Tryon, "Is the universe a vacuum fluctuation?" *Nature* 246, 396 (1973); R. Brout, et al., "The creation of the universe as a quantum phenomenon," *Annals of Physics* 115, 78 (1978); D. Atkatz and H. Pagels, "Origin of the universe as a quantum tunneling event," *Physical Review* D 25, 2065 (1982), and by my lights the best, A. Vilenkin's superb "Creation of the universe from nothing," *Physics Letters* B117, 25 (1982).

Did God Design the Universe?

6.0 Cosmic Order

THE UNIVERSE IS NOT AN UNDIFFERENTIATED, MESSY MASS OF CHAOTIC, lifeless goo, some randomly fluctuating, undifferentiated glob. From the most distant galaxies to the beating of your heart and the grass upon which you walk, even within that grass, there exist worlds within worlds arranged just so. Ordered structures within ordered structures, each linked to the other with minute precision, all running as accurately as clockwork, the entire system perfectly in balance.

Why does the universe not just fly apart, or fall in on itself and collapse into nothing? The sun rises and sets and then rises again and again, the tide rolls in and the tide rolls out, our cells divide and carry on their fine-tuned tasks. An apple never turns into a tiger, the tiger remains a tiger, the whole Earth rotates on its axis and revolves around the sun more accurately than the finest Swiss clock. Things change but they do so with a gentle precision found everywhere in nature.

Tornados come, earthquakes shake the ground, on occasion stars blow up. But the structures without which we would not even be here continue to persist in an orderly fashion. Each creature has its place and its function. The universe may be a torrential maelstrom but it is no destructive hurricane. The whole of existence is so precisely balanced that if the world could speak to us it might well say, "I am no accident!"

Ancient scriptures tell of miracles that supposedly happened a long time ago and far away; but here all around us are ten thousand miracles all at once and we are each an eyewitness. The wondrous sight is the scene before our eyes. How could all this be but a heap of random accidents, sprung spontaneously without a guiding hand, a random and spontaneous emergence from nothing? How blind do you have to be to not see that here, now, surrounding you on all sides, within us and without us, is the glorious handiwork of the greatest of all artists, arranged by a cosmic designer of divine proportions?

Suppose you found an ancient cave and inside it a painting. Would you think the pattern on the wall just happened to appear there by accident? What if the painting is not just a primitive scribble but, say, of the likes of Da Vinci's Mona Lisa? Furthermore, suppose that, instead of rocks you find many statues of the likes of David, Venus, and so on. You look up at the ceiling; the fresco there matches perfectly the stars of the heavens. Would you not be convinced, if you found yourself inside such a cave, that the objects in it do not just happen to be there by accident but were put there, created by someone on purpose, the result of conscious design?

If a lump of matter shaped like a man—a statue—would warrant the conviction that the figure did not just form naturally but had been created by design—and it would—how much more certain would we be of the existence of the designer if the lump of matter not just had the shape of a man, but moved and talked, laughed and cried, and had ideas? But, in an important sense, isn't that what we are? If it would be ludicrous to suppose that the statue rose up by itself from the floor of the cave as a randomly growing stalagmite, an accidental formation that just happened to have grown into that shape, how much more ludicrous would it be to suppose that we are but the result of some such random process? If the existence of the statue implies the existence of a sculptor, the existence of the painting the existence of a painter, what are we to conclude on the basis of the presence of a whole race of humans? After all, we ourselves are the lumps of matter existing not just in some cave with a picture of the heavens on its ceiling, but on a spinning globe inside a fully functioning cosmos, where the heavens themselves move in cosmic harmony. Surely this implies the existence of a designer of unimaginable skill and power, an artist of divine proportion, the author of all creation: God.

6.1 The Birds and the Bees and the Argument from Design: Is God the Author of the World?

So goes the moving testimony of the Yes-Believer who, convinced that the universe exists and is well ordered, professes also to be convinced, on the basis of such order, that God exists. Again we have an overwhelming object presented as evidence: the universe—not just its existence but its well-ordered structure. As we've just seen, however, no evidence by itself can provide us with the conviction that God exists unless it is presented in a good argument. As evidence for the existence of God, the well-ordered structure of the cosmos is only as good as the argument. Does the argument stand up in cross-examination?

The argument, call it B1, goes something like this:

B1
$\Big\{$
1. "Q is well ordered" implies the existence of a well-ordered P that gave rise to Q, and P   Q.
2. The universe is well ordered.
3. Therefore, there exists a well-ordered something that gave rise to the universe.

We put the P   Q qualification in premise (1) for the same reason as in argument A1; otherwise, B1 has no chance of successfully linking the evidence—the existence of a well-ordered

118

universe—to the existence of God. Once again, the conclusion, (3), does not lead to the existence of God but, at best, to the existence of "a well-ordered something." We would thus need a second argument to convince us that the only sort of well-ordered something that could have given rise to the universe is God.

Is this all starting to look very familiar? It should. The form and structure of this sort of argument, called "The Argument from Design," is the same as the argument we considered in the previous chapter, "The Cosmological Argument."

The first problem with the Argument from Design, B1, is with premise (1). Is this premise true? It depends in part on what we mean by "well ordered." A beehive exhibits definite patterns of symmetry. Is a beehive well ordered? Certainly it is not just a random hodgepodge; each cell is the same shape, contoured to fit with the others, and so on. Is this the kind of order that we will need to become convinced that God exists?

Here the answer must be no. Bees, we have good reason to believe, are not conscious of what they are doing but act purely on instinct. The beehive exists without designer or architect and there is little reason to think that a spiritual super-bee was its designer, some bee-god who was the grand architect of all bee-hives. The unconscious activity of bees can account for the well-ordered structure of the beehive. (Notice that if, at this point, the Yes-Believer says, "But what about the existence of the bees, or of anything, to begin with?" then we have left the Argument from Design and are back to the Cosmological Argument.)

What is needed is some sense of "well ordered" establishing the existence of a conscious designer. We know plants can produce other plants not because they've thought about leaves, stems, and photosynthesis, planned ahead, and so on, but because of the blind forces at work inside plants. Similarly, animals produce their offspring not by conscious planning but by instinct. Even human birth, which used to be a complete mystery to humans, is today understood to be a natural biological process; having discovered how sperm and egg meet, how genes work, the structure of DNA, and so on, reveals inner workings that are very machinelike; indeed, the molecules and cells making up all life as we know it work individually much the way insects do, without any conscious intention, following blindly the forces of nature.

So the first problem with the argument that tries to link the design found in nature with God is that nature itself provides us with plenty of examples of well-ordered structures that come about as the result of simpler and more basic forces. To get to God, we would need to find patterns that could not possibly arise randomly and spontaneously out of chaos. But, once again, today we have startling new testimony from physicists who can show how it is possible that complete randomness can bring about the sorts of structures we see. The family of propositions has once again grown, leaving "God designed the cosmos" in the graveyard. Likewise, the evolutionary theory offers evidence that order arises out of random variations. To be convinced that God exists on the basis of the structures we see would require our being *convinced* that quantum physics and evolutionary theory are mistaken.

6.2 Contemporary Physics and the Anthropic-Cosmological Principle: Did the Universe Design Itself?

But how could the patterns we see around us have come about by themselves? Consider the following. Suppose you find a deck of cards, perfectly arranged by suits from lowest to highest card. You would assume the deck had not been randomly shuffled but that someone had ordered the cards that way. Let's use the deck of cards as an analogy for the universe. This brings in several important factors. First, the cards can be shuffled infinitely many times. If the cards are shuffled enough times, sooner or later the well-ordered sequence will arise purely by chance. This shows how it would happen that the cards come up ordered, but it makes such an order a very, very rare occurrence.

Imagine, though, that *we are the cards*. Further, imagine that only cards in a specifically ordered sequence—say, where you have only Royal Flushes—can be conscious. In that case, the only time the randomly shuffled royal flushes could have the opportunity to ask, "Why is our universe (the deck of cards in which we exist) so perfectly ordered into royal flushes?" would be when in fact the deck happened to precisely thus order itself. All other random shuffles go unobserved. Only well-ordered shuffles are observed.

An imaginative, farfetched story? No; a recent scientific theory called "the Anthropic Cosmological Principle" claims to help us understand the existence of the order we observe by providing the missing component, the missing piece in the picture puzzle. That missing component is not God, as some used to think. Rather, it is *us*. You and me, the self-conscious orderings of random fluctuations out of nothingness:

> The central problem of science and epistemology is deciding which postulates to take as fundamental. The perennial solution of the great idealistic philosophers has been to regard Mind as logically prior, and even materialistic philosophers consider the innate properties of matter to be such as to allow—or even require—the existence of intelligence to contemplate it; that is, these properties are necessary or sufficient for life. Thus the existence of Mind is taken as one of the basic postulates of a philosophical system. . . . [D]uring the past fifteen years there has grown up amongst cosmologists an interest in a collection of ideas, known as the Anthropic Cosmological Principle, which offer a means of relating Mind and observership directly to the phenomena traditionally within the encompass of physical science.
>
> The expulsion of Man from his self-assured position at the center of Nature owes much to the Copernican principle that we do not occupy a privileged position in the Universe. This Copernican assumption would be regarded as axiomatic at the outset of most scientific investigations. However, like most generalizations it must be used with care. Although we do not regard our position in the Universe to be central or special in every way, this does not mean that it cannot be special in *any* way. This "Anthropic Principle" . . . [is that] *The Universe must have those properties which allow life to develop within it at some stage in its history.*
>
> An implication . . . is that the constants and laws of Nature must be such that life can exist. This speculative statement leads to a number of quite distinct interpretations of a radical nature: firstly, the most obvious is to continue in the tradition of the classical Design Arguments and claim that:
>
> (A) *There exists one possible Universe "designed" with the goal of generating and sustaining "observers."*

121

This view would have been supported by the natural theologians of past centuries. . . . [The physicist John Archibald] Wheeler has a second possible interpretation. . . .

(B) *Observers are necessary to bring the Universe into being.*

This statement is somewhat reminiscent of the outlook of Bishop Berkeley and . . . it has physical content when considered in the light of attempts to arrive at a satisfactory interpretation of quantum mechanics.[1]

Add to this the "creation of universes out of nothing" scenario of contemporary quantum physics, and you get a universe that, as contemporary physicist Alan Guth once put it, is a "free lunch":

. We can . . . construct a cosmic scenario that reveals the astonishing scope of the new physics to explain the physical world. . . . Recent discoveries in particle physics have suggested mechanisms whereby matter can be created in empty space by the cosmic gravitational field, which only leaves the origin of spacetime itself as a mystery. But even here there are some indications that space and time could have sprung into existence spontaneously without violating the laws of physics. . . . Discussing this scenario, the physicist Alan Guth remarked: "It is often said that there is no such thing as a free lunch. The universe, however, is a free lunch."
Does such a universe model have any need for God? . . . The "free lunch" scenario claims all you need are the laws—the universe can take care of itself, including its own creation.[2]

Again, keep in mind that we are not concerned with proving that the scientific hypothesis is correct. All we are doing at present is trying to move the Yes-Believer, who claims to be convinced that God exists on the basis of the order found in the universe, from what is a dogmatic, false, and *mistaken* position, to a more open-minded position. It is a dogmatic position because it is based on ignoring the sorts of things we are here considering; it is false and mistaken because, in so far as the Yes-Believer thinks, "I am convinced that God exists because the universe is so well ordered," the Yes-Believer is wrong: this is not really a conviction but, at best, elaborate self-persuasion based on an emotive response to the order found in the universe.

6.3 Back to the Double Standard?

The problems do not end here. Suppose we were to accept the Argument from Design and its conclusion. What reason do we have for thinking that the well-ordered structure that gave rise to the universe—if indeed there is one—is God? Presumably, the idea is that nothing well ordered can exist without having come about as the result of some even more highly ordered thing and that's how you get to God. But then, as before, we must ask: Who, or what, designed God?

In other words, according to premise (2) in argument B1, anything that is well ordered must have come about as the result of some other well-ordered thing. It is our amazement and our inability to understand how something could simply exist perfectly in balance without someone making it so that supposedly forces us to accept the idea that God did it. But if we are puzzled by all the order in the universe, how much more puzzled we should be by the even higher order that supposedly is the nature of God! We start out thinking that you can't just have something like the universe perfectly ordered simply by its own nature; it must have been created that way by God. But then we imagine God as being even more well ordered than the universe, simply by virtue of God's own nature.

> *Question: How did God get to be like that?*
> *Answer: Always has been.*
> *Question: Why?*
> *Answer: That's God's nature.*
> *Question: How do you know, then, that's not the nature of the universe itself?*

Again, as before, we might suppose that the universe is not the sort of thing that can order itself, where as God is. But such a double standard, though possible, cannot be convincing unless one can show what the universe, by itself, can and cannot do. According to the best experts we have on the nature of the universe, there is plenty of reason to think the universe can do what the double standard says it can't. So once again it seems the propositional framework has been expanded, in this case by science, and it can no longer support the concept of God in its privileged, formerly secure position at the center of the mystery.

Today it would simply be presumptuous on anyone's part to simply decree the limitations of the universe and thereby evoke the old concept of a God that, magically, does not have such limitations. To conclude that God exists on the basis of such an argument is no longer convincing, if ever it was. It is, at best, a fifty-fifty proposition. To believe on such a basis that God exists means you are not really convinced of God's existence. You have allowed yourself to be persuaded, without evidence.

Notes

1. John D. Barrow and Frank J. Tipler, *The Anthropic Cosmological Principle*, Oxford: Oxford University Press, 1986, pp. 1–23.
2. Paul Davies, *God and the New Physics*, New York: Simon and Schuster, pp. 214–217.

Can You Experience God?

7.0 Memory, the Past, and the Temporal Extension of Experience

IT IS ONE THING TO TRY TO CONVINCE SOMEONE ELSE OF WHAT YOU yourself are convinced. You need only present the evidence that convinced you and then the arguments showing that the evidence supports the belief to the required degree. Suppose you get a speeding ticket but you are convinced you weren't speeding. You looked at your speedometer and it said "35," the speed limit was 35, you had the speedometer checked, and so on—still, you fail to convince the police officer and the judge. You don't have reasonable evidence or a good argument. Failing to convince them, however, you do not thereby convince yourself that you must have been speeding. Rather, you conclude that you were missing the sufficient evidence or your argument was not very good.

Likewise, there are people who claim to be convinced that God exists not in virtue of some argument or theory but because they have directly experienced God. Suppose Abraham, a Yes-Believer, believes on the basis of some such experience. Abraham doesn't just have some evidence and a good argument for the existence of God. Abraham has himself personally, directly experienced God.

The wonderful thing about experience is that it is immediate and direct. The problem with trying to base conviction solely on experience is that experience doesn't last very long. Right now, for instance, what are you experiencing?

Look at the date. Your present experience is occurring on that date. Remember back to some date in, say, 1992. Your present experience is occurring right here and right now, not back then. Suppose you had a headache then and you have a headache now. This headache is not that headache. Suppose you had the thought "I'm hungry" then and you think "I'm hungry" right now. This hunger is not that hunger. Likewise, this thought that you are having right now exists here and now; the thought you had back there and back then, no matter how similar to the one now, exists back there and back then—not now! You may have a memory of that previous thought, that previous headache, and so on; but your memory is, at best, a *recollection* of an experience, not that very experience.[1]

Try to remember some time when you were swimming. Take a moment to do this. When was it? Where was it? Was anyone with you? What bathing suit were you wearing? Picture the scene. Try to remember the actual event of your swimming.[2] Do you see a swimmer—yourself?

Then ask yourself this: When you were actually swimming did you see yourself swimming? Of course not. You were in a headless perspective from which you saw hands moving and water splashing. What this sort of example vividly shows you is that memories are not directly recorded events but, rather, reconstructed ones, recreated replica events, they are not the past but *mental models* of the past. Your memories may be accurate renditions—good models—of the actual events. Or they may not be. But memories are not themselves the actual events. They are renditions—models—and not only are they always fallible, they are *never* the thing they render.

So although experience may connect you directly to the thing experienced, your experience does not reach beyond the present moment. Memories do not connect you directly to the experience remembered. This means that to be convinced of something directly and solely on the basis of your own experience, the experience must be occurring right now, at the very moment when you are making the conviction claim—whether to someone else or to yourself.

Many mystics have claimed to be convinced that God exists on the basis of their own direct experience. But unless you are having that experience at the moment in which you make the statement "God exists," the claim that you are convinced that God exists solely on the basis of your own experience is mistaken. Not that you haven't experienced God directly—you may well have. But then you need some reliable way of connecting yourself back to that experience. Your experience might warrant conviction while that experience was going on; but unless you can establish now that the experience was true and actual, that you have remembered it correctly, and so on, you are not right now on the basis of that past experience convinced that God exists. At best, you only think you are.

How long does an experience last? Certainly your present experience does not reach back an hour. Suppose you have been reading this book for one hour. These letters which you are now experiencing are not the letters you were experiencing an hour ago. The page you were on an hour ago, and that experience, are not presently being experienced. Presently you are experiencing this page, this paragraph, this sentence, these words. Somewhere within this short duration your present experience extends, but its duration is well under a minute. At most, any experience lasts but a few seconds.

So the first problem with supposing that you have no need for evidence and argument to be convinced that God exists, because your knowledge is based on direct experience of God, is that direct experience does not reach very far. Even people who are experientially rather than intellectually oriented tend not to realize this. They have a naive view of experience. They do not realize that without theory and interpretation you cannot get very far. Without theory and interpretation you are limited to being convinced only about what you are presently, at the

127

moment, experiencing. Using your immediate and direct experience, you have no way of reaching any other moment but the one going on right now. To move beyond the present moment you need some sort of reasoning that involves concepts and theories, whether implicitly or explicitly.

7.1 Interpretation and Representation

The problem with claiming to be convinced that God exists on the basis of one's own experience does not end there. There is the additional problem of interpreting your experience. But here we must again pause to ask: What *is* experience?

Most people do not realize that their eyes are not windows, their ears are not tunnels. Light, for instance, does not go into your eye, travel up the optic nerve, and enter the brain. The brain lives in complete darkness! Inside your brain it is as dark as inside a mainframe computer. So where are the images that you now are seeing? If we opened up your skull, we would not see little images among the neurons. No image, no light whatsoever, travels past the back of the eye.

Perception—the visual component of experience—is something whose creation the brain itself is actively involved in. No one has yet solved the mysterious problem of exactly how the brain, which lives in darkness, is able to stimulate itself into having the phenomena we call "perception." But we do understand that perception is an active, not a passive process. And the images the brain synthesizes—the ones you are now perceiving—we have good reason to believe somehow correspond, in varying degrees, to the objects out there in the world. But the visual images themselves, of which the perceptions consist, are not the objects out there. They are, at best, accurate internal representations of objects. Your experience is thus a model, like a computer simulation of the world. It is a good model, a superb simulation. It is a marvelously rich and realistic Virtual Reality, run by the brain similar to the way a computer processes video images in its circuits, in the language of pure logic, without any pictorial representations.[3] But just because the Virtual Reality we call "perception" in some degree corresponds to what is, literally, the scene *before* your eyes,[4] it is *not* what is "before your eyes." It is only a model, albeit a very realistic one.

Similarly, sound does not travel into your ear. After air pressure hits the eardrum, impulses, which themselves cannot be heard in any ordinary sense (they are as silent as the optic nerves' firings), travel along nerves to the brain where the auditory perception is somehow created. But your ears are not open tunnels through which sounds enter your brain. Your brain itself creates the heard sounds you hear as such. The difference between dreaming and waking sounds is that, when you are only dreaming you hear a train whistle, there is no train whistle within earshot, no air waves hitting your ear that were sent on their way by a passing train. When you are awake, i.e., dreaming with your eyes open, and you hear the train, there are soundwaves outside your ears on which that is based. In both cases, however, the *perceptual* impetus of the perception, as such, comes from inside the brain, not the soundwaves outside the ear.

Your tactile sense, too, is created by the brain's representational system; what we call "touch" is not direct and uninterpreted touching of objects "out there." What the fingers holding this book, for instance, feel at most is only pressure; yet *you* feel an object, a book.

What does all this have to do with the direct experience of God? Well, given the representational nature of experience, it seems that *any* experience of *anything* is, at best, a representation of the thing experienced. The experience is not the thing. It is, at best, a good representation, an accurate model. Whether some experience is a good representation cannot be determined on the basis of that experience alone. So what model will you use to check the model? An argument is still needed and will always be needed. A theory is still required and will always be required. Evidence still needs to be presented. Where there are models and theories there are alternatives. Where there are alternatives there is a need for careful philosophy. Which model—which representation, which interpretation—is best cannot be determined on the basis of which one happens to be the one you are psychologically most attracted to.

7.2 Abraham's Dilemma

The difficulties get worse. Take one classic example of a person supposedly having the direct experience of God. According to the famous story in the Bible, God tells Abraham to sacrifice his son. Abraham believes it is God talking. Is Abraham justified in believing that the voice he hears is God's?

Perhaps Abraham feels 100 percent psychological confidence—there is no doubt whatsoever in his mind that the voice he hears is God talking. In that case, Abraham has the psychological feeling of confidence that it is God talking. But the psychological feeling of confidence toward some proposition, p, as we've already seen, by itself counts for nothing in terms of evidential justification for p. Abraham believes he is talking to God but unless he has more than just a feeling that this is God, he is not really convinced this is God. He only thinks he is convinced. He is fooling himself. It might, indeed, be God. The question, however, is on what grounds Abraham could be convinced of this.

Is the voice extra deep? Extra moving? Does what it says come true? Well, even in that case, it might not be God. It might be the devil. It might be a powerful extraterrestrial trying to gain control of people. It might be Abraham's own brain playing tricks with him. He may be losing his mind. It may be any number of things. The point is that, by itself, a voice does not come with identity papers certifying whose voice it is.

Suppose Mary has a vision. She's in the hospital when God appears to her and tells her that she will get well by tomorrow. The next day, Mary gets well. Is she now convinced that God exists? Or is it merely emotional persuasion? Well, how is she convinced that what she saw was real? Did the person in her vision have a name tag? Long hair? Glowing eyes? Does she have sufficient evidence that this was not a hallucination? An evil demon? A dream? Multiple personality?

Keep in mind: The point is not that Mary's "experience of God"—the vision, the voice, etc.—could not be God. It could. The problem is how to establish, on the basis of such an experience, that Mary's belief is not just belief by emotional persuasion but belief by evidential conviction. Clearly, if you had some such experience you would have *some* direct evidence for the existence of God. Most people do not have such experiences, they certainly are not very common. But would it be *enough* evidence to justify Mary's being convinced that God exists? This question cannot be settled by wishful thinking. It requires doing some philosophical thinking, analysis, and interpretation.

130

The great twentieth-century philosopher Bertrand Russell once remarked that it is very clear what sort of experience we would all readily acknowledge would qualify as reasonable evidence to warrant a conviction that God exists. It wouldn't necessarily prove it; the experience would just clearly qualify as *probable* knowledge in the sense we've discussed. What is the experience? Well, he said, if at noon tomorrow everyone hears, in his or her own language, say, the Ten Commandments, or a voice identifying itself as God, then that would be reasonable justification to warrant a conviction. Anything less than that would not count. But there is no such experience.

7.3 Mystical Union with God: Can You Have an Interpretation-Free Experience?

What about mystics, some of whom have claimed to have had *special* kinds of extraordinary experiences that, unlike ordinary experience, require no interpretation? According to these mystics, it is only on the basis of such "interpretation-free experience" that one can be convinced that God exists. Is there such a thing as an interpretation-free experience?

There may be. The problem, again, concerns one's claims to knowledge. A light, no matter how bright, is just a light. A voice, no matter how deep or profound, is just a voice. Likewise, anything you *say* about any experience is just a bunch of words. Words are not the thing but, at best, representations of the thing. Thus it seems difficult to imagine how, if one had an interpretation-free experience, one could describe it in words or think about it without thereby interpreting it. And once one interprets it, the experience ceases to be interpretation-free.

How then could one be convinced of anything on the basis of such an experience? Suppose you had such an "interpretation-free" experience of God. What was it like? The moment you say anything about it—what God is like, what God said, what God wants, and so on—you are interpreting. Are you interpreting correctly? Perhaps. But on what grounds are you convinced?

It seems that, if one had some such mystical experience, one would have to leave the question of God outside the realm of warranted conviction, even of justified belief. No one could ever truly be convinced or in any degree justified on such grounds. Why? Because if there is nothing at all you can say about X, it is not clear what it even means to say you are convinced of X.

Suppose I say I had an interpretation-free experience of Zwabongo. What was it like? I can't say. What is Zwabongo? I can't say. And so on. Well, are you now convinced, then, that Zwabongo exists? It cannot be clear, even to me, that I am convinced. Converted by emotion, perhaps (of *what*, though?), but not convinced (of *anything*) by evidence. And we have decided to use words like "S is convinced that P" to mean "convinced by evidence," not emotional persuasion, self-deceptive trickery, or clever manipulation. On those very real grounds, it must be acknowledged that we cannot be convinced that God exists solely on the basis of direct experience.

If there is a God, the conviction is not yet earned. Thus far all we have, at best, is belief by emotional persuasion, without evidence. All we have is make-believe.

Notes

1. For a fuller treatment of the ephemeral nature of experience and its implications for the problem of personal identity, see our chapters "Who" and "Experience" in Kolak & Martin, *Wisdom Without Answers*, 2nd ed., Belmont: Wadsworth, 1991.
2. This example is from Julian Jaynes, "Consciousness and the Voices of the Mind," in Kolak & Martin, eds., *Self & Identity*, New York: Macmillan, 1991.
3. For an exploration of the philosophical implications of this in terms of a souped-up version of the brain in the vat problem, see my "Experiment II" in Kolak & Martin, eds., *The Experience of Philosophy*, Belmont: Wadsworth, 1993.
4. I here follow David Lewis's immensely clever but subtly deceptive locution in his "Veridical Hallucination and Prosthetic Vision," *Australasian Journal of Philosophy*, 58/3 (1980), 239–49.

Is It in Society's Interest That We Believe?

8.0 Prudential Justification and the Moral Appeal: Does Yes-Belief Provide a Foundation for Ethics?

SOME YES-BELIEVERS DEFEND THEIR BELIEFS NOT WITH REASON AND EVI-dence for the existence of God, which they may agree is not readily forthcoming, but with a moral appeal. According to them, it is not a question of *whether* God exists. Rather, we have a moral imperative to believe that a cosmic arbitrator of right and wrong exists, that in the end all wrongdoers will be punished and our good deeds rewarded, and so on. Without belief in such an absolute moral center, society would fall apart.

"If God is dead," wrote the existentialist philosopher Jean-Paul Sartre, "everything is permissible." And then, echoing Nietzsche, he added, "God *is* dead." According to the moralist's argument, it is Yes-Belief, in and of itself—independently of the evidential justification for the existence of God—that provides people with a basis for accepting and upholding ethical rules of moral conduct. The convincing argument for Yes-Belief, according to the moralist's position, is based not on evidence for God's existence but, rather, on the evidence for the claim that Yes-Belief is a basic and necessary condition for *our* existence as a society.

In other words, by providing a divinely ordained ethical system for moral conduct, it is Yes-Belief itself that—regardless of the particular religion from which it is derived and regardless of whether God really does exist—makes the world a better place than it would otherwise be. Without the idea of some sort of God who is absolute arbitrator and judge to serve as our conscience, an all-seeing divinity who decides what is right and what is wrong, we would give in to our individual, selfish needs at the expense of society. People would be even more selfish and cruel than they already are. Having definite beliefs about God's commands tempers our baser, dog-eat-dog instincts with a sense of community, charity, love, salvation, and so on.

The idea, then, is that Yes-Belief is not justified on evidential grounds concerning the nature of truth but on moral or "socially prudential" grounds (we will consider personally prudential grounds next). That is, independently of whether there really is a God, it is socially prudent—it is in the interest of society as a whole—to accept and encourage individual Yes-Belief: without individual Yes-Belief, ethics would be impossible. According to this view, even questioning people's beliefs about whether God really exists may be to tempt disaster; not because we have enough evidence to be convinced that God exists and will punish us but because we have enough evidence to be convinced that raising doubts about the existence of God makes us less likely to be obedient to rules of behavior necessary for the survival of society as a whole.

So: Accept the existence of God as a service to your society. You should believe not because there is reasonable justification that the belief is true but because there is reasonable justification that, without this belief, society would be worse off. And, ultimately, if society is worse off, your chances of survival—and the chances for your offspring—will be lessened. So ultimately it may be in your self-interest to do what is in the interest of society.

But now we must ask: What *is* the evidential justification for the moral worth of Yes-Belief? This question often puzzles the moralist, as if getting off the evidence justification track concerning God's existence is a carte blanche for just throwing evidence to the wind, making any claim you wish and then supposedly being convinced that you are justified in making it! It is one thing to be persuaded into accepting the existence of God, on faith, without any evidential justification. It is quite another to be persuaded into accepting, on faith without evidential justification, the Social Prudence Argument for Yes-Belief, and then claiming instead to be convinced. The argument may be structured, roughly, something like this:

1. It is imperative that you do what is best for society.
2. Belief is God is best for society.

Therefore,

3. It is imperative that you believe in God.

According to such an argument, Yes-Belief regarding the existence of God is an *imperative* that provides the foundation for ethics and makes people more moral. In other words, one is asked to forgo evidence for the existence of God in lieu of moral considerations. Few would quibble with the first premise. Of course, we all would like what is best for the human race. But this gives quite a leeway as to what is actually viewed as best by different individuals. There is no entity, "The Human Race," that communicates with its individuals. What is best for the human race, in so far as it is talked about or communicated, must always come from the mouths of individuals. So what is "best" must always be tempered by: best according to whom?

Notice that the Social Prudence Argument for Yes-Belief cannot—though it often nevertheless does—make appeal to what is best according to God. What is at question is whether belief in God is warranted, even on socially prudential grounds; to resolve the "best according to whom" problem by appeal to the dictates of a particular religious system merely begs the question. One could say that it doesn't matter which religious view of "best" you follow, so long as you follow some. But, first, this then makes what is "best" arbitrary. Second, is the view you pick really what is best? Many religious views of what is best have led their societies to ruin and even extinction.

The problems with the second premise are even greater. What is the evidence for the second premise—for the prudence of Yes-Belief? The argument says: Believe not because you think it is an educated guess that God exists but because it makes society better. Well, what is the evidence for the premise that it will make society better? The question now is not whether there is convincing or reasonable evidence that God exists but whether there is convincing or reasonable evidence that Yes-Belief makes for a better society. Or are we supposed to accept, also *without evidence,* that it is better for society if we believe that God exists than if we don't? What could convince us that it is better? Where's the evidence? What's the argument for *that?*

What is often odd about arguments that shift from evidential justification for the existence of God to prudential justification is that *the evidential justification for the prudential justification is missing.* It's a sleight-of-hand trick, shuffling the problem into the background so that we can't immediately see it, as if now suddenly to become convinced of something—rather than merely converted by emotional persuasion—no evidence is required. At some point, however, that prudence must itself be justified on evidential grounds. But the evidential justification of that prudence is missing.

Suppose Scottie says, "Leprechauns exist." Doubtful, you ask for evidence and get nothing but an appeal to Irish myths and some stories. Seeing that you are not persuaded, Scottie adds, "Why worry about evidence? Believing in leprechauns will bring you good luck!" In other words, supposedly it's not a question of evidential justification but of prudence. Believing in leprechauns is just the smart thing to do, it's good for you, it will bring you luck. Well, but *will* believing that leprechauns exist really bring good luck? Leprechauns may be beyond the reach of evidence. Real world casinos are not. "Leprechauns exist" might not be testable; "Believing in leprechauns will bring you luck" is *very* testable.

Likewise, even if we suppose that the existence of God is beyond the reach of evidence, whether believing that God exists can be the basis for a system of ethics or make us more moral is certainly *not* beyond the reach of even the most basic and ordinary kind of evidence. Whether Yes-Belief is prudent on ethical grounds is a straightforward question, testable by evidence. It is a question about ethics and about us; in particular, it is a question of the impact of certain beliefs on our moral lives. There are two separate questions: (1) Can Yes-Belief, of any sort, provide a convincing foundation for ethics? (2) Does Yes-Belief make people more moral?

Assuming now the Yes-Believer believes the answer to one or both questions is Yes, the first question may seem ridiculous— what do you mean, can ethics be based on beliefs about God? Isn't it *obvious* that it can? It already is, isn't it? Here the Yes-Believer who believes that the moral argument for belief is convincing is in for a surprise.

8.1 The Divine Command Theory: Does Morality Depend on Religion?

The view that a system of ethics is based on divine commands has been called "The Divine Command Theory." The theory says, basically, that whether some action is right or wrong, good or bad, and so on, depends on whether God approves or disapproves of it.

When one thinks of whom our society considers to be its "moral experts," this view may have some initial plausibility. After all, when moral issues arise, the priest, the minister, the rabbi, the ayatollah, the rinpoche, the lama, are often called on for moral guidance, as somehow it is self-evident that they are the real experts on ethical matters. Even our political leaders speak of having to defer to a "divine guidance" supposedly found within their deepest religious commitments, as if they too rely somehow on God for moral arbitration.

Such behavior seems to imply that Yes-Belief already is, as a matter of fact, the basis of our system of ethics. So the question of whether it *could* form such a basis seems, at best, moot: It already does. But what is far from clear is not only whether it really does but *whether even in principle it ever could.*

Before we get to the many serious difficulties with the Divine Command Theory, one immediate problem is: the divine commands of *which* God? The Muslim God? The Hindu God? The Christian God? Even within any particular religion—for instance,

137

within Christianity—is it the "divine commands" in the Old Testament or the "divine commands" in the New Testament that we should follow, the Protestant "divine commands" or the Catholic? And so on.

The Yes-Believer might respond: Whichever God you have been raised with, that is the God whose divine commands you should follow. Although this may add some arbitrariness to your system of beliefs, it does give you a definite, particular system.

The problem with this answer is that immediately a slew of other difficulties arise, having to do with matters of interpretation. First of all, you weren't raised with a particular God. You were raised with a particular view of God. Presumably, no God raised you. Parents did. And they did not get their dictates, presumably, directly from God but, if they were religious, from their religious authorities. In other words, if you had a religious upbringing you were raised with someone's interpretation of God. You were given certain commands to follow. Just because you were given those commands does not make them divine. Your parents, or your parents' religious leaders, might have been persuaded through emotional manipulation, indoctrination, and conversion into accepting those commands as being divinely inspired rather than having been presented with sufficient evidence to evidentially justify the belief that those commands are indeed divine. Nobody's say-so makes it so: Without evidence, this is merely belief by conversion.

Now, for the next problem: Where is the evidence that the particular moral dictates of any religion are divine commands? It is very doubtful that there is any such evidence. Most of today's moral issues are not even *referred* to explicitly in the "divine scriptures" in which the supposedly "divine commands" have been preserved. This means that various decisions are left in the hands of religious leaders to decide, based on their interpretation of the scriptures, what the rules are—which leads to lots of changes over time. For instance, to take but one contemporary example, there is presently a deep, worldwide moral commitment on the part of the Catholic Church against abortion based, supposedly, on a divine command according to which a person's life begins at "the moment of conception." Few Catholics today realize that their church's position on this is of relatively recent vintage. For centuries the church claimed, apparently using the arguments of St. Thomas Aquinas, themselves based on Aristotle's views, that the human soul is not present "at the moment of conception." The church formally accepted this as its official view in 1312 at the Council of Vienna, *and that is still its official, though not publicized, view.* How then did it get to its present, "public" position? When did God change God's mind—and, at that, *unofficially?*

> . . . in the seventeenth century, a curious view of fetal development began to be accepted, and this had unexpected consequences for the Catholic view of abortion. Peering through primitive microscopes at fertilized ova, some scientists imagined that they saw tiny, perfectly formed people. They called the little person a "homunculus," and the idea took hold that from the very beginning the human embryo is a fully formed creature that needs only to get bigger and bigger until it is ready to be born.
>
> If the embryo has a human shape from the moment of conception, then it follows, according to Aristotle's and Aquinas's philosophy, that it can have a human soul from the moment of conception. The church drew this conclusion and adopted the conservative view of abortion. The "homunculus," it said, is clearly a human being, and so it is wrong to kill it.
>
> However, as our understanding of human biology progressed, scientists began to realize that this view of fetal development was wrong. There is no homunculus; that was only an invention of mistaken science. Today we know that Aquinas's original assumption was right—embryos start out as a cluster of cells; "human form" comes later. But when the biological error was corrected, the church's moral view did not revert to the older, more consistent position.[1]

There is a deep irony here. Some years earlier, the church had refused to acknowledge Galileo's new theory about the motion of the Earth, choosing to hold steadfast to its supposedly divinely inspired official view based on scriptures, according to which the sun, the moon and all the other planets revolve around the Earth. The Earth, according to the Bible, does not move. It sits at the center of the solar system. Because of this, the church suffered a great embarrassment at the hands of science. In the case of abortion, this time the church apparently decided to get on the scientific bandwagon, perhaps hoping to avoid having to suffer a second devastating blow from science. As every child is taught today in grade school, Galileo was right and the church was wrong. Today there is no question but that the Earth goes around the sun rather than that the sun goes around the Earth. You too were probably taught this at a very early age. Well, one can only guess at the "Bible meeting" behind closed doors with whoever had decided that this time the church should go along with the scientists. Of all the times to go wrong, this time, when the church was finally on the side of science, science had somehow managed to make one of the most egregious blunders of its career!

What the example of abortion shows so vividly is that while the attraction of having "absolute" standards based on direct commands from God *might* be a good thing to have, there is no reason to think that the commands issued from the mouths of religious authorities are divine. In fact, there is lots of evidence to the contrary.

8.2 Socrates Resurrected

The difficulties do not end there, but they began more than twenty-five centuries ago when Socrates dealt the first devastating blow against the Divine Command Theory with one of the most famous philosophical questions of all time: Is an action right because God says so, or does God say so because it's right?

This question poses a grave dilemma for the religious moralist. Perhaps the answer is, "It is right to do X because God says so." This means God's say-so is the *cause* of it being right to do X. Suppose God says, "Be kind to others." What then makes kindness right rather than wrong is not the kindness itself. Rather, it is the fact that God *says* kindness is right that makes it right to be kind. If not for God's say-so, kindness would not be the right thing to do. It wouldn't be wrong, either; it would just be morally worthless; there would be no intrinsic value to kindness independently of God's say-so. Suppose God says,

> "Avenge the children of Israel of the Midianites . . . therefore kill every male among the little ones, and kill every woman that hath known man by lying with him. But all the woman children, that have not known a man by lying with him, keep alive for yourselves."

Then, in that situation, killing the male children of your enemies and keeping the female ones for yourself would be the right thing to do.

On this view, no act has any intrinsic value in and of itself; everything has but extrinsic value derived from the fact of God's command. But isn't kindness good *intrinsically*, regardless of what God or anybody else says? Likewise, killing children seems a nasty thing to do, not to mention killing the male children and keeping the female virgins "for yourself," regardless of what the creator of the universe, or anyone else, might command. To claim, "But surely God *wouldn't* command such a thing" misses the point entirely. First, *the command above to kill the males and keep the virgins for yourself is taken verbatim from the Bible.* Second, and even more importantly, is God's say-so to do X really the *cause* of X being right, or is X being right the cause of God's say-so? It can't be that whether X is right or wrong is in this way arbitrary. Surely, then, it must be the latter: God says "Do X" *because* doing X is the right thing to do.

Thus, to avoid making a divinely inspired ethics arbitrary, we are led to take the second horn of the dilemma: God says "Do X" because doing X is the right thing to do. In that case, however, God's say-so has nothing to do with whether X is right or wrong, good or bad. Whether X is right or wrong, good or bad, and so on, must be based on something else.

For instance, consequentialist moral theories define whether a particular action is right or wrong based on the consequences of the action. If it leads to good consequences, it was right; if it leads to bad consequences, then it was wrong. (This of course raises the problem of what is meant by "good" and "bad.") The other way is nonconsequentialism: Define right and wrong action based on whether the action is done in accordance with a good rule. (This also raises the problem of what is meant by "good.") These, of course, are standard sorts of ethical questions. God's likes or dislikes have nothing to do with it. So if you believe that God commands you to do X—even if your belief is true—this cannot be a convincing foundation, the basis, the cause, of X being the right thing to do. Nor would it be correct to say that you did X because you were convinced that doing X is the right thing to do. You did X not because you are convinced that X is the right thing—which would make the act moral—you did X because you were persuaded to do it without being convinced that it is right. In other words, your doing X is not a moral action at all. It is either arbitrary and therefore immoral or a conditioned response and therefore also immoral.

Thus, the Divine Command Theory cannot, even in principle, provide a convincing foundation for ethics. And, as I've just suggested, one could claim that actions done in accordance with divine commands are *immoral.*

To sum up, then: On the divine command theory, when it comes to moral issues, God's say-so—even if we knew what it was (and we don't)—is either the *cause* of something being right or an *effect* of something being right. If the cause, then the "rightness" itself is arbitrary, and therefore of no moral worth in and of itself; if the effect, then the "rightness" is valuable in and of itself, thus causing God merely to acknowledge it, in which case God's acknowledgment is superfluous to what it is that *makes* the action right, and therefore God's say-so is unnecessary. The Divine Command Theory thus either makes morality arbitrary or it makes divine commands superfluous. It is therefore self-defeating.

8.3 Does Yes-Belief Make Us More Moral?

The second sort of difficulty with trying to make up for a lack of evidential justification of Yes-Belief with appeal to moral imperatives concerns the question of whether beliefs about God do, in fact, make people more moral. That is, regardless of whether God's approval and disapproval can determine whether particular actions are right or wrong, isn't it the case that *believing* that God approves or disapproves is essential to our being moral? Again, it *may* be. Or it may not be. But we cannot be convinced that it is so unless we have evidence that it is in fact true that beliefs about God do in fact make people behave better.

So again we have to look for the evidence. The evidence does not fare well for the moral prudence view. In fact, the evidence is in the end rather incriminating; it is like putting up an alibi for your defense designed to save you and the alibi ends up incriminating you. The problem is that the Yes-Believer now appeals to the edification of human beings that has resulted from Yes-Belief. We then examine this claim and find how Yes-Belief has contributed, instead, to the destruction of human beings.

There has hardly been a war in which Yes-Beliefs about God did not play a fundamental, perhaps even a key role. Whether the war is between Catholics and Protestants, between Christian crusaders and Muslim "infidels," Hindus against Muslims, Hindus against Buddhists, Christians against Jews, or even between countries of "mixed" religious denominations, a crucial motivating factor has always been, and continues to be, the belief that yes, there is a God, and "God is on our side." Indeed, what better way to justify horrible atrocities than by claiming to have the absoluteness of God on your side? Hitler claimed that were it not for his belief in God he would never have dared do what he had done; a Catholic pope declared by divine infallibility that Indians don't have souls and therefore it is all right to torture and kill them; the list goes on and on.

Surely, then, it is far from obvious that Yes-Belief *is*, in fact, good for society. In fact, there is plenty of evidence pointing in exactly the opposite direction. That is not to say that we can say with certainty that Yes-Belief is good or bad, one way or the other. Rather, the Yes-Believer's assertion that believing in God or believing that God exists is convincing on grounds that it just obviously makes people morally better, is false. It may even make them worse.

Indeed, the research psychologist Stanley Millgram suggests a frightening possibility: that breaking the biological rule against killing your own kind is made possible precisely through obedience to authority.[2] Millgram designed and carried out one of the most shocking and important experiments ever made on human behavior, revealing the extent to which ordinary people like you and me are ready to kill other innocent people simply out of obedience to authority. Insofar as God is represented in each culture as the supreme authority, and as so many wars are religious wars, there is some reason to think that religion in general and the concept of God in particular may be one of the leading causes of human suffering.

8.4 Does Belief Make You a Better Person?

What about you, personally? There may be no convincing evidence that Yes-Belief makes society better, but doesn't Yes-Belief make y*ou* better?

Well, first, it seems that in this case what is true at the social level is also true at the personal level. What reason do we have for thinking that Yes-Believers are better people than No-

Believers? One thing we could do is start by taking a survey, say, of the prison population with regard to beliefs about God. What such data tend to show, however, is that, on average, the percentage of Yes-Believers on the inside is the same as the percentage of Yes-Believers on the outside. There is no reason to think that exposure to religion on a regular basis, as part of growing up in a religious family, will affect your chance of ending up in prison. Among the population at large, there have been notoriously evil Yes-Believers as well as notoriously evil No-Believers. But also there have been tremendously wonderful human beings who were No-Believers, and equally great people who were Yes-Believers. In general, Yes-Belief seems to have nothing to do with how you treat your fellow human beings. (It should be noted, too, that 40 percent of all clergy profess to be atheists, based on surveys taken at the end of their graduation from divinity school. The percentages vary widely, of course, but some divinity schools have been 100 percent atheist, such as Harvard Divinity School during the heights of their famous "God is dead" movement.)

But perhaps it's not a question of morality; Yes-Belief might not make you a better person morally, but it might *be* better for you. It might. Or it might not. Once again the question is a straightforward question about evidence. Does Yes-Belief make you feel better about yourself, give you hope, make you more successful, and so on? Although this may be very difficult to ascertain, it is neither impossible nor is it merely a subjective matter. The answer depends on what the facts are about your life. You might *believe* that Yes-Belief makes you feel better about life than does No-Belief. But you might be wrong. To find out, you would need to be convinced by evidence that you are, in fact, better off as a Yes-Believer than you would be as a No-Believer. This evidence is not forthcoming.

8.5 Personal Self-Interest: Pascal's Wager Refined

Yes-Believers sometimes claim to be convinced by the rewards open to Yes-Believers; if God exists, Yes-Believers will go to heaven and No-Believers will go to hell. So what about such *personal* self-interest? As we've already seen, two different sorts of arguments can be made. One concerns the quality of your life, the other the quality of your *after*life.

In life, you have a choice: Yes-Belief, No-Belief, or Non-Belief. As a Yes-Believer or No-Believer, you go through life believing either that God exists or that God does not exist. As a Non-Believer you go through life without any beliefs about God, one way or the other. As a Yes-Believer, perhaps you're obliged to go to church or temple, pray, and so on. As a No-Believer or Non-Believer, you're not. The difference, in terms of what it costs you to believe that God exists, is not monumental. Why not take a chance and put your faith in God? Otherwise, if you don't, when your life ends—what will you say then?

Perhaps in the end there is just nothing. But even then, if there is just death and then worms, what have you lost by believing? Almost nothing. On the other hand, if there isn't just nothing—if there is a divine judge, an ultimate arbiter, a God waiting for you at the end of the proverbial tunnel—what will you say *then*? Think about it: your *every* move. Everything you ever did. Everything you ever *thought*. *Everything*. And there stands God, creator of the Cosmos, *knowing*.

Clearly, God either exists or does not exist. Suppose God does not exist. Death comes. If you were a Yes-Believer, you were wrong. The loss? You may have wasted time in church and in prayer. If you were a No-Believer, you were right. The gain? For a brief instant you may be able to say "I was right," but it is rather doubtful whether you will even have time to smile. On the other hand, suppose God does exist. Then the Yes-Believer has something to cheer about—eternity in heaven. That's quite a reward. The No-Believer is out of luck.

Thinking about it in this way, as the great mathematician and philosopher Blaise Pascal did, it seems the choice is clear: Believe, Believe, Believe! It would be sheer stupidity not to. You have hardly anything to lose and everything to gain. What could be more reasonable than that? The famous "Pascal's Wager" seems like a sure bet.

As in the social prudence case, once again prudential reasons act as a substitute for reasonable evidential justification. This time, however, the benefit is not to society but to you. And, once you make the calculations, the possible benefit of Yes-Belief so outweighs the possible inconvenience of Yes-Belief that it would be unreasonable not to believe.

Pascal's argument goes something like this. Basically, you have two choices: either you believe that God exists (Yes-Belief) or you don't (No-Belief and Non-Belief). There are two possibilities: God exists and God does not exist. So there are four possible combinations of outcomes:

1. Yes-Belief + God exists
2. Yes-Belief + God does not exist
3. No-Belief + God does not exist
4. No-Belief + God exists (ouch!)

(The Non-Belief choice amounts, in Pascal's Wager, to the same thing as No-Belief.) Now, what is the probability of each of the two possibilities concerning whether God exists? It doesn't really matter, so long as there is even the *slightest* chance that God exists.

Let's suppose the chance that God exists is very, very small—we'll give it an evident probability of .01. This means that the evident probability that God does not exist is .99, a virtual certainty. If you think Pascal is giving up too much to the No-Believer, that surely the probabilities are better than that, don't worry. You can make the probabilities for the existence of God as small as you want—it doesn't matter how small. As long as there is some—*any*—chance that God exists, Pascal's Wager says that by far the most prudential self-interested choice is Yes-Belief. Now, what is the payoff for either bet? Again, the numbers themselves don't matter. It's their ranking relative to each other. Let's start with outcome (1). If you are a Yes-Believer and it turns out that God exists, provided you were a fairly decent person, you get immortality; eternity awaits you in heaven. How much of a payoff is that?

Well, no matter what finite number of units of happiness you would ascribe to a year of blissful life, an infinite number of blissful years will make that payoff, in terms of happiness, virtually *infinite*. (Life in heaven might begin to get tiresome after a billion years of unlimited happiness and having everything you want. But how bad could it be? Seems immortality plus being able to get everything you want would be pretty good.)

What about outcome (2)? In this case, all that time spent in church, synagogue, temple, praying, and so on, whatever your belief demands of you, has been wasted. Let's suppose you find the cost, in terms of happiness, tremendous; going to church is, for you, sheer torture. How bad a torture is it?

Let's give some numbers to pain you've experienced. Missing a movie costs you negative units of happiness, say –3. Falling down the stairs and breaking your arm, –20. And so on. Going to church, praying and believing, for you, is such bad torture that if there is no God, having believed would have cost you –100 units of happiness.

Payoff (3), on the other hand, gives you some satisfaction. The satisfaction will be, at best, but brief: As you're going over the edge into the abyss of eternal death, nothingness forever, you laugh at all the fools who wasted their time believing, and this gives you +100 units of happiness. It doesn't last very long, of course, but you go out laughing.

Payoff (4), on the other hand, is bad news. Think of when you burned your hand on the stove. Now imagine a really hot stove, hotter than any you've ever experienced. Now imagine your genitals on that stove. *Imagine them there for all eternity.* That's how hot Hell is! Plus you have to shovel coal under the Devil's whip and all that sordid, nasty stuff. Whatever finite number of negative units you ascribe to such torture, you'll have to undergo it *forever.* Some payoff. How bad is it? It is virtually infinitely bad. Figure 6 shows how Pascal's Wager looks.

		Outcomes 1	2	
		God exists	God does not exist	outcome value:
	probability of outcome:	0.01	0.99	
A	you believe	value: ∞ payoff: ∞	value: -1 payoff: -100	∞ + -1 = ∞
B	you don't believe	value: -∞ payoff: -∞	value: +1 payoff: +100	-∞ + 1 = -∞

value = probability × payoff

FIGURE 6.   Pascal's Wager

147

As you can see, it doesn't make much difference what the finite numbers are. No matter how you look at it, given those choices, Yes-Belief is clearly the dominant choice. To calculate the value of any bet, you multiply the probability of the outcome times the payoff. The value of Choice A, if outcome 2 occurs, is

$$-100 \times .99 = -1$$

For outcome 1, the value of Choice A is:

$$\infty \times .01 = \infty$$

For Choice B, the value of outcome 2 is:

$$100 \times .99 = 1$$

For Choice B, the value of outcome 1 is

$$-\infty \times .01 = -\infty$$

The outcome value for either choice, A or B, is derived by adding the values of the two possible outcomes:

$$A: \infty + -1 = \infty$$
$$B: -\infty + 1 = -\infty$$

Some choice! A is of infinitely positive value, B is of infinitely negative value. What could be more obvious than that it is in your personal self-interest to be a Yes-Believer?

If you are a staunch No-Believer who is reading this part of the book for reinforcement of your beliefs, and you have finally seen the light, then mend the error of your ways, go to the Belief Chart, and mark off a more suitable position for yourself—surely this can persuade you to get a little closer to (0,0)?

You might think that, surely, this is a cold and ruthless way of relating with your creator! Pascal's Wager has often been criticized on just such grounds: God, if God exists, surely will not be looking for calculating believers who place their faith in God the way gamblers place their chips in a casino.

In fairness to Pascal, however, who also happened to be one of the inventors of the roulette wheel, it should be kept in mind that this argument was designed precisely for the disbelieving gamblers, the skeptical aristocracy, the rich atheists whom Pascal saw all around him, people who, having dispensed with any rational arguments for the existence of God, had also dispensed with a spiritual life, forsaking all questions of cosmic proportion in favor of the vain pursuit of self-interest. He saw a bunch of cold-hearted intellectuals who were treating life itself as if it were but a huge casino and to them he said, all right, you want to play games? Want to place a little wager? Here's a wager! Self-interest, is that all you live by? Then consider this!

Furthermore, the often heard response that God would not accept such self-interested belief from anybody is based on taking Pascal's Wager out of the context in which it is given. Pascal does not say that the belief his wager will produce is of the proper type that God will recognize and admire. Rather, the wager may prompt you to live a more pious life. As we've already seen, you can't *make* yourself believe by converting yourself through emotional persuasion. Pascal, a brilliant mathematician, realized this. *But you can alter your beliefs by convincing yourself using evidence.* Thus, if you see what lies in store for the No-Believer, you can convince yourself with Pascal's argument. This can make it possible for you to go through the motions: The cognitive attitude is now in place, functioning as true. Going through the motions is by itself not good enough, but nor is it the end of the process; the psychological attitude will follow. Eventually, Pascal argues, you will come to see the merits of Yes-Belief in its true light, with a cognitive attitude and a psychological attitude properly based on it, which would otherwise be beyond your means to attain simply by direct emotional appeal to your own belief mechanism.

Suppose you are an elementary school teacher shipwrecked on an island with your third-grade class of juvenile delinquents. You went on a boating trip, ran into bad weather, and by the looks of it you'll be marooned with the little idiots forever. As it happens, the boys hate the girls, the girls hate the boys, and they all hate each other.

One day, you tell them about love. They stone you. When it comes to the question of love, they are staunch No-Believers. You explain to them about what will happen one day; they will get interested in the opposite sex, there will be love and holding hands and gentleness; there will be sex. They laugh, they taunt you and refuse to believe anything you say about love.

The situation gets worse. One day, fearing they will never learn, you devise a plan. You decide that the children are to play-act as if they do care about one another. They are to be civil and polite, even though they do not feel it. You set them up in such a way that they must play house, etc. even though they think the members of the opposite sex are utterly uninteresting and worthless.

Somehow, you must get them to go through the motions. So you bribe them, you do whatever you have to do to place them in actual life situations that then, once they are in those situations and see what they are like, make it possible for them to convince themselves by using the evidence before their eyes.

Of course, going through the motions is not love. But if you can get them to go through the motions long enough, certain things will begin to happen in their minds that could never happen otherwise. The little boy and the little girl have to actually be alone together at the shore, before the vast distances in the starry heavens, and when the waves roll in and tickle their feet they may feel a certain connection to the cosmos and to each other that no amount of explaining in the classroom could ever achieve. They have to actually experience it for themselves. You need both the head and the heart.

Make room for love in your heart and love will find a way in. Make room for faith and there will be no need to go in search of God. Like a gentle breeze through an open window, God will enter. Pascal was merely trying to open your window.

8.6 No More Bets: What's the Final Verdict?

Three problems immediately present themselves. First, the concept of God who punishes sinners for all eternity is held only by some religions. Unless you are convinced that *that* type of vengeful God exists, you cannot really be convinced that it is prudent for you to believe in that type of God. And thus the level of your evidential justification for the belief that Yes-Belief will get you to heaven is predicated upon, and cannot exceed, the degree of your evidential justification for the existence of *that* type of God rather than of the many other available concepts of God. Indeed, who is to say that the only people in hell aren't those who believed out of fear that God exists!

In other words, it could be that God—who, after all, if there is a God, gave you a mind with which to reason and weigh evidence—can and will forgive everything except one thing that really makes God furious: weak, self-interested souls who grovel and cringe and toss their beliefs, like trinkets, to whoever is likely to be the winning bet. Hell could be a place full of believers who sold their soul's divinely given reason to emotional persuasion! Maybe God hates that. Second, which God are you supposed to believe in? Pascal's Wager has the same flaw as the Divine Command Theory. There are too many conflicting religions to make such beliefs practical, not to mention impossible! Even if you limited your beliefs to just the major religions, you would have to spend most of your time trying to keep up with going through all the motions, running from the various churches, synagogues, and temples. According to one set of beliefs, you must do X— say, eat a certain type of food on a particular day, or not, light candles, or not, and so on—whereas according to a different set of beliefs you must do just the opposite. What will you do? Eat and not eat? Light candles and not light candles? That's impossible! Either way, you're doomed to sin.

So, finally, to be convincing, the view that Yes-Belief is better for you, like the belief that Yes-Belief will make you more moral or will make society better, requires, ultimately, some evidential justification. We've already seen in what ways the evidential justification for the existence of God is missing. What all the prudence arguments do is bait us with supposedly something that takes the place of the missing evidence: a moral imperative to believe.

We've seen this move before. It's very common. It even has a name. It's called "bait and switch."

Notes

1. James Rachels, The Elements of Moral Philosophy, New York: Random House, 1986, pp. 51–52.
2. See Millgram's profound *Obedience to Authority*, New York: Harper & Row, 1974, excerpts reprinted in Kolak & Martin, eds., *The Experience of Philosophy*, 2nd ed., Belmont: Wadsworth, 1993, pp. 28–35.

Is There Convincing Evidence Against the Existence of God?

9.0 The Problem of Disconfirming Evidence

IT IS ONE THING TO BELIEVE SOMETHING WHEN YOU HAVE SOME EVIDENCE but not enough to warrant a conviction. You make an "educated guess": after considering the available information, you make an *evidential leap*. In Chapter 1, we defined faith as when your psychological confidence exceeds your evidential justification. In that sense, faith means your emotions are suggesting something is true—something you would perhaps like to be true—even though you don't have the evidence for it; the gap is filled in by intuition, by wishful thinking, or somehow with your own psychological Yes attitude. By *evidential leap*, however, I do not mean faith. I mean going beyond what the evidence warrants not with your feelings but with your probabilistic calculations. How reasonable an evidential leap is depends on how wide the chasm is between what you are convinced is the case and what, by extrapolation, you are convinced the likely case may be. If the chasm is too wide, at some point trying to leap across it becomes not just unreasonable but suicidal. An evidential leap—calculating and then guessing where the best place is to try to jump the cliff—is one thing; a leap of faith—hurling yourself off the cliff in the hope Superman will come to the rescue—is quite another.

What, then, are we to make of the gap between ourselves and the available evidence for the existence of God? Is it a case like that of our friend the drunkard, where at the same time while I believe *in* my friend's rehabilitation, I believe *that* there is but little chance he will actually pull through? Well, in such a case I'm merely choosing to "play along," not for the sake of the truth but for the sake of my friend. It's nothing like that with God. It cannot be that I am trying to do God a favor by believing in God against all evidence. God is hardly the sort of entity that, unless God gets our moral support, God will get depressed and go on a destructive binge (though many cultures used to explain natural disasters in exactly this way and sought to appease God through sacrifice). So believing in God without evidential justification would, at best, be a favor to society or a favor to myself (the prudent view of Yes-Belief), which we have already considered and found unconvincing. Such moves merely sweep the question of evidential justification under the rug of *supposedly* evidentially justified prudence until the question of evidential justification is simply forgotten—the old bait and switch.

But now the problem for the Yes-Believer gets even worse. Going "beyond" the evidence—making an evidential leap—when you are reasonably justified in doing so is one thing; continuing to believe that something is the case *contrary* to the evidence before your eyes, going *against* arguments to which you are forced to make elaborate rationalizations—faith—that's altogether something else. At some point, Yes-Belief ceases to be both rational and even prudent and becomes mere dogmatic stubbornness that can degenerate not just into unreasonableness but into blatant irrationality of the worst sort. As an illustration, consider the following story.

You're a parent. Like many parents, at Christmas you play along as if there really is a Santa Claus. You never really thought much about it, everybody does it, it's cute, it's funny, your son

Alvin loves it, and so on. You assume that as he gets older and grows up, he will stop believing.

But suppose, further, that Alvin continues to believe, not just in a playful "pretend" way but really, Alvin believes there is a Santa Claus! In school, he argues with the other children. His arguments are still naive but, you must admit, you are quite proud of how he manages to hold his own against the other children, even against the teacher.

Alvin becomes a teenager. He continues to believe fervently that Santa Claus exists. That's when you decide enough is enough. You've been playing along, sort of, but now you realize the time has come to tell your son the truth. So, on Christmas morning, you tell Alvin that there is no Santa Claus.

His reaction is somewhat strange. He doesn't say anything at first. He stares at you, very seriously. He asks where all the presents have been coming from. You explain you bought them at the store. He doesn't believe you. He wants to know why you are playing these cruel "head games" with him. Are you going to be like all the other parents, who at some point decide to deceive their children into thinking there is no Santa Claus? You show him the receipts for the presents. Convinced that the receipts are real—which gives you some relief—Alvin now wants to know why you would go to all the trouble of replacing the gifts Santa brought with store-bought replicas!

You're no longer angry. You're frightened. You ask him where he thinks Santa gets the presents. "Magic," he answers. According to him, you are one of the evil grownups he has read about, who when they get old forget about the magic, who refuse to believe, who in that cold and heartless way adults have of existing try to kill the magic with lies and deceptions.

You say this is ridiculous, there is no magic, you don't get presents from magic! You have to work for them. It takes money. Money doesn't grow on trees and presents don't just pop in from nowhere at the North Pole! Alvin says the presents don't just pop in, Santa's elves make them with magic. You say no, the presents are from the store. He asks where the store gets the presents. "Toy factories!" When Alvin asks if you have seen them, you say yes, of course you have. Without even realizing it, you lied. Alvin shakes his head. Where are the factories located, he wants to know—do you have addresses? Have you ever been to a toy factory, ever even seen one? He gets you to admit that really you haven't, not really—you "just know."

"Aha," he says. "You mean you believe on faith that there is no Santa?"

You explain that this is not so. All right, so maybe you haven't yourself been to the toy factories but you know there are some, you will look together in the Yellow Pages, you will go to a toy factory. Alvin concedes the point. He says, all right, let's suppose there are toy factories. Where do these toy factories get the presents? You tell him they don't "get them," they *make* the toys there!

"Aha," he says, "You mean the elves work there?"

Perturbed, you explain that no, not elves, not Santa, it's ordinary people who use ordinary materials . . . Alvin interrupts you. He asks where this "ordinary material" comes from. You tell him, "The Earth!" When he asks where the Earth comes from, you tell him how it came from the sun. He grins. "You know this? You've seen the Earth come from the sun? What a ridiculous idea!"

"It's evolution," you explain.

"Oh? How does it work?"

You try explaining what little science you know. You tell Alvin about evolution, about how stars and galaxies condense from interstellar dust, how the whole universe is expanding, how it all started with the Big Bang.

Alvin grins: "See how far you have to go to hide the magic?"

Now you are furious. Yet you keep trying to reason with him, hoping he will come to his senses.

Finally, you grab him by the shoulders. "Look, Alvin. Just tell me this. Ever seen Santa?"

"Of course," he says. "Many times."

"Where!"

"At that place even you believe in: the mall!"

"That wasn't Santa Claus!"

"Why the beard and the red suit and the `ho, ho, ho's?'"

"The beard is fake."

"Ever pulled on it?" he asks.

"Of course not!"

"Well, then how do you know?"

Suddenly, you realize what the ultimate, devastating piece of evidence is with which you will be able to sway Alvin.

"Remember last year," you say, "when we went to Macy's and there was a Santa in the parking lot, one outside the door, and another one inside? Remember how I laughed about it?"

"I remember, of course." He smiles, staring at you suspiciously.

"Well, how do you explain that Santa was at three different places at the same time?"

Alvin nods smugly: "*You* explain it!"

"What do you mean?"

"It's obvious, isn't it? You saw the evidence yourself. Three Santas! Obviously that *proves* it—Santa is a divine being."

You tell him how crazy all this is, that you and he and everybody knows for certain that no person could be at three different places at the same time, that's absolutely crazy. "Have you lost your mind, Alvin?"

"You're the one who's crazy," he says. "You should hear yourself! Or do you go deaf on Sundays?"

"What are you talking about? What do Sundays have to do with anything!"

Alvin shakes his head. "How many times have you heard the preacher explain it? The Son, the Father, and the Holy Ghost! How many persons? One, right? Yet you just said how it's completely crazy that a person could be more than one place at the same time. When the Son was on Earth, the Father was up in heaven, right? Don't you even know how to listen, how to reason? Or are you like most parents, completely irrational? Make up your mind, will you? What are you, schizophrenic or something?"

More than one moral can be drawn from this story. One is that there is something wrong with Alvin, though it is far from obvious what it is. It seems he "just doesn't get it." But is it so clear at what point Alvin is going beyond the evidence that has been presented to him?

A less obvious moral is: Given all the Santas you've seen, shouldn't *you* be convinced in the existence of a magical being who is in many different places at the same time? Why *don't* you believe that Santa is real? By what evidence did you come to this? You do, after all, see Santa everywhere at Christmas—just like Alvin. He, like you, certainly hasn't stopped reasoning. Alvin is reasoning very well. (The story even has a happy ending. Alvin becomes a philosopher.) You've never checked a Santa's credentials, never pulled on a beard—and probably never will. Even if you did pull on a beard, what would that prove? And even if the Santa says his name is John Smith, ho, ho, ho, couldn't *that* be the clever disguise?

The point is not that you couldn't, in principle, verify the truth with absolute certainty. (Though you couldn't.) The point is that you neither have actually verified it *even a little nor will you ever*. Like everybody else, you rely on hearsay and say-so, which you just pick up and never think twice about. The glue of belief holding you to "commonsense reality" is strong.

When that glue holds you to a "crazy reality," that's when we say there is something wrong. The problem is that we seem neither to have a ready solvent for this glue, nor are we able to say just what it is that distinguishes the "real reality" from the "crazy reality," except perhaps the number of people who are in one rather than in the other! But of course if that's the only difference . . .

Unless we are willing to end up like Alvin, we must be ready, willing and able *at some point* to give up our beliefs in light of disconfirming evidence and restrain ourselves from rationalizing. And so when we look at the possible evidence *against* the existence of God, we must be careful not to place our Yes-Belief into an invulnerable cocoon from which nothing could ever dislodge it. If we wish to achieve the purpose with which we started—getting ourselves into a neutral state of unknowing—we must be on the lookout for the sort of errors made by Alvin in the story above.

9.1 The Problem of Evil

So, is there any disconfirming evidence for God, that is, convincing evidence against the existence of God? Yes, there is: the universe. Not that it exists but that there is evil in it. Ironically, the very thing that supposedly fingers God as the divine creator—the universe—ends up being used in an argument against the existence of such a being. How can that be?

Whatever your concept of God, God is taken to be more advanced, in every way, than ourselves. We have some degree of (relative) knowledge; God knows much more than we ever could, and what God knows is true *absolutely*. We have some degree of wisdom; God is much wiser. We have some degree of strength; God is much stronger. We have some degree of moral worth; God is far more worthy. And so on. This sort of anthropomorphic reasoning has led some to believe that God must be *perfectly* wise, *all* knowing (*omni*scient), *all* good, and *omni*potent.

But when we take a good, hard look at the world around us, what do we see? Is this the sort of place about which we could reasonably say that, more than likely, this is the work of a creator who is omnisicent, omnipotent, and perfectly moral? The world is far from perfect. Wars, hunger, starvation, cruelty, suffering of all kinds . . . the evidence seems overwhelming that our world is *not* under the divine guidance of a benevolent, omniscient, and omnipotent creator. Looking at all the evil in the world, what are we to conclude but that this cannot possibly be the work of an infinitely powerful benevolent being who has a deep concern for human welfare?

This, the so-called "Argument from Evil" against the existence of God, might go roughly as follows. Let us call the originating source of the universe, "God."

1. There is unnecessary evil in the world.
2. Either "God" could have made the world with less evil in it but didn't want to, in which case "God" is not all good and therefore not God, or else "God" wanted to make a world with less evil in it but couldn't, in which case "God" is not omnipotent and therefore not God.

Therefore,

3. God does not exist.

Similarly, if "God" doesn't care one way or the other (which would be the case if "God" turned out to be a natural physical phenomenon, such as the physicist's concept of superforce), "God" is just a blind force, like gravity, which disqualifies it from being God. What, though, is the measure here of "perfectly good," "omniscient," and "omnipotent?" How do we even conceive of such a being? This is often considered to be a problem but we shall get around it as follows. We shall use ourselves as a test. God must be, if God is omnipotent, omniscient and all good, superior to us. Had we been the designers of the cosmos and, with our limited creative powers and resources, we could have made a better world than now exists, then this is a convincing argument against the existence of a being superior to ourselves who created it.

9.2 Could We Have Done Better Than God?

Steve believes society is run by special, gifted human beings superior to us in every way. These wise geniuses, the great and noble authorities, are in charge of designing and running civilization. Steve believes this because, according to him, it can't be that people like himself could possibly be the ones who created civilization. It must have been done by those vastly superior minds at the top. Who else but the supremely gifted people could have designed the financial system, the media, the political, academic, social, and religious institutions?

Jane disagrees. She says Steve's view is based on never having looked soberly at how bad things really are. Examine the inner workings of civilization up close, she says, and you'll see how things are actually run and who really is in charge. She points out how bad most governments are, how economic systems take advantage of the poor, how academic institutions do a terrible job of educating the people, and so on. It is simply ludicrous, she says, for Steve to believe that human institutions are the brainchilds of superhuman beings! Her reasoning is that, in most cases, *she finds it very plausible that she herself, had she been in such a position, could have done a much better job of it.*

Some things work well but most things barely work at all; the sheer incompetency, she says, is staggering. More often than not, people who hold positions of authority are perfectly ordinary. For many years Jane herself has looked seriously into the question of why the world is so messed up. Like Socrates, she has discovered that the only reason why the flaws and imperfections are not even more blatantly obvious than they are is that what nearly everybody everywhere is most skilled at is *pretending*. To keep their positions, the president, the pope, the scientist, the professor, the general, the doctor, all those "at the top" and "in the know" pretend to know more than their limited knowledge allows, to be far wiser than they actually are, to exaggerate their moral scruples, etc. It's not that the authorities aren't smart or don't know things. It's that they always overstep their boundaries with pretense and self-deception. And since they are in a position of power, that only aggravates the various problems, leading to a sort of inflation of ignorance, making the world even worse.

"I may be just plain old Dorothy," she says, "but they're the Wizard of Oz!"

Steve suggests to Jane that she must have missed something. Maybe the great minds have a truly amazing secret plan and that's why they put in all the flaws. Perhaps the flaws are not even flaws; after all, the great minds might be so superior that what to us look like flaws, to them are perfections. And so on.

It is at this point that Steve, like Alvin in the story above, seems to be using his ability to reason not to steer toward the truth but, rather, to rationalize by steering the evidence in the direction of something he would like to be true. This is bad reasoning. It is not that, when you rationalize, you have stopped reasoning or are reasoning *badly;* indeed, what makes rationalizing so insidiously unphilosophical is that, typically, in order to rationalize, good reasoning ability is absolutely necessary. But good reasoning skills can be used for getting at the truth or distorting it, even hiding it. Just as a skilled lawyer can use reason to manipulate a jury, so clever people can sometimes use reason to manipulate others, even themselves, into believing something that they would like to be true but for which they do not have reasonable justification. Perhaps Steve has some need to believe in the "great minds"; perhaps it is his way of avoiding responsibility, letting himself off the hook by saying, in effect, "I can't do anything about the world's problems, I'm just ordinary, it takes those great superior minds, let them do it."

What this story illustrates is that we must be on guard not to use our own cleverness to rationalize away what we don't want to see. What the Argument from Evil says is: Look at the world. Does it seem to you that a great cosmic mind is in charge, an absolute knowing mind that created such suffering, so much evil? Couldn't we ourselves, with our limited resources, have done a better job if only we had the power to create a world using wishes, as God supposedly does?

In other words, looking at our world, what do we see? Does what we see around us suggest a superior, kind and benevolent, conscious mind at work? Or do we see a bunch of imperfect human cogwheels in an insectlike machine, a world without eyes for suffering, running on chaotic forces, devouring each other in a blind rage to survive?

But here it seems a Yes-Believer can turn this line of reasoning back against itself as a defense against the Argument from Evil. It's not that had we the power we could have made a better world, *we do have power and we made this world.* We're the cause of the problem. If it were only up to God the world would be perfect. But God loves freedom even more than perfection. And so God chose to forsake a perfect creation so that we could be free.

In other words, all this supposedly once was a Garden of Eden, a place free of all evil. The evil we see all around is not the work of God. It is our own doing. God gave us free will to choose, knowing that we sometimes would choose badly. After all, wouldn't it be an ultimate sacrifice on God's part to make us free creatures who sometimes err rather than making us into obedient robots who always have to do the right thing but who have no freedom of choice?

9.3 Free Will and Responsibility

This so-called "Free Will Defense" against the Argument from Evil can only succeed if (1) we do have free will and (2) the sort of free will we have places the responsibility for our actions squarely on ourselves, not on God.

For the Yes-Believer who believes on moral grounds if it turns out that we do not have free will of the proper sort, this position will turn out to be even more *un*convincing. Remember, our purpose is not to defend our prejudices but to move ourselves into the neutral starting position, (0,0), on our Belief Chart. Let us therefore consider the following criticism, not just of the Free Will Defense but, in general, of the concept of free will.

Imagine God, before the big bang, preparing to actualize the universe. Like the novelist or filmmaker who has not yet begun to write the novel or make the movie, God has as much time as God wants to consider everything in advance: plot structure, characters, general story line, all sorts of various alternatives to each scenario, etc. Unlike ordinary novelists, filmmakers, and other artists, who have only the time and imagination to consider but a few alternative possibilities in their creations, God can glimpse as many *possible* worlds as God wishes before actualizing one—*this* one, this world, this one actual world that God in fact chose to actualize among a slew of alternative possible worlds. Doesn't this imply that God—not us—is responsible for all the evil that occurs, in the same way that in a novel or a film it is the writer and the editor, not the characters, who ultimately are responsible?

Imagine an infinite library whose books contain each and every possible combination of letters in the English language. Throw out all the meaningless ones. Every book ever written, even books not yet written, can be found somewhere on its shelves. The book you are reading right now exists somewhere in that library, as does a book exactly like this one except that in this sentence there are two commas instead of only one. *But if God exists, the library we have just imagined is not imaginary but real, in the sense that all actual books and all possible books are accessible to the mind of God.*

In other words, God must actualize the world from an infinite number of possible worlds, each of which differs from the one next to it by one detail. In one possible world, Adam decides to eat the proverbial apple. In the next possible world, everything else is the same except Adam decides not to eat the apple. Well, if God wanted Adam not to eat the apple, God should have actualized the second of these worlds and not the first! It would certainly be idiotically sadistic of God, who has every possible version of *Moby Dick* to choose from, to choose to read one that he does not want to read—and then punish that version of Ahab for not being a different version of Ahab!

Novelists with lots of time and money typically go through more than a hundred drafts before they publish. Filmmakers with large budgets typically have a ten-to-one shooting ratio; this means they shoot ten takes of every scene and then use only the best one. God, we are to assume, has no budget problems and is in no hurry. This means that no scene can take God by surprise; it would never be that God is forced to use some unwanted scene in the actual universe because God's budget ran out! Even Francis Ford Coppola wields that kind of power in his films. Surely God would be even more obsessively creative than Coppola on an infinite budget. God's "shooting ratio" would be *infinity* to one—God chooses each "actual scene" from an infinite variety of "possible scenes."

Thank you for taking the time to review our book. We hope you find it suitable for use in your classes.

However, if you do not choose to adopt this text, we encourage you to use this pre-gummed postage-paid label to return it to us. Simply moisten the back and affix it to the parcel.

Your cooperation will help keep textbooks affordable.

SPECIAL FOURTH CLASS RATE

POSTAGE DUE COMPUTED BY:
DELIVERY UNIT IF NO SPECIAL
SERVICES (OR)
ACCEPTANCE POST OFFICE IF
SPECIAL SERVICES ARE
REQUESTED (See 919)

POSTAGE
MERCHANDISE RETURN FEE
INSURANCE FEE (IF ANY)
SPECIAL HANDLING FEE (IF ANY)
TOTAL POSTAGE AND FEES DUE $

MERCHANDISE RETURN LABEL

PERMIT NO. 1   FLORENCE, KY 41042
WADSWORTH, INC.   7625 EMPIRE DR.

POSTAGE DUE UNIT
U.S. POSTAL SERVICE
FLORENCE, KY 41042-9998

God can see much better than Coppola can see into his own creative imagination to know in advance how each and every thing will turn out. Indeed, in many concepts of God, God does not even have to use intelligence to calculate the future; God directly *sees* the future in the way that our filmmaker sees all the takes hanging on the cutting room wall before splicing them in. The difference is that God sees not just versions of actual futures, God directly sees versions of all possible futures; in other words, God's powers of imagination are such that, unlike the novelist who has to give the character a chance to develop, unlike the filmmaker who has to shoot a possible scene to see whether it will work, and so on, God knows well in advance how each and every possible event will turn out once God chooses to actualize it.

But then the problem is this: If God can see what I will do tomorrow before it happens, then tomorrow is fixed. If God can see it, it is already there. It will do no good to say that God sees only "possible," not "actual" futures; for if we were to ask God right now if God can see what Smith will have for breakfast tomorrow, and God says, "I have no idea, I can see only possible futures," then God is not much better than the fortune teller on Main Street. You and I can "see" plenty of "possible futures" too. It's seeing into actual futures that counts.

God, unless God is as blind as we are about what will happen, must *know* what will happen in the world *even before God creates the world*. But if God knows what Smith will have for breakfast tomorrow, in what sense is Smith *free*? The morning comes. "Wonder what I'll have today," says Smith. "Cheerios or corn flakes? Ah, freedom of choice . . ." But of course God has known for the last fifteen billion years that Smith will eat Cheerios today.

In other words, it seems free will and the existence of God are incompatible. To see why more clearly, consider the following. Smith is contemplating whether to murder Jones. Presumably, at this point Smith is free to decide. What does it mean to say that Smith is *free* right now to kill or not kill?

Presumably, it means Smith has a *choice* among more than one alternative. That's what "having a choice" means; if I offer you just *one* card and I say, "Here, pick a card, any card," either I am a comedian or a very bad magician. Obviously, I am not offering you freedom of choice! If there is any choice involved on your part, it is *whether* to take the one card I am offering. It is not a choice among alternative cards. Thus, either because I am funny or because I am stupid, I have misused language: I used the phrase "pick a card" as if it meant "choose among several cards," when really what I should have said, if my intentions were not to deceive you, is: "Here, take this card." You can decide not to take the card but in this case you have *not* decided to not "pick" a card—you have decided to not "take" a card. You cannot, even in principle, decide not to *choose* a card if there is no choice among cards being offered.

In other words, how can you decide not to *choose* a card if there is only one card offered? You can't. There is no choice of cards. There is just the one card, period. What I am offering you is: Either take the one card which *I* have selected for you or don't take the one card which *I* have selected for you. This is not a situation in which you have *selected* a card. It is not a situation in which you can, even in principle, *freely choose* a card. For you to be able to freely choose, there would have to be at least two cards in my hand.

To act freely means, necessarily, that one could have done otherwise than one actually did do. This, in turn, requires a plurality of actualities from which to choose. One cannot "pick a card" unless there is more than one card, such that if you pick card A you could have done otherwise than you actually did do, namely, you could have picked B. If there is no B, only A, you didn't really pick. You could have mistakenly *thought you picked* a card; for instance, you tell a blind man to "pick a card, any card," and he takes a card from your hand not realizing it is the only one. He didn't really pick the card. You did.

"But he could have chosen not to take the card." Again, yes—provided that there is an alternative such that he could have done otherwise than he did do. If his brain has been wired in such a way that whenever he is offered a card he takes it, then he did not really choose to take the card, either; for that to have been his choice, it is necessary that he could have done otherwise than he did actually do.

So whether we are free depends on whether we could do things otherwise than we actually do them. But if God exists, then God knows absolutely what we will do before God even creates the world; if God knows what we will do at each and every moment before God even creates the world, that means from the very beginning there is just the one thing per moment that we do. The moments follow each other so quickly that we have the illusion that we are choosing; but moment per moment, God knows absolutely what the actual event will be, and God knew absolutely from the very beginning of the cosmos what would be occurring at any particular moment.

So: Let us imagine God before the big bang. There God is, composing the universe in whatever way God has of composing things. Like a good filmmaker, God makes a storyboard in God's mind. Not that God would have to do this, but God could do this and we are assuming that God is at least as conscientious a creator as your average Hollywood filmmaker. Hopefully, God is in many ways superior.

There, in God's screenplay, is the fateful moment when Smith murders Jones. If God exists, God knows about the murder. God isn't looking into the world at the time of the murder and thinking, "Oh, my God, look at that—another murder. Why didn't I think of this, why didn't I foresee this? Oh, no, what shall I do now? Quick, get me my eraser!" God, even a rather modest sort of God, would have foreseen each one of the moments presently occurring even before the universe began to unfold, including me writing these words and you reading them.

Sitting in God's study before the beginning of the cosmos, God foresees what will happen: whether Smith will or will not murder Jones. Whatever it is that happens, God will not be surprised! God could at any time write down on a card what it is that Smith will do at any moment in time. Suppose, in fact, that for every event that occurs in the universe, God has made an index card and filed it away. This would take a lot of index cards but we are, after all, talking not about some adolescent kid with a video camera who wants to make the greatest story ever told, nor even about Francis Ford Coppola making *Apocalypse Now*, but about God. Even Francis rarely gets to a scene and says, "Oh, my God, look, Kurtz is being assassinated in this scene. What do we do now? Help me, somebody, what do we do next?" He's got a fairly detailed storyboard. It doesn't have everything spelled out in advance but it has a lot.

Likewise, it is difficult to imagine even a mediocre writer getting to the end of a novel and gasping, "Oh, no, look at how it turned out. This is terrible, just terrible. I wanted them to go to Disneyland and live happily ever after and now look what they did, they went to Tahiti and committed suicide." God's mind is, we are assuming, at least quite a bit better and more detailed than that of human writers and filmmakers.

Now, suppose it's Friday. Smith hasn't yet "picked" what he will do on Saturday. "Picking" what to do is like picking a card. It means that, necessarily, there must be more than one card being offered or else it is not really a choice. So: How many index cards are there in God's filing system (or in God's mind) about what Smith actually will do on Saturday? Does God not have an index card for that event?

Presumably, God can look to see what Smith will do before he does it. How many index cards *for that particular actual event* are there? It makes no sense to say that there are more than one. Smith will not do more than one thing at that one time. It would be pointless for God to have two index cards for what Smith will do on Saturday—either murder or not murder. When Saturday night rolls around, there is only one thing that Smith will do. Smith may go for a walk or take Jones to dinner where they make up. Or it may be that Smith will kill Jones. (Or something else.) We don't know which it will be. And we do know, what God would also have to know, that Smith won't, at any moment, have dinner and not have dinner, go for a walk and not go for a walk, kill and not kill. But God knows even more: God knows which one of the things that Smith *might* actually do is the *actual* thing that Smith will do. God may have lots of filing systems with lots of cards, but in the drawer marked "Actual Universe" there is only one card for that event. *So go ahead. Pick a card. Any card.*

Now of course there may be no God. But we are assuming, right now, that there is a God who knows what Smith will do before Smith does it. So then we ask: First, does Smith even *have* free will? To have free will would require that you are in a situation in which you actually can choose among alternatives. Unless there are actual alternatives from which to choose, there is no choice. There is only the action that occurs without any real choice, without real freedom.

Second, suppose Smith decides to kill Jones. To say that the choice was a free one means Smith could have done otherwise. But what Smith actually will do on Saturday is already written on an index card, locked up in God's mind since the beginning of the universe. Does Smith have the power to make whatever God wrote on that card *false?* Smith's freedom would require of God, who presumably does not have false beliefs, to have some false beliefs. Or it would require of God, who presumably is some sort of absolute knower, not to be a knower at all.

Well, does Smith perhaps have the power to change what is on that index card? God would still have known how Smith would change it and that change itself would already be accounted for on God's index card. The idea that Smith can freely choose seems to vanish in a drawerful of index cards; the requirement of vague possibilities disappears in a precise cosmic mind that knows no uncertainty. And so when Smith pulls the trigger we must ask who is responsible: Smith or God?

What all these cases suggest is that God, if God exists, is the finger behind each and every trigger of every gun that has ever launched a bullet into someone's flesh. This is hardly a person of superior moral worth; this is a murderer that makes Hitler look like an amateur, concentration camps like playgrounds!

Think of it this way. Suppose an omniscient magician offers you a fanned-out deck of cards and says, "Pick a card, any card." What would this ceremony be for, except perhaps deception? The omniscient magician knows what card you will pick before you pick it. The other cards the omniscient magician offers are not really an offering but a deception. The *real* magician, if the magician was not just a real magician but also honest, would never say, "Pick a card, any card." The real magician would offer you one card and say, "Here, you will now take this card!" You would then, if the magician really were omniscient, take that card. You couldn't help it.

This truly would be amazing—but that's not the issue. The question is, who chose the card? Not you. The magician. Likewise with all the events that occur in the cosmos. If God exists, all the things you and I do are not our choices. We are but God's actions actualized.

This radically alters any ordinary conception of human choice, free will, good and evil, right and wrong, and so on. It leaves no room for the existence of any kind of moral God. Indeed, it raises the question of whether God thus conceived could have any sort of freedom. After all, it seems the same constraints limiting our choice would limit God's choice. To see why, imagine another filing cabinet next to the one labeled "The Actual Universe," one that has the awesome title "The Mind of God." If God has access to all the events, possible and actual, in the universe, it stands to reason God also has access to all the events, possible and actual, in God. How would God *choose* to actualize one universe from all the possibilities? God knows what choice God will make before God even makes it—when was that choice ever made? Never.

Suppose God chooses on Tuesday to make a world on Friday. Friday comes. God makes a world. When did God choose to make the world? On Tuesday. But did God know on Monday that God would choose on Tuesday to make a world on Friday? In that case, when Tuesday rolled around God had no alternative but to do as God knew God would do. On this view, *even God, if God exists, cannot be free to make any choices!*

On the other side of the coin, if we wish to have the concept of free will as ordinarily conceived, then necessarily, it seems, there can be no ultimate knower, no God. It is then precisely the absence of God that would make human freedom possible.[1]

9.4 Acts of God

A second reason why the Free Will Defense fails is that it completely fails to take into account the existence of natural evil. Earthquakes, floods, tidal waves, tornados, hurricanes, plagues, cancer, and so on—what have these to do with free will? They may have some other function, such as to keep us from being "spoiled" by having to live in a utopian world, or something like that. But then one needs a different sort of defense, not free will. And then the difficulties only pile up.

For instance, let us suppose all the natural evil in the world is put there by God so that we might be informed about the difference between good and bad things. Without darkness we would not know light; without natural evil we would not know good.

There are many difficulties with such a view. We need but point out only a few of them. First, let's take as an example a philosophy professor who is neither omnipotent nor omniscient nor all good, but who has some limited power. The philosopher knows many things and is to a certain degree a good person—better than some, worse than others. Suppose, furthermore, that the philosophy professor decides to use this limited amount of power, knowledge, and goodness to design the best of all philosophy classes.

It is not good when students fall asleep. The professor must come up with a way to keep them alert and so the professor hangs heavy objects from the ceiling that occasionally, at the flick of a switch, fall down and crush the unwary student. Sometimes a flame thrower shoots out from near the blackboard and if you are asleep and don't move out of the way, it incinerates you. What would you put on the student evaluations—that this was a good professor or a bad professor?

You say to your classmate, "You know, this professor is really a monster. Forget this class." Your classmate says, "Come on, the philosophy professor knows what's best! Philosophers just teach in mysterious ways. Philosophers know what they are doing!"

The problem, of course, is that you do not yourself need to be omniscient and omnipotent to know, using your own limited power, knowledge, wisdom, and goodness, that this professor is bad news! Likewise, as a philosophy professor, I can use my own experience to know that no teacher in his right mind would use such methods (except on special occasions). It would be primitive and brutal. Similarly, to argue that God has made all the world's disasters because God is the best of all teachers is, using what I know about good teaching, simply ludicrous.

Furthermore, even if some such suffering were necessary through natural disasters, at some point one would have to ask: Why so much of it? Would not three birth defects a year, leading to three poor innocent children who have to suffer through life, be enough? Do we need 100,000? One hurricane every seventy years would be plenty. An earthquake a century would probably suffice to remind us that the Earth sometimes moves. Do we need 50,000 deaths a year by auto accident? Wouldn't 5,000, or 500, or even 5 serve just as well? And so on. At what point does believing that there is a guiding hand keeping us from disaster become as ludicrous as Alvin believing in Santa Claus?

There is also the question of why the suffering is so extensive. An earthquake occurs in Mexico. A little girl is crushed by a falling wall—almost. Her legs are crushed and she is pinned up to the chest beneath the rubble. There is some flooding and as the water slowly rises, the paramedics, emergency workers, even the girl's parents are trying to help her while the CNN television crew films the entire scene. The little girl cries; so do her parents. She tells of her pain and her fear. Her face finally disappears under the water; the paramedics keep the oxygen on her for a little bit but then all the workers have to leave, dragging away the screaming parents. Before our eyes, after many hours of unbelievably horrible agony, the little girl pinned beneath the wall drowns.

Where was God? Supposedly, God is very powerful. Suppose that for some reason known only to God, the little six-year-old girl had to die. Could she not at least have died quickly? If God had moved the wall a little bit as it fell, one way or the other, the little girl's life would have been spared or she would have died instantly. If there was a God—not even an omnipotent, omniscient, and all-good God, but a fairly powerful, knowledgeable, pretty good God—one of these two choices could easily have been arranged. The fact that they were not shows that even such a semi-omnipotent, semi-omniscient, semi-good God probably does not exist.

There are plenty of events in the world where even someone like Superman, who is at best an extremely modest version of God, could have prevented some suffering or at least lessened it. If looking at the world we can see that even benevolent, super-powerful creatures like Superman don't exist, then we know, *a fortriori*, that God does not exist.

Of course sometimes people do escape by narrow margins. But we are not discussing here whether there are "miraculous" events. Even if, on occasion, wonderfully good things happen in a concentration camp, this is no evidence that the concentration camp was designed by a benevolent being. A prisoner is cured of cancer by one of the concentration camp guards. Three prisoners are given their freedom. Four children are showered with gifts. An old woman wins the concentration camp lottery and gets to go to the movies. Six hundred thousand go up in flames. Put it all together, the concentration camp is a nasty place.

Now, no one is saying that the world is as bad as a concentration camp; rather, taken as a whole, we are trying to determine whether anything like a God has had an overseeing and guiding hand in the world's design. The best available evidence is convincing: The answer is No.

To respond with "God works in mysterious ways," as a defense against the Argument from Evil, is, at best, a deceptive rationalization that misses the point entirely. It would be one thing if the amount of natural evil in the world were such that we, using our best available evidence, were in a state of uncertainty as to whether this is too much or not enough. We are not in such a situation. Ask yourself this: If you were even *almost* omnipotent, knowing what you know now, if you were entrusted with having to improve the world would you be able to think of ways to do it?

I certainly could. The first thing I would do is make human beings less vulnerable. Not necessarily completely *invulnerable*, just less vulnerable than they are now. Thicker skin, stronger bones, and so on. I would make them less prone to developing diseases like cancer, AIDS, and so on. When designing a car, if you have unlimited resources you use better materials, ones that will make the car last longer before it wears out and less prone to scratches, accidents, malfunctions, breakdowns, and so on. Similarly, computer manufacturers are limited by their resources; if you have thousands of billions of dollars to spend in making your computers, you will make better ones than if you only have one billion. God, if God existed, would be in a position relative to us of having unlimited resources. If using our limited resources we could design a better world, then by all reason no creature superior to us had a hand in its design.

A different sort of defense using the "God works in mysterious ways" line of reasoning is to say that God really is completely beyond our understanding. Words like "good" and "evil," "right" and "wrong," and so on, simply do not apply to God. Our minds cannot even begin to comprehend the mysterious and unfathomable workings of the mind of God. Again, this may be so, but as a defense this throws out all evidential justification for anything concerning God. If God is in this way completely unfathomable, then we can make no pretense to understanding God. Certainly it would dispense with all orthodox religious views of God, since they would have no way of understanding what God really wants or what God is really like.

Does God think killing innocent children is good or bad? We can't say: God's mind is impenetrable. Does God think religion is good or bad? We can't say: God's mind is impenetrable. Note that pointing to what some bible says concerning the matter won't do now, since what this document might *mean* is completely and utterly incomprehensible. If whether the particular bible in question captures what the real God really wants is difficult to establish, how much more difficult is the Yes-Believer's task of finding out what God wants if God's real intentions are completely beyond our reach? If to ask, "Does God exist," means we are asking whether there exists something of a certain sort that we can know about, think about, reason about, ask about, and know what it is that we are asking, then to make this sort of move is tantamount to answering "No!"

9.5 Why Aren't We Angels?

Suppose that, in light of what has been said above, we ask why the world, if it was created by God, is not a utopia. Why, if God knows everything we will do before we do it, did God not choose to actualize a world in which we all freely choose to do only good things? Presumably because it would be impossible to have all these things simultaneously. Not even God could actualize a world like that.

But what is truly amazing about this sort of response is that, supposedly, *there in fact does exist such a state of affairs actualized by God*. Where? Heaven! Angels aren't robots. They have free will. Yet they don't do bad things. Heaven is a possible world. But there are no tornados and hurricanes and mutilations and birth defects. *Why doesn't God just stick to making Heavens, populated by angels?*

In fact, shouldn't we also ask why, if there is a God, this God makes inferior creatures such as ourselves? Does God need little playthings to toy with, to threaten, even when God knows before we are even created how we will behave? It's like creating windup toys and then yelling at them and smashing them when they just go where they are wound up to go. If God exists, wouldn't it be more appropriate for God to make some colleagues? Or is God like all those bad teachers and bad parents who want to teach you and want you to advance—so long as you do not exceed them?

One true mark of a great creative artist is that the artist succeeds in creating things equal or greater, not lesser, than the artist. In other words, if God demands so much of us, should we not ask of God, if there is a God:

"Ask yourself, oh God, whether there is not a moral imperative for God to make more Gods!"

Notes

1. For a much fuller treatment of these and related topics, including the effect of possible worlds analysis on the problem of foreknowledge and free will and a counterexample to Plantinga's position that relies on the Stalnaker-Lewis semantics, see my "Causality, Responsibility, and the Free Will Defense," in Kolak & Martin, eds., *Self, Cosmos, God,* Fort Worth: Harcourt, Brace, Jovanovich, 1993, pp. 286–299.

What Is the Role of Authority?

10.0 Is Appeal to Religious Authority Justified?

SOME YES-BELIEVERS IN THE DIVINE APPEAL TO HIGHER *HUMAN* AUTHORITY. The appeal goes something like this:

All right, so maybe I'm not really convinced that God exists. Maybe I don't even have enough evidence to make my belief an educated guess, not even a hunch. Perhaps I'm not even convinced that believing in God is good for society or good for me. But I do know that certain authorities who must on any account be regarded as experts on matters religious, such as the question of the existence of God, the status of the evidence and arguments for the existence of God, and so on, repeatedly encourage people to trust what they say. And, in the final analysis, they all say God exists. I therefore believe because they believe. I am not qualified to make judgments

about such matters. They are. They know best. It is reasonable
that I listen and obey.

The first problem, as already noted, is that a large number of
religious authorities are atheists. That notwithstanding, such appeals are only as good as the track record of the particular authorities in question who claim that God exists and that you
should believe, and they really *do* believe what they claim. The
question then is: Have these authorities been honest with people
in the past? Have they always done what is best for society and for
individuals? Have they always been honest in what they present
as truth, never deceiving, never tampering with the evidence,
never being the tools of corruption? And so on.

Here one need not refer to the religious wars that have existed throughout history in all lands, the torture by religious leaders of innocent people, the suppression of the truth, the burning
of witches, the Inquisition, and so on. One need only ask the
following question: Has the Yes-Believer been made aware of all
the problems with the arguments for the existence of God in
general, and religious belief in particular, both in terms of evidence and of faith, that have been presented in this book? Typically, the answer is No.

Suppose you were raised a Catholic. You've gone to church,
to Sunday school, to catechism, and so on. You believe on the
basis of some appeal to authority. Well, many of the problems
thus far raised about the traditional arguments for the existence
of God—the problems with the Argument from Design and the
Cosmological Argument, as well the difficulties for belief posed
by the Argument from Evil, the philosophical difficulties with the
concept of free will, and so on—have been around *for centuries.*
Of course, until recently, for people to question the existence of
God was widely considered heresy. Until recently, heresy was
punishable by death. These facts hardly speak well for appealing
to religious authorities. Why?

Because rarely, if ever, do religious authorities present criticism of their views, teach new developments, encourage followers to study and compare in depth their religions with others,
and so on. Sometimes they do, but very rarely, and usually such
questioning is carefully manipulated to keep the faithful from
straying from the flock. Most people are shocked to find that a
large percentage of clergy, by their own account, are atheists. If

the religious authorities were more open and honest, rather than manipulative, such views would come as no shock. The issue is not whether this is proper or improper behavior on the part of religious leaders on their followers. Rather, the question is whether the nature of religious education succeeds in justifying an appeal to authority.

10.1 Scientific Authority vs. Religious Authority: Is There a Difference?

Suppose you're a science student from a little-known country, "Authoritaria," who has come to the United States to go to school. Like all Authoritarians, you've been educated in physics. When the theories of relativity and quantum mechanics come up in discussion, you politely inform your fellow students that while it is all right for them to believe in these theories, any calculations required of you must be done by you using Newtonian mechanics. You've been told that you might encounter "other points of view," and that is fine, but you have been told by your authorities to keep to the Newtonian system because that is the true nature of the cosmos.

Your fellow students call up your old teachers and find out they really did tell you this; furthermore, the teachers claim it was all for your own good. Science, they say, is constantly changing and they believe that it is better to stick to tradition than to go with whatever Johnny-come-lately theories currently happen to be in vogue. The students approach you and show you all sorts of problems with classical Newtonian physics, how Einstein's relativity theory helps solve some of them, and so on. Next, they present difficulties with Einstein's own view, which quantum mechanics nicely solves; they then point out various difficulties with even the latest formulations of quantum theory. At this point, unable to respond to the various criticisms of your received view, you again evoke an appeal to authority, as follows.

Neither the other students nor you, you claim, know more than your respective authorities. At some point they, your fellow students, have accepted what their authorities have told them, and you have accepted what your authorities have told you. You tell them that physics is too complicated to be understood by students and so you have to wait until you yourselves become sufficiently informed to make the sorts of judgments that now must be deferred to your respective authorities.

But suppose that your fellow students respond with the following. It turns out that for the last three centuries your authorities have not been ignorant of the developments of relativity and quantum mechanics. On the contrary; in Authoritaria the physicists in power have suppressed their critics by imprisoning them, burning them, intimidating them, and so on. You are shown that this has been the case. What would you conclude?

It is true that, in science as in religion, there is appeal to human authorities. One can claim to be speaking for God, just as one can claim to be speaking for the universe itself. But such claims are just that—claims. Without reasonable evidence, such claims are neither convincing nor justified. *But that is not the problem.* Even if none of us could ever tell whether what the authorities are saying is true, the problem is that when it comes to the question of the existence of God, we *can* tell whether a particular set of authorities have been honest with their followers, and to what degree. *This* is not a question of faith but of public record.

Scientific authorities sometimes lie. Sometimes they deceive. Sometimes they are very slow to bring about change in their systems even when such change is warranted. But, by and large, they have no track record of murder, torture, evoking "divine infallibility," and so on—though they are sometimes known to get rather defensive when questioned. Indeed, scientists as a group have a good enough track record that someone who has no taste for actually inquiring into matters scientific might reasonably wish to appeal to scientific authorities and say, "All right, on this particular question I will for now just have to trust you and take your word that it is so until I am ready to find out for myself."

Scientists do have a pretty good track record, too, of admitting what they don't know, of changing their mind in light of new evidence, of revising their theories, of informing their students of the latest developments, and so on. It's not just that no Einsteinian has ever put a Newtonian on the rack for being a Newtonian; Einsteinians have actually, as a matter of public record, not only endorsed but supported and elected to positions of authority anti-Einsteinian quantum physicists! Einstein himself furthered the careers of physicists who disagreed with him vehemently. Not one quantum physicist has ever blown up the house of a believer in the continuum hypothesis. Believers in the big bang theory have not waged a war against believers in the steady state theory. Indeed, Fred Hoyle, staunch supporter of the steady state theory, made headlines when he publicly announced that his theory was no longer as good as the big bang theory. This would be a little like, say, the pope announcing that the Bhagavad Gita is by far a better book than the Old Testament! In general, when in science evidence is found to the contrary of some accepted view, typically the destroyer of the old theory is heralded as a hero, and the results are anything but suppressed. They are published in journals and disseminated to the public, often with great reward to the critic of the former view. Can the same be said of religious authorities?

The point here is not that appeal to scientific authority is a good thing or evidentially justified. It may or may not be. In the next chapter we'll see whether it is. The point is that not all authorities are created equal.

Scientific authorities *may*, perhaps, in certain situations, be trustworthy. It depends. There are problems, qualifications, all sorts of difficulties, and one must proceed very carefully. A history of suppression of evidence, manipulation of belief, and so on, would throw that authority into question. And it is precisely this sort of comparison that makes appeal to religious authority not just questionable but unreasonable.

Can Science Solve the Mystery?

11.0 Do Scientific Theories Dispel the Need for Religious Explanations?

MANY PEOPLE DO NOT BELIEVE ANY KIND OF GOD EXISTS. SOME PROFESS TO be convinced of this, perhaps not in the sense of being convinced with absolute certainty that there is no God, but at least in the same sense as they are convinced there is no Santa Claus, no phlogiston, no ether, and so on. In other words, using our terminology, they profess to have a warranted conviction that God does not exist. If this is how you categorize yourself, then you have the strongest type of No-Belief. So certain are you in your belief that you feel certain, beyond any reasonable doubt, that there is no God. You are the strongest type of No-Believer: a No-Knower (in the relative sense, of course).

We've already seen why such a position, though sometimes erroneously called "nonbeliever," insofar as it involves having

179

beliefs about something—in this case, believing that God does not exist—*is* a type of belief. Whether it qualifies as (relative) knowledge, an educated guess, a hunch, or faith depends not on how strongly you believe it—your level of psychological confidence—but the basis on which you believe it—the level of evidential justification, consisting in reasonable evidence and arguments, and how you came to your belief.

Many of the people who place themselves into the category of No-Believer or, even more strongly, No-Knower, do so on the basis of their confidence in the ability of science to provide a high degree of certainty in an otherwise uncertain world. Science dispels the silly superstitions that arose from religious myths and provides the groundwork for answering questions about the nature and origin of the world by gathering evidence and using the light of reason.

Now, science may or may not be a vehicle to truth. Right now that is not the issue. The question is whether a No-Believer with regard to the existence of God is actually convinced that God does not exist, on the grounds that science can dispel the mysteries for which God would be otherwise required. In other words, it is not so much a problem with the extent and limitations of scientific method and the status of scientific truths; rather, the question is about how the Non-Believer came to have the belief that God does not exist.

That is, how—and whether—the likes of Albert Einstein and Richard Feynman are convinced of what the universe is and how it came to be, and whether the mysteries previously requiring God are now dispelled, are interesting and relevant questions. So are the questions of how—and whether—the pope, the minister and the guru are convinced of what they profess to know; even how—and whether—Jesus Christ, the Buddha, Mahavir, Joan of Arc, and Mohammed can be convinced of what they think they know. These are deeply interesting questions. But the issue at present is not their convictions and beliefs but the No-Believer's views. If you're a No-Believer, is your belief that God does not exist the type and level of belief you think it is?

Some people claim they were convinced of the existence of God through direct revelation. Hardly anyone claims to get scientific convictions in this way. So presumably if the No-Believer has scientific convictions, they were acquired by going to school or by reading. Many of our beliefs are acquired this way. Take, for instance, your belief that Christopher Columbus, going against accepted public opinion of the time (according to which the Earth was flat), boldly sailed westward trying to reach India and that's how, by accident, Columbus discovered America. This belief is taught to children by teachers who teach us many of the things of which we think we are now convinced.

But the words "taught" and "convinced" are here being used rather loosely. We've already considered what it means "to be convinced." It means that you have a belief, which is a propositional attitude, such that the proposition is true relative to other such propositions, and your psychological attitude is based on a cognitive attitude, not the other way around—a cognitive attitude based on a psychological attitude. If it is the other way around, then you are not really convinced of that belief, you have merely been converted. What then does it mean "to teach"? If it means "to condition someone into having a particular psychological attitude toward a particular proposition," then it means the same thing as "indoctrination." Conditioning people's attitudes is just that—conditioning. It is like obedience training.

If you are given just the results of some inquiry, whether historical, scientific, religious, or philosophical, and not the *method*, what you have is, at best, a belief by persuasion. It isn't (relative) knowledge; it is not belief by conviction. To see why, let's consider your belief that Columbus discovered America. It may be very odd even to call him the *discoverer* of a land where millions of people already had lived for thousands of years. (Not to mention Leif Ericsson, who sailed there before him.) It is also odd that in fact Columbus never even set foot on the mainland but only on some of the Caribbean islands. Yet, apparently, Columbus insisted even after he had been back and forth many times that he had found a passage to India and that he had, in fact, landed in India! That is why American natives are still today called "Indians." But all this pales in comparison to this next item. Probably you are very familiar with the story of how Columbus had difficulties in getting his trip funded because people thought the Earth was flat. Supposedly, everyone was convinced that you couldn't sail west to India because you would fall off the Earth. The fact is, however, that hardly anyone in Columbus's time believed the Earth was flat. On the contrary, the precise circumference of the Earth had been already known for fifteen centuries, since the Greeks. Well, then what really happened?

Apparently, Columbus was a very bad geometer. He did his own calculations and came up with a circumference of the Earth that was about one-sixth of the actual circumference. The geometers in the court where he tried to get funding knew Columbus was grossly mistaken and advised the queen that Columbus was completely wrong. The argument between the court geometers and Columbus was *not* whether the Earth is round or flat but, rather, how big it is in circumference. And Columbus was way off—way, *way* off. Yet, he managed, by using his powers of persuasion, to seduce the queen to his side—apparently in more than one way.

Why were you not taught this version of the historical events by your teachers? Did they not know the truth about the nature of the disagreement between Columbus and the court—that it was never a question of whether the Earth is flat or round? If your teachers did not know this, then they were ignorant and thus unreliable. Did they know the truth but thought it would make a better and more dramatic story for schoolchildren if they lied about various details, such as people's beliefs about whether the Earth was round or flat? In that case, your teachers were deceivers and thus not trustworthy.

Now, the point here is not that your teachers don't know anything, or that you don't either. Rather, the question is whether you can be convinced enough of a belief to have relative knowledge—for our present purposes, the truths of science—by being conditioned into believing it. What the Columbus example shows is how untrue the "truths" you were "taught" by the method of conditioning can be.

But, surely, the truths of science are not as vulnerable as the truths of history! Here it is the No-Believer's and No-Knower's turn to be shocked.

11.1 Copernicus vs. Ptolemy, the Church vs. Galileo—A Philosophical Recount: Who Really Won?

To examine the nature and methods of science, which so often are presented as a counterpoint to the nature and methods of religion, let us turn again to what we've already discussed and what most people today would regard as one of the most basic and incontrovertible types of known facts that there are: that the Earth goes around the sun. Unlike the roundness of the Earth, which has been accepted for thousands of years, the belief that the Earth moves around the sun is of relatively recent vintage. The Greeks, for instance, believed that the Earth was at the center of the solar system. For many centuries, this was taught as official doctrine. Ptolemy's geocentric system, according to which the sun, the moon, the planets, and the stars all revolved around the Earth was even accepted by the Catholic Church, which committed itself to the view that the Earth was indeed motionless and at the center, as the Bible decreed to be the truth according to someone who should know: God.

It was Copernicus who first challenged the Aristotelian-Ptolemaic geocentric system with a heliocentric one. Copernicus put the sun at the center. Fearing repercussion from the church, Copernicus put a disclaimer at the beginning of his work because to challenge church doctrine was heresy punishable by death. Some years later, however, Galileo declared the Copernican heliocentric system to be not just a possible truth being speculated about in theory, but the *actual* truth.

The trials and tribulations that Galileo underwent because he dared to contradict accepted church doctrine are well known, and we shall not go into them here. The question that concerns us is with your indoctrinated belief regarding the solar system. Who was right, Ptolemy or Copernicus? Does the sun go around the Earth, or does the Earth go around the sun? What do you believe, *and why do you believe it*? Probably, if you are like most people, you think you believe the Earth goes around the sun because this is known by scientists to be true. It may indeed be true, and it may be known to be true by scientists (in the relative sense, of course). But why do *you* believe it?

Nineteenth-century schoolhouses in the U.S. had ominous signs over the blackboard that read "Fear God!" Religious pictures, such as scenes from heaven, various saints, and the hierarchy of the angels, were not uncommon in nearly every school across the country. These religious icons have since been replaced with pictures of great scientists like Albert Einstein, Thomas Edison, Madame Curie, George Washington Carver, and so on, and various charts such as the hierarchy of the elements. And what elementary school classroom today does not have at least one picture of the solar system, with the sun at the center and all the planets going around the sun?

Probably it was some such image that first introduced you to the Copernican-based heliocentric view of the solar system. How convenient for the teacher in charge of indoctrinating you with this belief; all she had to do was point to the great mural on the wall and say, "There . . . *see?*" This pointing, of course, is just a ritual that simplifies having to go outside and demonstrate how in fact this is known to be true, right? Because of course, in principle, one could, right? One just doesn't have to, right?

After all, can't we, in principle, go outside and look directly at the solar system and *see* whether the Earth goes around the sun or the sun goes around the Earth? Probably you believe some scientist must have had some such experience, or else surely this would not be so widely disseminated with such absolute authority. Galileo must have looked through his telescope, an astronaut must have looked out the window, or *something.* Surely, somebody must have actually looked and saw the great truth that the great men like Copernicus and Galileo discovered, namely, that the Earth indeed can be observed to move and to go around the sun.

Well, let's think about it. Could we, if we wanted to and had all our technology at our disposal, go and *see* whether the sun goes around the Earth or the Earth goes around the sun? Of course it would be silly and we'd be laughed at if we actually went to anyone, doubting what everybody obviously knows, and said we just want to see for ourselves. It would be like going to pull on Santa's beard in the department store to try to verify if that's the real Santa. You'd have to be a little crazy to do it. So let's be a little crazy—even though we're certain that the Earth has been seen by somebody to move around the sun. Let's doubt the obvious, let's pretend we really are crazy enough to doubt what is so obviously true. Well, of course we don't really doubt this scientific certainty, but if we did, how could we go to see the truth for ourselves? Science, after all, is based on experience. The empirical method will allow us to see that the Earth goes around the sun, surely.

We step outside and look up. What do we see? The sun rises, then sets. The moon rises, then sets. The stars move across the heavens . . . so far, everything seems to be moving around the

Earth. Not very convincing for the sun-centered view! We had better go up in a spaceship.

We go to Florida, we get in a rocket, and we lift off. We go straight up until we are in a synchronous orbit around the Earth. Many satellites are in such a synchronous orbit, meaning that (according to the heliocentric theory) they move at the same speed that the Earth revolves, thus remaining in the same position over the Earth. Like tall radio and television towers, these satellites are used to bounce signals from one side of the Earth to the other.

Now, inside our spaceship, looking down from our synchronous orbit, what do we see? Below us is the Earth, with the Florida coastline visible beneath a layer of clouds. The Earth is perfectly motionless. We look up. The sun, the moon, all the planets, and all the stars are seen to move around the Earth!

Well, of course, we are in Earth's reference frame. It's like being on a moving train and throwing a coin up in the air. It doesn't just fly away and smash against the back wall because the momentum of the train has been imparted to the coin. If the train is moving 70 miles an hour westward, the coin is moving 70 miles an hour westward and continues to do so even when you toss it up; that's why it lands back down in your hand, which also is moving 70 miles an hour westward.

So, obviously, up in our spaceship above the Earth, what we must do is start moving about. We fire our thrusters and start orbiting the Earth. We look up. What do we see? The sun, the moon, and all the stars—*still going about the spinning Earth below.* Well, obviously, then, to see with our own eyes what the *real* movement of the solar system is, we must leave Earth's reference frame and go to the sun. We fire our thrusters and retro-rockets and fly away until we are in a synchronous orbit around the sun (the air conditioning is very good). What do we see?

Lo and behold, we now see the sun perfectly still beneath us and all the planets and stars moving about the sun. Finally! Copernicus and Galileo vindicated! But hold on. We now fly to Mars. From our orbit around Mars, what do we see? The Earth, the other planets, the sun and all the stars revolving around Mars. So Mars is at the center. No, wait . . . what is going on?

Well, the truth must then be this: Whatever reference point in the solar system you're looking out from, that place will seem to be still and everything else will seem to be moving around you. But what, then, are the *true* motions of the planets and the sun? Do they even have a *true* motion in some absolute sense? Even if they did, *you can't—even in principle—see it just by looking.*

But isn't that exactly what the church officials said? Their argument with Galileo was that you couldn't tell just by looking. And guess what? The church was right!

Maybe Columbus isn't all that we've been deceived about. Maybe science itself is starting not to look so good. The history books themselves, who wrote them? The science camp or the religion camp? How did we come to believe what the famous disagreement was between Galileo and the church and, further-more, *that Galileo, who supposedly was right, won, and the church, which supposedly was wrong, lost?* Even more remarkable, why don't today's church officials know this (and they don't—they will be as surprised to hear of what you're reading in this chapter as most scientists will)? Have perhaps they, too, been duped by this scientific-historical put-up job?

According to the church at the time, facts about the true nature of the world, including the solar system and the universe, are not available to us without revelation from God. It wasn't that, at the time, you couldn't go up to have a look, as some scientists today may want you to believe (and may even them-selves, wrongly, believe to be the case). The problem wasn't that back then people didn't have airplanes and spaceships. We are in a position to go up and look all we want! The problem is that looking doesn't settle it: There is no position in the universe from which to look.

You might think the problem is that what really is needed is a better vantage point. We would have to leave the solar system. All right, let's lift off from Florida and never stop. We just keep going up, up, up . . . finally, we're beyond the orbit of Pluto. We look back at Earth. What do we see?

We see the Earth as a stationary dot, and all the other plan-ets, including the sun and the stars, revolving around the Earth! Unless we shifted our reference frame to some other position, say, Alpha Centauri, which then will be the one and only still object in the whole cosmos, our point of view will remain locked in to the Earth's position and everything else will be seen to move around that point. Indeed, as Einstein showed, there is no absolute vantage point in the universe where we could stand to see what the "true" motions of anything are. (That is why his picture is in all the schools.) The only absolute thing about motion is that it is relative.

At this point, one is apt to wonder: did we ever come to prefer the Copernican picture to the Ptolemaic one? One apparently obvious answer that presents itself is that the Copernican model is by far the more accurate. For instance, it is well known that the "inner" planets, the ones between the Earth and the sun, do not exhibit retrograde motion, whereas the "outer" *planets*, the ones beyond Earth's orbit, do. This puzzle was well known even to the ancients. Plotting the motions of the planets—which means, literally, "wanderers," so named because they moved against the background stars—night after night, ancient observers saw that some of the planets, like Mars, Jupiter, and Saturn, would on occasion "backtrack." The planet would slow down, then start moving backwards, then forward again—hence "retrograde motion."

Copernicus's system easily explains retrograde motion. If the Earth also is moving around the sun, and it is closer to the sun than, say, Jupiter, it has got a shorter distance to go and hence will "catch up to" and then "pass" the position of Jupiter. But Ptolemy's system explains this too. Since Ptolemy (around 150 A.D.) developed his system to account for the seen motions in the heavens, it should not be surprising that he accounts perfectly well for retrograde motion. He does it with "epicycles." Each planet, such as Mars, does not just go around the Earth in a circle, but circles its own orbit around the Earth. The orbit of Mars around the Earth would be represented as something like Figure 7.

Each of the planets, and also the moon and the sun, moves about the Earth along its own eccentric circle (the deferent), while its epicycle circles its deferent. Using several such epicycles, Ptolemy was able not just to account for the positions perfectly, but to predict future positions. His system was accepted by the entire Western world for more than thirteen centuries.

Then how *did* we ever come to pick the Copernican system, first published in 1543, over Ptolemy's? The next most obvious answer that presents itself is that Copernicus's system must be simpler and should therefore be preferred on grounds of simplicity. But nothing could be further from the truth.

Either system can get you just as well from the Earth to the moon. Not only does the U.S. Coast Guard still use Ptolemaic

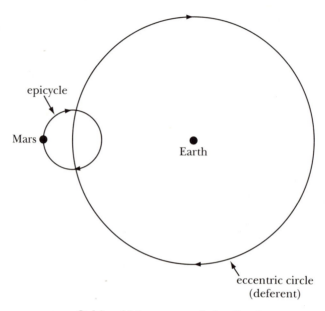

FIGURE 7.   Orbit of Mars around the Earth

calculations because they are simpler, it is not even clear *which system uses fewer epicycles!* What, you say? That's preposterous! Isn't Ptolemy's system the ugly one with all the crazy epicycles?

Here once again you are in for a shock. Not just because Copernicus's system also had epicycles. *Because the best scientific, historical, and philosophical experts, the great knowers who have access to and have studied the actual scientific documents, cannot even agree as to who had how many!* Let's check a few sources and see, for ourselves, what the experts actually do say:

> Copernicus reduced the number of epicycles from 80 to 34. (Burtt, *Metaphysical Foundations of Modern Science*)
>
> Copernicus uses altogether 48 epicycles—if I counted them correctly . . . Brought up to date by Peurbach in the 15th century, the number of circles required in the Ptolemaic system was not 80, as Copernicus said, but 40. In other words, contrary to popular, and even academic belief, Copernicus did not reduce the number of circles, but increased them (from 40 to 48). (Koestler, *The Sleepwalkers*)
>
> [Copernicus's] full system was little if any less cumbersome than Ptolemy's had been. Both employed over thirty

circles; there was little to choose between them in economy. (Kuhn, *The Copernican Revolution*)

[Copernicus] used 34. (Crombie, *Ancient and Medieval Science*)

Copernicus reduced the number of circles required to explain the apparent movements of the heavens from the 80 or so used in the elaborate versions of the Ptolemaic system to 48. (Mason, *History of Science*)

Copernicus used 17 epicycles. (Margenau, *The Nature of Physical Reality*)

Copernicus used 80 epicycles. (Harre, *The Anticipation of Nature*)

Copernicus used no epicycles. (Bohm, *The Special Theory of Relativity*)

[Copernicus] used 40, as opposed to 240 for Ptolemy. (Motz and Duveen, *Essentials of Astronomy*)

Copernicus succeeded in reducing by more than half the number of arbitrary circular motions which Ptolemy had been obliged to postulate. (Armitage, *Copernicus*)

The introduction of the revolution of the earth about the sun never managed to do away with more than five epicycles. (Dijksterhuis, *The Mechanization of the World Picture*)

Copernicus used no epicycles. (Kaplan, "Sociology Learns the Language of Mathematics" in Wiener, *Readings in the Philosophy of Science*)

May I please have the envelope? And the winner is:

The popular belief that Copernicus' heliocentric system constitutes a significant simplification of the Ptolemaic system is *obviously* wrong. . . . the Copernican models themselves require about twice as many circles as the Ptolemaic models and are far less elegant and adaptable. (My emphasis. Neugebauer, *The Exact Sciences in Antiquity*)

Really reinforces your faith in science and history, doesn't it?

But look, we're not talking here about superstring theory, quantum electrodynamics, wormholes, virtual vacuum fluctuations, the many worlds interpretation of quantum mechanics, to mention but a few of some of the latest "scientific sobrieties" that help science to "see the truth." We're talking about something as simple and supposedly as incontrovertible as whether the Earth goes around the sun or the sun goes around the

189

Earth—*a question of "brute scientific fact" supposedly settled centuries ago and taught to schoolchildren as "straightforward, scientific facts" that have been settled centuries ago in a land far, far away . . .*

Right now, at this moment, do you have an answer to the puzzling, perhaps even disturbing, questions presently being raised? Probably you don't. Are you going to rush to the library to examine the above sources or even the originals? Probably you won't, any more than you'll pull on Santa's beard next time you see one at the mall. You might even repeat what you've just read without checking any of it. Even if you did go look up the sources, will your feeling of certainty that the Earth orbits the sun change? Hasn't it been so indoctrinated into you, the "scientific facts" so driven into your mind by persuasive authorities that questioning such "obvious" and "incontrovertible" facts as the movement of the Earth seems ultimately preposterous, a waste of time, perhaps a bit like *intellectual blasphemy*?

The philosopher Paul Feyerabend, a critic of science, remarks:

> Scientific "facts" are taught at a very early age and in the very same manner in which religious "facts" were taught only a century ago. There is no attempt to waken the critical abilities of the pupil so that he may be able to see things in perspective. At the universities the situation is even worse, for indoctrination is here carried out in a much more systematic manner. Criticism is not entirely absent. Society, for example, and its institutions, are criticized most severely and often most unfairly and this already at the elementary school level. But science is excepted from this criticism. In society at large the judgment of bishops and cardinals was accepted not too long ago. The move towards "demythologization," for example, is largely motivated by the wish to avoid any clash between Christianity and scientific ideas. If such a clash occurs, then science is certainly right and Christianity wrong. Pursue this investigation further and you will see that science has now become as oppressive as the ideologies it had once to fight.[1]

So if you think you're convinced that God does not exist because science has replaced the old myths with new, clear-cut, incontrovertible facts about what the world is and how it came to be, then think again. When you examine the scientific "revolutions" since the seventeenth century, it quickly becomes very clear that every view that has ever been held by anybody has turned out to be either false or deeply questionable. At the time it was held, however, people took the (now defunct) view to be the final truth. The scientists of the time claimed, while their theories might not be absolutely perfect and account for everything, they were "on the verge." Today, scientists still talk this way, claiming the theories that are the latest fad have them "on the verge" of understanding everything. But the theories don't get closer and closer, they shift completely! And then the new theory has them "on the verge" again.

Today we are in the same boat. Whatever is taken to be the truth according to our evidential framework of propositions is heavily biased toward the ever-receding present—and apparently recedes with it. Based on what has happened to past (relative) truths, we have, it seems, good reason to believe that much of what science now claims to be true will someday be unmasked and revealed as false by future scientific views that will also, at some later future time, themselves be revealed as false. But all along the way, of course, the scientists will keep chanting, like a mantra: "We're on the verge! We're on the verge!"

Science might well be the best way to truth. And that truth might be that God is not necessary to explain the world, that God does not exist except as a myth. But if the propositions we believe about the world arrived in our minds via having our psychological attitudes indoctrinated into us by scientific authorities, then we are not convinced of those propositions. We are indoctrinated. We are members of the faith of what may be the greatest religion that has ever yet existed: the Church of Science.

Note

1. Paul Feyerabend, "How to Defend Society Against Science," in Kolak & Martin, eds., *Self, Cosmos, God,* Fort Worth: Harcourt, Brace, Jovanovich, 1992.

Why Is There Something Rather Than Nothing?

12.0 What Is the Question About?

WHAT IS THIS QUESTION ABOUT? EVERYTHING. IT ASKS: WHY EXISTENCE? Why does anything exist? Why isn't there just nothing?

It has been said there are two sorts of people: those for whom this question, at some point in their lives, arrives, and those for whom it does not. Have you ever asked this question of yourself? Seriously: All this, what makes it exist, here, now, like this? Here you are with a book in your hand on a planet going around the sun, well, anyway, on a planet, in a solar system, in a galaxy, somewhere in the vast cosmos . . . where is the totality of all this happening, why is all this here, how did it come to be?

Some say, "God did it." Presumably, those who are No-Believers regarding the existence of God believe that all this—the whole of existence, the entire cosmos and everything in it—can best be accounted for by some sort of scientific explanation. We might not know all the details, and there may be gaps in our theories, but according to the No-Believer the scientific answers fare better than God. So in the interest of moving ourselves to the ideal starting point on our chart, the center of the neutral zone at (0,0), let us do a comparison test to see whether the current scientific answers really do fare better than the answer "God did it."

12.1 Quantum Genesis: Beyond the Big Bang?

According to the most widely accepted scientific answer, the universe began about fifteen billion years ago with the so-called "big bang." (The "big bang" started as a tiny dot of existence, the tiniest little dot imaginable, and it was *completely silent*, since there were no sound waves. So why do the scientists give it that name? Is it perhaps because "the teeny, tiny silence" wouldn't as easily convert?) Until recently, science could explain up to the big bang but no further. What about *before* the big bang? There was no "before," since not just space and matter but also time itself began with the moment of cosmic birth, before which there was absolutely nothing: no time, no space, no matter, no energy— not even black emptiness, since "blackness" is something and emptiness itself implies a container.

Recent cosmology, however, as we've already noted, does not end where the universe begins. It reaches beyond the beginning, into the very heart of nonexistence itself, where from the womb of nothingness it supposedly brings forth the ultimate answer why:

> . . . the entire cosmos simply comes out of nowhere, completely in accordance with the laws of quantum physics, and creates along the way all the matter and energy needed to build the universe we now see. It thus incorporates the creation of all physical things, including space and time. Rather than postulate an unknowable singularity to start the universe off. . . the quantum spacetime model attempts to explain everything entirely within the context of the laws of physics. It is an awesome claim. We are used to the idea of "putting something in and getting something out," but getting something

for nothing (or out of nothing) is alien. Yet the world of quantum physics routinely produces something for nothing. Quantum gravity suggests we might get everything for nothing. . . . Does such a universe model have any need for God? . . . one traditional cosmological argument for God proceeded on the assumption that everything must have a cause. Quantum physics has confounded this claim.[1]

So genesis according to quantum mechanics goes something like this: Before the beginning—before the big bang—there was Nothing. The Nothing became something. Why? On the view of some physicists, such as Steven Hawking, Alan Guth, and John Archibald Wheeler, the ultimate answer to the ultimate question is: "The nothing is unstable." Thus, Alan Guth's remark, "The universe . . . is a free lunch."

This sounds extremely odd and paradoxical. How can one speak of a *nothing* and then say it is unstable? If there is nothing there, how can "it" be unstable or stable? (There is no *it!*) *What* is unstable? We might be able to understand how, for instance, one might say that having no money, no house, no food, and so on, makes you unstable, provided there is someone there, you, who is penniless, homeless, and hungry. This is certainly not a very stable position to be in. But if there is no one there, then homelessness is not there either, nor is the pennilessness.

And yet, these scientists insist, it makes sense to talk of an unstable nothing. If you ask them *why* the nothing is unstable, they will tell you: Because that is its nature! But how can *nothing* have a particular nature? Here the incredulities begin to pile up so quickly that for a little intellectual repose one might just as well turn to the concept of the holy trinity. Indeed, in describing the various paradoxes of quantum mechanics, the contemporary philosopher of physics Allen Stairs, who believes that "reality itself has a richness that, so to speak, 'spills over' when one attempts to contain it within a single point of view," aptly remarks:

> The sorts of analogies that are apt to occur to the nonreligious reader are religious paradoxes, for example, the Christian doctrine of the Holy Trinity—that God is one Being, but three Persons—or the more general idea that God is transcendent and yet immanent. Both are attempts to express a conception of a reality that cannot be captured by a single, nonparadoxical description.[2]

Certainly we can ask, at this point, whether the scientific answer is any better than the religious answer. After all, science prides itself on being rational, the product of logic, reason, and—most importantly—the so-called "experimental method." But here the extrapolations are so many steps removed from any possibility of empirical verification that one wonders whether one is in the domain of science or religion.

12.2 God and the Ultimate Question

So: Why is there something rather than nothing? The biggest answer to the biggest question, according to religion, is God. Does the religious answer fare any better? Well, supposedly God explains the occurrence of the big bang. What, though, explains God? According to most religious views, unlike the big bang, which came from nothing, God did not come into existence from nothing. God has always existed. *Why* has God always existed? Unsurprisingly, the religious answer here parallels the scientific answer: Because that's God's *nature*. That is, just as it is the nature of the nothing to be unstable, it is the nature of God to be permanently permanent!

Why is it God's nature to exist permanently? Why is it the nature of the nothing to give rise to something? Here science and religion fall prey to the same fate. The question "Why is there something rather than nothing?" swallows them both.

A quantum physicist, a priest, and a philosopher sit next to each other on a plane, arguing about the ultimate question: Why is there something rather than nothing? According to the scientist, the best answer is that "the Nothing, which is essentially unstable, nothings itself and gives rise to the universe." The priest disagrees: "God, who is eternal, creates the universe," is the best answer.

They turn to the philosopher sitting between them. What do you think, they want to know? The philosopher shakes his head, "You've both misunderstood the question. It asks: Why is there something—anything at all—rather than nothing? God is not nothing. God is something, a *very big* something. So the religious answer says, in effect, that the reason there is something rather

195

than nothing is that 'the Big Something made the Little Something!' How ridiculous! And look at the scientific answer. Instability is not nothing. Even the potentiality to make a universe because there is nothing else there and this nothingness is unstable, is not absolutely nothing! Absolutely nothing would be neither stable nor nonstable. So the scientific answer says, in effect, that the reason there is something rather than nothing is that out of the Little Teeny Weeny Something, An Almost But Not Quite Nothing—so we'll call it 'Nothing' for short—came the 'Big Something!' How ridiculous!"

"So what's *your* best answer?" asks the quantum physicist.

The priest nods angrily. "Yes—what's *your* best answer, tell us!"

The philosopher shrugs his shoulder. "I'm glad to see you two have finally found something to agree about."

"Very funny," says the physicist. "At least I have a scientific theory. What do you have?"

"Yes," agrees the priest. "And I have theological theory. What do you have?"

"The most important thing of all." The philosopher grins. "I have the question."

12.3 A Brief Interlude: Death and the Ultimate Question

Before we return to why there is something rather than nothing, let us briefly consider our own impending meeting with what may be our own personal nothing. For the fact is that, for many people, the sorts of "ultimate questions" we have been asking are irrelevant. The search for the ultimate is, ultimately unnecessary; the ultimate answers, so they think, await us. No matter where we go and what we do, we're all headed right for it at full speed, straight ahead, at the end of the tunnel of life: the tunnel of death. What's the point of wondering now, while you're alive and in a state of uncertainty, when all the time you're on your way to your death and then, at the end of the tunnel there is either just the end of the tunnel or there is an opening where all our questions will finally be answered?

Thus, for many people, whether God exists is tantamount to asking: Will I survive my bodily death? Or is the universe but a cold and uncaring place, with no concern for us and our brief existence, the final answer being just a big fat No to us and to everything? When the end comes, is it the end of consciousness, are we but food for worms? Or do we somehow live on? If there is no God, our prospects are bleak. If there is a God, then there is hope.

For such people, who view the questions of God and death as inseparable, it *might* be of utmost importance that we try to find out what the truth is—provided that the truth is affirmative. If the truth is that there is no God, only this brief life and then worms, the truth may be too depressing to live with. The fate of all living things is eventually to die; the sun will explode, the Earth will be destroyed, the whole universe eventually will end or die slowly by entropy. What would be the point of living, struggling, building for the future, even raising children? So if it turns out that there is no God, don't tell us about it. Give us our hope, so that we may live our lives as best we can, without making all we do meaningless.

In other words, suppose you're on a crashing plane. There's still a little time left and there's plenty of material, so on the plane you build another crashing plane, you put your children on it and fire it off. As the next plane slowly begins to crash, your children build a crashing plane, put their children on it, and fire it off. Suppose we lived in some such strange world. Suppose, further, that we knew sooner or later the resources would be gone and there would be the final crashing plane and no survivors. Why go through all the trouble?

If there is something to this line of reasoning, then obviously there may be a deep ulterior motive for not looking openly, without prejudice, at whether God exists: *fear*. If the truth is that death is the final end and then there is just nothing, we don't want to see it. We'd rather have our illusions.

This objection to pursuing our journey of course is predicated on the assumption that seeing the truth, if the truth is that God does not exist and that therefore death is the end, would be bad for us. It would make our lives even worse. Is this assumption true? Many assume that it is. But can we find out?

Well, the first thing to notice is that the question of life after death and the question of whether God exists are not the same question. Conceivably, one could have life after death even if God does not exist. This may seem surprising until you think about it: If it is conceivable that there could be life before death even if God does not exist (and it is), why should it not be conceivable that there is life after death even if there is no God?

The view that you can't have an afterlife without God is a lot like the view that you can't have a universe without God. But what would explain the existence of the afterlife? Well, what would explain the existence of the universe? Indeed, how could anyone think that the afterlife, which would be a strange, mysterious, and inexplicable phenomenon, *plus* God, an additional strange, mysterious, and inexplicable phenomenon, taken together would be less inexplicable than taken separately? Which is more mysterious: (1) a tiny eternally burning flame or (2) a tiny eternally burning flame dancing on the surface of an eternally burning fireball?

Second, the truth, whatever it might be, may have its own rewards. There are plenty of people, some of them deeply religious, who do not believe in an afterlife, some of whom do not even believe that there is moment to moment survival (Buddhists), who by many accounts seem much happier, less fearful, and generally healthier psychologically than some people who are devout believers not just in moment to moment survival but survival for eternity, who for some odd reason seem—in spite of their belief in immortality—full of fear, sorrow, and pain. Could it be the Buddhists are correct, that the greatest cause of human suffering is attachment? Well, maybe. But the point here is merely that it is not at all obvious that believing in an afterlife makes you better off. And it may just be that the opposite is the case: Giving up belief in one's own permanence may be liberating.

It seems, therefore, that we ought to pursue the truth and see whatever it may bring us. Good or bad, exciting or depressing, we want to know what the truth is. The truth is hard enough to find without our worrying what it may do to us if we get it. That's a formula for ostriches.

Death is your very own personal ultimate unknown. How you relate to your death is how you relate to the unknown. It is interesting and perhaps disconcerting how we humans deal with death. We have so wrapped this phenomenon with myths, stories, rituals both religious and scientific, that it is difficult even to begin to approach the topic philosophically.

It is here that we can see clearly the motive for beginning our philosophical journey at (0,0). Philosophy means being in a state of unknowing, not for the purpose of remaining where you are, or living in ignorance, but for journeying into the unknown. How else to meet the unknown, except with unknowing?

Let us now rejoin the scientist, priest, and philosopher. The plane crashed, killing everyone aboard. But the story does not end there.

As it turns out, there is an afterlife. Resurrected, the scientist, the priest, and the philosopher walk together into the hereafter, joined by other resurrected souls from the plane crash. They celebrate happily in a beautiful field of glowing flowers; there is endlessly flowing elixir, singing and dancing, beautiful music. After a while, our three friends sit down together at one of the picnic tables.

"So," says the priest, raising his glass. "The Bible was right after all!"

"How do you figure?" asks the philosopher.

"Well, it's obvious, isn't it? Here we are. We died. And yet we live again. Obviously, a miracle—the work of God!"

"Ridiculous," says the physicist. "Obviously, Wheeler, Everett, and DeWitt were right[3]—the many worlds interpretation of quantum mechanics is true! We've obviously branched off into a parallel world. We did die back there in the plane crash. But according to the many worlds interpretation, there are an infinite number of branches to the world. When you die in one world consciousness ends there, in that world, but branches into another. This whole place can be explained by the laws of quantum physics. We've branched, that's all. Consciousness makes a 'quantum leap' to the next most similar world when a branch ends. This is that quantum leap." He turns to the philosopher. "What do you think?"

"I think," says the philosopher, "you're both wrong."

The two look at him, angry again.

The priest shakes his head. "How can you be so blind? Obviously, God has been vindicated. Order and design are here at hand. Why do you continue to deny God?"

The scientist shakes his head. "Obviously, quantum physics

has been vindicated. Everything *is* possible—this crazy world is the proof! Why do you continue to deny science?"

"Wait," says the philosopher. "Don't you remember what we were discussing before the crash? Look, first of all, let me ask you: Everything you see around you, the endless, cloudless light above, the infinite plane on which these beautiful gardens grow, those dark trees, these perfect bodies—what is all this?"

The priest looks at his own hands. "Souls," he says. "Made by God."

"Spiritual quanta," says the physicist. "Created out of random fluctuations."

"But look, don't you remember, the question is why—"

"Hello there," interrupts a young man. "Come, join me with the others and let us sit together at the feet of our lord. All is bliss, all is bliss, praise the lord!" He points to the crowd of people gathering around an angelic being in a white robe with long hair who has begun to speak.

"Who is that?" asks the scientist.

"Don't you recognize him?" asks the young man. "That's God!"

"Alas," says the priest, sneering at the scientist and philosopher. "What do you say now?"

"I say let's see the fellow work some miracles," says the scientist, boldly. "Let's see him prove it!"

The philosopher shakes his head. "What proof is there in miracles? He could be a very powerful being. He could even be the devil. In fact, this place might not be the afterlife at all! Now that I really am thinking about this, who is to say that we weren't beamed onto some spaceship, and all this is some sort of clever experience-inducing hologram? Perhaps the aliens are studying us to see how our psychologies work so that they can figure out what it will take to enslave the entire human race by clever super-advanced technological trickery—"

"There you go again," laughs the priest. "Don't you see how far you have to go to deny God? I mean, all this—isn't this good enough for you philosophers, miraculous enough? I say let's go listen to what God has to say."

"Hold on," says the scientist. "Though our dead philosopher's thinking, I must admit, is mighty 'exotic' at the moment—in fact, he's way beyond all reasonable limits—he does have a point. After all, many people on Earth have sworn that they are God. Why should the afterlife be any different—if this is indeed the afterlife! I don't see any labels on things. And even if there were labels all around, saying 'Welcome to Heaven,' how would we know they were genuine? And how, after all, are we supposed to recognize God? Is God going to be wearing a name tag?"

The priest stands up. "Now look, I say if that is God over there, and he can resurrect us from the dead and do anything—"

"You mean," says the philosopher, "maybe he can make us *see* anything? What if all this is an illusion of some sort?"

"What if, what if! What if just by looking into our eyes he makes us know, beyond any doubt, with absolute certainty—"

"You mean," interrupts the philosopher again, "if he is able to magically reset our psychological levels of confidence? Even on Earth, hypnosis and drugs can do that! How difficult would it be, for creatures that can do all this, to get into our brains and reset a few of our neural networks, replace our psychological and cognitive attitudes to whatever they want?"

"Suit yourself." The priest turns away. "I'm going over there to see what God has to say."

"Good riddance to you," says the physicist. He looks up at the philosopher. "Why don't we sneak off into the woods, see what's there, try a few experiments? Maybe I could rig up some gizmo and find out what kind of world this is—"

"Hold on, both of you," says the philosopher. "Let's stick together. If the priest wants to go listen, let's go listen. Together."

They agree to join the crowd. The being in the glowing robe speaks beautifully and says wondrous things; he explains that this place is heaven, the place where dead souls are resurrected. He tells them that beyond the field is the City of God, which they all can enter if they wish and there, with him, spend all eternity. Suddenly, he stops and looks at the three sitting just behind the crowd.

"I can hear your troubling thoughts," he says. "You, priest, why is there doubt in your heart? And you, physicist, who have trained yourself to trust your senses above all things, why do you not trust what is before your eyes? And you, philosopher, who have sworn to guide your fellow beings on the path to truth, why do you corrupt their souls with doubt?" He points at them accusingly. "Stand up! Show yourselves before me. What have you to say for yourselves?"

They stand up. The priest is first to speak. "Forgive me, lord. If you can see into my heart, then see that I have faith in God, shaken though it is."

The being turns to the physicist. "And you? What do you have?"

"Can you see into my heart?"

"Yes," says the being.

"What do you see there?"

"Faith in your science," says the being, "though it too is shaken."

"You are correct," admits the physicist.

The being smiles. "Don't worry, my children. You are all equally welcome into the Kingdom of God." He stands up. "Arise, all, and follow me—"

"Wait a minute," shouts the priest. "What about him?" He points to the philosopher. "You didn't ask him."

"That's right," says the physicist. "Why did you leave him out?"

"He too is welcome," says the being. "You are all welcome. You are all, equally, the children of God—"

"So why won't you tell us what is in his heart," the physicist insists.

"Because I can see what you cannot see! Your friend's heart, I am sorry to say, is empty. I did not wish to embarrass him. He is a poor and quivering fool who has nothing." Smiling, the being locks eyes with the philosopher. "Do you admit you have nothing?"

"I admit I have a question."

"A question!" With a roar, the being slaps his hands together and lightning cracks across the sky. He laughs loudly. "All right, then! Let us hear your question!"

The crowd turns and stares at the philosopher, who remains looking steadfastly at what is before him; throwing his stare back into the eyes of the man in the robe, the philosopher asks:

"Why is there something rather than nothing?"

The being, unwavering in his calm certitude, grins smugly. "That's your question?"

"It's one of them."

"All right, then I will give you your answer, the ultimate answer to all your questions."

"What's that?"

"God!" shouts the being. "The ultimate answer is God."

"Why is there something rather than nothing?" repeats the philosopher.

The being frowns. "Apparently, you didn't hear me."

"Apparently," retorts the philosopher, "you didn't hear *me!*"

"Enough of your insolent irreverence! This is your last chance to enter the kingdom." With a wave of his robed arm, the being summons the crowd to follow him. "All of you who wish to follow God, come with me to the City of God—follow me!"

Rejoicing happily, the people arise, fearless and secure, and follow the robed man. The priest, the scientist, and the philosopher remain standing together, alone in the field of spectacularly glowing flowers, watching the crowd wind its way toward the light at the horizon.

"So," says the priest. "What now?"

"I don't know." The scientist shrugs. "But we stay together."

The philosopher looks at the woods on either side of the glowing field. "What about the woods?"

"I've always loved trees," says the priest.

"The woods, yes," says the scientist. "Me too." He looks at his two companions. "But we have no map. The woods stretch in all directions. Where do we go?"

The philosopher surveys the huge trees with their gnarled limbs, thick with leaves, the labyrinth of plants and shrubs.

"There." The philosopher points to the deepest, darkest shadows. "That way."

"I'm afraid," says the priest.

"Me too." The scientist turns to the philosopher. "You?"

"Very." The philosopher returns their smiles. "Let's go."

And together they forge a path.

The point of this story is simple. Many people imagine that the unknowns of this world can all be resolved in some ideal, heavenly world where everything is known. The story suggests that there is no such world. Not that there isn't a heaven or an afterlife—there may well be. Rather, if we do persist beyond the grave, if you think about it you will see that so will our questions. Philosophy will still be necessary.

So: Why is there something rather than nothing? To say that the universe springs from the mind of a mysterious God, whose nature it is to exist forever and who is essentially stable, is not an answer to the question. God is a Big Something, and the question asks why anything—big something or little something—why does something exist at all? Or, to say the universe springs from a mysterious and unstable nothing, whose nature it is to not exist because it is *essentially* unstable, also is not an answer to the question. An unstable nothing is a little something: instability. The question remains unanswered.

Take your pick. Or don't take your pick. But don't make the mistake of thinking one make-believe answer is so superior to the other make-believe answer that your make-believe about ultimate answers is anything but a fifty-fifty proposition. That (0,0) place on your Belief Chart should be starting to look like a mighty attractive place to be—the position of no position.

But you're *not* nowhere. You're centered, at the crossroads from which all paths are equally open to you. You are not blind. Your eyes are wide open. And so is your mind. Now when you move the movement is all yours. With each step, you have to decide which way to go and why. You have to think and to choose. The responsibility for each and every step, even if you follow someone else's footsteps, is yours and yours alone.

Starting from the position of no position and taking the first step you move through the world, on your own, for the first time. That is the way of philosophy.

Notes

1. Paul Davies, *God and the New Physics*, New York: Simon and Schuster, 1983, p. 216.
2. Allen Stairs, "Quantum Mechanics, Mind, and Self," in Kolak and Martin, *Self & Identity*, New York: Macmillan, 1991, p. 472.
3. See B. S. DeWitt, "Quantum Mechanics and Reality," *Physics Today* (September 1970) and B. S. DeWitt and N. Graham, *The Many-Worlds Interpretation of Quantum Mechanics*, Princeton: Princeton University Press, 1973.

What Is the Ultimate Mystery?

13.0 What Is This Question About?

THE UNIVERSE DOES NOT CONSIST JUST IN MATTER FLOATING THROUGH space and time. Well, maybe, ultimately that is what it is, as some scientists believe; but also we're here, we exist. So the universe is not *just* that. The universe also, at the very least, contains the *illusion* that there is more to the universe than just lumps of matter illuminated in the vast darkness by the light of burning matter, the stars; there is also, within that part of the universe we call ourselves, the illumination of the existence of all things, including the universe and of ourselves, by the light of consciousness: the mind.

Whether illusion or reality, the mind asks: Who am I? How did I come to exist? Why am I here? What is the world? Where did all this come from, how did it originate? Why don't I know?

The mind is painfully aware that, for all its beliefs, all its answers, to itself the existence of all things, including itself, is ultimately an unanswerable unknown, a mystery. The mystery exists, here and now, as close at hand as it is inexplicable: the awareness of the mystery of existence within the mystery of existence, here, within us. We are it.

The question is: What is the mystery and how far does it extend? Are our unanswerable unknowns merely limitations of the human mind? Or does the mystery extend all the way from the innermost reaches of the mind to the outermost limits of the universe, perhaps even beyond?

Clearly, were it not for consciousness, there would be no awe, no wonder at the existence of the universe and ourselves. The universe would still exist, without answer, but also without question; the world would be dark, blind, soulless, unquestioned. Would existence then still be a mystery? Or is mystery just a psychological product of the human mind?

Here there is a surprising complementarity between religion and science. According to science, the ultimate mystery is ultimately resolvable: Everything, the totality of the universe and all things within it, including any of its unknowns, is comprehensible. It is just that we can't yet comprehend it. Insofar as this view rejects supernaturalism—the existence of forces that can have no natural explanation—it seems to be the opposite of religious views. According to religion, although we cannot comprehend everything, there is a God who can and does. It is comprehension in the supernatural realm, perhaps, reserved only for God, but it is comprehension still. The differences hide an incredible similarity: On both the religious and scientific views, the world is all there, even its incompleteness completely understandable, perfectly neat and orderly—even the laws of chaos can be understood, and so on. In that sense, both science and religion deny that the ultimate mystery extends beyond everything. God never says, "I have no idea, no concept, not even a theory with which to understand how anything is what it is, it just is!" The scientist never says, "Ultimately it is all incomprehensible, there are no ultimate truths, no ultimate laws, nobody could ever understand it fully because ultimately there's nothing to fully understand, it's all just floating on nothing!"

There is thus an important sense in which the world according to science and the world according to religion are the same world. The difference is just where all the answers are hidden. Either the ultimate answers to the ultimate questions are hidden in the world itself, waiting to be discovered or invented by the right scientists, or else the ultimate answers to the ultimate questions are hidden beyond the world, in God, waiting to be revealed, perhaps, to the right souls.

Within the light of consciousness, in the awareness of existence, the darkness of the world, its unknownness, presents itself to itself, self-luminous. Ultimate answers may forever be beyond us, in God, or they may be forever hidden from us, in the world. In either case, ultimate questions are here, now, the unanswerable unknown within us. The question "What is the ultimate mystery?" asks whether the unanswerable unknown is local, psychological, or global, metaphysical. If the ultimate mystery is local, as science and religion both tend to proclaim, the mystery is not an aspect of the world, of existence itself, but only a product of the human mind. If the ultimate mystery is global, metaphysical, as I will argue in this chapter that it is, the mystery is in the world itself, wormed into the very heart of existence. If local, the sphere of mystery is merely the limit of our world, not the limit of the world; if global, the sphere of mystery extends everywhere, through the known and the unknown, beneath the bottom and above the top and in between, beyond even the farthest horizons.

13.1 Questional Attitudes: What Is the Unknown and What Is the Mystery?

To inquire into the ultimate mystery, we must begin by asking what our ultimate questions, in and of themselves, tell us—what does the existence of mystery within us itself say? Does it tell us anything revealing about ourselves, about the cosmos, about God? What *is* this mystery in and of itself, this awe and wonder about the existence of all things, including ourselves? Why does it exist, within us? Are we the only ones in whom the awareness of the unknown lives? Or do other species, perhaps even ones living on other planets across the vast cosmos, know the unknown too? Is that why a lone wolf in the wilderness howls at the moon?

Human language turns such primordial howls into questions. Like hooks thrown forth, the questions launch outward. We don't just howl at the moon, we build a scaffold and reach it. Part of that scaffold consists in propositional frameworks that make possible the transmission of information from one brain to another. Recall that a proposition is a linguistic representation of a purported fact. Add to the proposition a psychological attitude and you have a belief. What, then, are questions representations of? And are there psychological attitudes that, when added to questions, make for a counterpart to beliefs— "questional attitudes"?

Well, when I ask, say, "What time is it?" I am using language to represent an unknown within my propositional framework. Thus, questions are linguistic representations, within a propositional framework, of possible holes—possible unknowns—within that framework. But just as propositions need not be inscribed with a Yes or No attitude to exist in a propositional framework (in which case they are not beliefs), so too questions need not be inscribed with any psychological attitude to exist within that framework. For instance, "How many books are there in the Library of Congress?" That's a question about which at the present I have no psychological attitude whatsoever. Similarly, when I asked above what time it is, I knew the time and so that question wasn't even really representing an unknown within my propositional framework. That's why I say that questions are linguistic representations of *possible* unknowns. I can and do sometimes use that question to solicit a proposition into my framework, such as "It is two o'clock," when some such proposition is needed and requested but missing. In that case, the question does not occur merely as a linguistic representation, it comes wrapped in a psychological attitude. When it does, the question is not just a question. It is what I call a "questional attitude," the linguistic representation of an *unknown.*

So the logical relationship between beliefs—propositional attitudes—and unknowns—questional attitudes—is that they serve complementary functions in the cognitive apparatus: Beliefs (propositions inscribed with psychological attitudes) and unknowns (questions inscribed with psychological attitudes) are the tools of thought. Your propositional framework contains propositions *plus* questions. The questions add and subtract propositions as well as being the vehicles for the psychological attitudes, including the repositioning and resetting of cognitive attitudes. Like propositions, which come in two varieties—true or false— questions also come in two varieties: answered and unanswered. Whether a question is answered or unanswered depends on its cognitive attitude with the propositional framework in which it exists as a representation of a possible unknown.

The psychological attitudes involved in believing that something is so consists, in varying degrees, of psychological confidence. The psychological attitudes involved in questioning whether something is so, or what it is and why, and so on, consist, in varying degrees, of the opposite feeling: psychological nonconfidence, that is, psychological insecurity. And just as the psychological attitude part of a propositional attitude comes in varying degrees of two basic flavors—Yes and No—so too the psychological attitude part of an unknown also comes in varying degrees of two basic flavors: secure and insecure. It is important to remember that in both cases the psychological attitudes— unlike the cognitive attitudes, which are all or nothing (True or False for propositions, Answered or Unanswered for questions)— aren't all or nothing; feeling secure or insecure about some question comes in degrees.

When you wonder about something, what is going on in your mind? A questional attitude—an unknown—is insecure. This means that the question is unsettled within the propositional framework, to some degree unsettling you. You feel insecure and so we say you're "searching for an answer." Within your mind there is movement, something unfixed and stirring. What is moving? What is the movement through? The unknown—the questional attitude—is not secure, it is wandering about within the propositional framework and, psychologically, you feel yourself wondering. You're trying to secure the question with an answer, anchor it somewhere within your propositional framework, perhaps with a new propositional attitude. Questioning, wondering, thinking, as activities of the mind, consist in unknowns— questions inscribed in the psychological attitude of insecurity— being used as a vehicle for consciousness within the framework, to *wander* about through the conceptual landscape. Sometimes an answer is found. The questional attitude—the unknown—is then secured; the question is for now answered. The insecurity ceases; the question remains, to be used again when necessary, but that particular linguistic representation of a possible unknown is no longer wandering about. What has been stirred up has, for now, been settled. This is why a good philosopher is insecure about *everything*.

Other times, an unknown stirs within you but no answer is found. You then go to a book or you ask someone. Suppose you ask someone. Suddenly, the unknown that has been wandering about within you wanders about within someone else, an insecurity within their propositional framework, probing the framework, seeking an answer. This is why most people don't like being asked questions. It literally makes them insecure.

Children, unlike adults, are unafraid of asking questions. They are taught answers but the questions themselves emerge from within them, untaught. Like true philosophers, children are not insecure about their insecurity. They revel in it. They engage directly with the mystery; they play. When you are insecure about your insecurity, when you are resisting the questions bubbling forth from within you, your unanswerable unknowns cause anxiety; the mystery evokes fear. When you are not insecure about your insecurity, when you do not resist the questions, your unanswerable unknowns cause wonder and amazement; the mystery evokes awe.

Suppose Marvin, who is three years old, amazed at finding himself existing, wonders, "Where do babies come from?" Within him this question is inscribed with some degree of insecurity; using our terminology, the status of his questional attitude is that of an unknown. But he is not embarrassed to ask it, he is amazed, he is in awe. Within Marvin's propositional framework, this unknown is unanswered; the questional attitude is therefore an unanswered *unknown*. But of course we can answer it. Marvin's unknown is therefore ultimately answerable. It is not an unanswerable unknown. Other questional attitudes, however, are not answerable; they are "unanswerable unknowns." When a questional attitude is an unanswerable unknown, I will call it a "mystery." In this way, when asking about "the mystery," I am not being "mystical." Nor am I inquiring into the psychological sense of insecurity. Rather, I am asking about a question's cognitive *attitude*.

Thus, in asking "What is the ultimate mystery?" I am not asking merely about your greatest psychological insecurity, though I am asking that. I am also asking what, within you, is the ultimate unanswerable unknown.

210

13.2 What Is the Ultimate Unanswerable Unknown?

Some unanswered unknowns, like Marvin's question in the example above, are limited to the particular propositional framework within which they are asked (they are limited to the person asking the question). Marvin's unknown is local, not global; ultimately, it tells us something about Marvin, his psychology, his stage of cognitive development. We can answer his question. It is not a mystery. Or is it?

Well, here the mind encounters a grave philosophical problem. When an unanswered unknown becomes answered and, therefore, (relatively) known, the mind loses the mystery. Why? First, remember what I mean by the mystery: an unanswerable question inscribed with an attitude of insecurity—an "unanswerable unknown." It is very difficult to be insecure about the question of where babies come from once you know where babies come from! The questional attitude is reset from a cognitive state of "unanswered" to a cognitive state of "answered," and the corresponding psychological state is reset from "insecure" to "secure." The issue has been settled within you. But has it really?

Well, in one obvious sense yes, it has. The sperm and the egg come together, exchange genetic material, and their DNA and RNA make a zygote. But where do the sperm and the egg come from? A good question—a good unanswered unknown—but Marvin didn't ask about the sperm and the egg. He didn't have such concepts yet formulated consciously in his mind. He can now go on to ask about them. The question he asked, however, has been answered. Indeed, to say that it hasn't been answered is to fail to distinguish between ancient people who believed God made babies in heaven and then put them into women, and contemporary people who believe that babies are made in the womb by DNA, etc.

In another sense, however, we can still ask: Ultimately, where *do* babies come from? Parents, who had parents, who had parents . . . who according to the scientific story evolved from apes . . . fish . . . amoebas . . . interstellar gas . . . the big bang . . . ??? Or, according to the religious story, God did it . . . but how? . . . why? . . . why God? Why that? So, ultimately, all answered knowns, whether scientific or religious, end in unanswerable unknowns. But do they, really? And, if so, what does it mean? Or are answers even to those unknowns ultimately forthcoming, somewhere, either from the world itself or from God—and, if so, what does *that* mean?

In other words, at the ultimate level, is there an answerable unknown or an unanswerable unknown? Is the world, the universe, existence, in and of itself, a nonmystery? Or, at the ultimate level, is there an unanswerable unknown—is the world, in and of itself, a mystery? How can we decide? We must inquire into whether we have reason to believe that some questions cannot be answered in any framework, known or unknown: Does there exist, at the ultimate level, an ultimate mystery, an *ultimately unanswerable unknown?*

Here we can notice an interesting categorical relationship between the domain of religious unknowns and the domain of scientific unknowns. Scientific unknowns are questions that presently are unanswerable within the scientific framework but, we have some reason to believe, will someday be answerable within that framework. It is just that we don't yet have enough data, the right theory hasn't yet been worked out, and so on. But it's just a matter of time. Religious unknowns, on the other hand, are questions that presently are unanswerable in any known framework but, ultimately, can be answered by God.

"Why does the universe exist?" used to be a religious unknown. Scientists, who used to call themselves "natural philosophers," like Isaac Newton, used to be convinced that questions concerning the ultimate origin of the cosmos would forever be under the domain of religion, never under the domain of science. Twentieth-century cosmology, as we've seen, has changed the status of this cosmic mystery, which used to be a religious unknown, into a scientific unknown (for which the big bang theory is just one possible answer). When the big bang theory was first put forth, scientists at the time were convinced that the question, "Why did the big bang happen?" would be forever beyond the category of scientific unknowns and thus should be placed in the category of religious questions. Only a few decades passed before this question, too, as we've seen, has been moved from the category of religious unknowns to scientific unknowns.

It would thus seem that the domain of religious unknowns is shrinking. It's not that scientific answers are replacing religious questions; rather, it is that, putting it more appropriately, religious *unknowns* are being replaced by scientific *unknowns*. It's how you approach the missing pieces, not how you fill them in, that differentiates science from religion. It's not just that science has answers and religion does not; after all, religion has as many answers, perhaps even more answers (in terms of sheer numbers) than does science. Notice, too, that again whether a question is a religious unknown or a scientific unknown is purely a factual, not evaluative, matter.

So perhaps Sartre overstated the case. *God is not dead; it's just that in our rapidly expanding universe God is rapidly shrinking!* But here I would throw in a word of caution to the No-Believer. As you may already have intuited in the previous chapter, and as I've been implying above, it's not so much that all the religious unknowns under the name of God are being dispelled from existence: rather, they are being shifted from the domain of religion to the domain of science.

This is not a new shift. In the seventeenth century, Galileo was a leading proponent of scientific materialism, the view that the entire cosmos, including us, could be understood in terms of matter and motion. Ironically, this view, called "The New Science" by its three major founders—Kepler, Galileo, and Newton—was in part the result of trying to understand the universe as a giant clockwork machine created by the great cosmic watchmaker, God. According to Galileo, for instance, God was not a mystery—an unanswerable unknown—beyond reach that could never be comprehended or understood; rather, God's nature is revealed to us in God's greatest handiwork: the universe. In other words, God, for the New Scientists, was an answerable unknown. Thus physics became mechanics—the study of matter and motion—and, gradually, the answerable unknown became the answerable known (in the relative sense). Supposedly, someday physics would show how the whole universe and everything in it was one vast, artfully created machine, revealing what God, the cosmic architect of space, time, and matter, is like.

Doubly ironic is that the real argument between Galileo and the Catholic Church was *not* that Galileo was denying the existence of God; rather, what made the church officials so angry was that Galileo claimed we could learn about the nature of God directly, by our own observation. Of course, this would imply that you don't need their religious institution (though of course you might need, instead, the New Scientist's scientific institution to

Chapter 13

help you see things "right"). The church officials did not like this because they claimed only "revelation" according to official church doctrine could give humans knowledge of God. Whereas according to the New Scientists, all you have to do is look—not at scriptures but at the world. In other words, using our terminology, we could say that the bone of contention between seventeenth-century religion and science centered around whether God was an answerable or unanswerable unknown. In either case, they agreed that the universe, existence itself—one way or the other—was an answerable known (either to the scientists, in the relative sense, or to God, in the absolute).

So, for the purpose of getting ourselves to the neutral starting position required for philosophical journeying, what I am now suggesting is the radical thesis that both Western science and Western religion have committed the same cognitive sin: obscuring our connection to the ultimate mystery.

The shifting of unknowns from the religious to scientific categories, for all its cognitive power, may be causing a short-circuit in the cognitive apparatus that complements the short-circuit caused by the resetting of cognitive attitudes through emotional persuasion. This time, what is being short-circuited is the brain's remarkable capacity not just to see the world via its own representations but also to experience the mystery via its own psychology. At the same time, the forced and artificial containment of unanswerable unknowns within the domain of religion, stubbornly keeping them away from the realm of scientific unknowns, causes the same sort of short-circuit; in this case, the preservation of the feeling of mystery without the appropriate cognitive attitude: the mystery not by conviction but by conversion.

Nearly all religions, past and present, have given to the ultimate unanswerable unknown within their own particular religious framework the same name: God. In that sense, they do acknowledge an ultimate unanswerable unknown, even though, on most religious views, the unanswerable unknown is limited to humans and does not extend to God. The science of today, however, does not even give it a name. In science, whose language is the formal language of mathematics and logic, what is not named does not exist. That is one of the nice, clean properties of formal systems: They contain only what they name. In that respect, formal systems are closed systems in which all propositions

214

are decidable (either true or false). This means that scientists, mathematicians, and logicians can talk forever and never mention what they don't want, because the undesirables are not in their language! In other words, they can purge their propositional frameworks, by artificial means, of any and all insecurity. We are for the moment exploring whether this is a good thing, whether it is even warranted.

There are lots of problems with taking such an approach to the world, the most obvious of which is that it brackets the mystery. The beauty and power of such formal systems, of course, is that even the problem of what they are leaving out is expressible perfectly well in the formal languages, as for instance in Godel's famous "incompleteness" theorem that shocked the intellectual world in the 1930s. The complexities of the theorem preclude our discussing it here, except to say that its conclusion—roughly, that no formal system, such as arithmetic, can be shown to be consistent within that system—may imply an ultimate limitation of the mind ever to fully understand itself and the world.

Note, however, that many scientists, as well as many scientifically minded philosophers, are quick to try to nip the unknown in the bud, lest it allow room for the mystery to enter. A famous example is Ernest Nagel:

> Godel's proof should not be construed as an invitation to despair or as an excuse for mystery-mongering. The discovery that there are arithmetical truths which cannot be demonstrated formally does not mean that there are truths which are forever incapable of becoming known, or that a "mystic" intuition (radically different in kind and authority from what is generally operative in intellectual advances) must replace cogent proof. It does not mean, as a recent writer claims, that there are "ineluctable limits to human reason." It does mean that the resources of the human intellect have not been, and cannot be, fully formalized, and that new principles of demonstration forever await invention and discovery. . . . It would be irresponsible to claim that these formally indemonstrable truths . . . are based on nothing better than bare appeals to intuition.[1]

The question we are presently pursuing is whether the scientific world view, in bracketing what has traditionally been a domain of religion—the mystery—may be doing something as harmful to the human mind as the damage done to the cognitive apparatus through religious conversion into the mystery. The issue is, in part, whether it is reasonable to suppose that scientific theories and observations, which at this point in human development are still definitely incomplete, may someday provide an objective account of why the universe exists and why it is the way it is rather than some other way. This would mean that what is presently among the greatest of all scientific mysteries—the greatest unanswerable unknown—will become an answerable known: All the big questions will be answered with true propositions about which the mind will have warranted convictions. In that case, the ultimate unanswerable unknown is merely a product of the human mind; the universe will then someday understand itself completely. (I say "the universe" to leave open the possibility that human evolution may be just a stage in the development of some sort of cosmic mind.) In that case, there is not even room for what the concept of God represents in our propositional frameworks. The ultimate mystery is merely about us, not about the world; it is but a figment of our imaginations, expressing, at most, the limitations of our own ability to understand the world.

Remember, again, that by "mystery" I don't mean just a psychological sense of insecurity, which at the extreme levels, if there is no resistance to it, evokes not fear but amazement and, ultimately, what Einstein himself called the most important capacity of the human mind: awe. I mean an unanswerable unknown. Likewise, by "ultimate mystery" I mean an unanswerable unknown that we have some reason to believe is not answerable in any framework and will never be because it is not a property of our frameworks but a property of the world.

The question, then, is whether there is reasonable justification for the view that the whole of existence and ourselves within it is, ultimately, a mystery. How can we find out?

Well, again, we cannot survey either the cosmos nor God. We cannot glimpse directly into the heart of being and see the origins of all things. To do so would require having an uninterpreted experience of ultimate reality which, as we've discussed, there is good reason to think is impossible. Indeed, it seems this is something even God could not have. Why? Well, suppose we ask whether God, if God exists, believes God exists. If so, what is God's evidence? God's own thoughts? God's own experience? God's own direct apprehension of God? Couldn't God conceive how it is possible that any of God's own events or actions or states are not as God conceives them? Even if God has no need for conceptions of any kind, isn't it possible that God could conceive of the possibility of God misinterpreting God's own states? If so, then God's interpretation of God—no matter how good an interpretation, even if a perfectly good interpretation—is still only an interpretation.

Ironically, it seems that ultimately, we are in the same boat as God. We cannot directly ascertain the truth about the world nor even about ourselves. We must interpret it. Unlike God's interpretation, which of course would no doubt be the best, possibly even most perfect, ours cannot be that. Like God, however, we too must, as before, try to ascertain the truth by looking as best we can at ourselves.

In other words, we cannot get, right now, to the outer limits of the world to be able to comprehend the extent of the ultimate unknown. So, if we are to address this question, we must go the other way: the inner limits. Reason can guide us as follows. If the ultimate unknown exists, it means that, ultimately, everything— the whole world, from top to bottom and inside out—is a mystery. Even at the innermost core of our being, what we are most intimately and in closest contact with, must therefore in some crucial, but perhaps obscured sense, be a mystery.

Well, what is the very closest, most familiar, most intimate part of ourselves, that to which we are most directly connected? Isn't it our own minds, the inner universe of experience, consciousness itself? So: Is there ultimate mystery? If there is, this time the evidence does not come from the existence of the cosmos but from the existence of us. Here, within the sphere we have already mapped out, we must inquire into whether that which is most familiar is, possibly, the most amazing thing of all. This time, reaching through the inner labyrinth we must look for evidence that what links us directly to the ultimate unanswerable unknown exists from the first step, even before the first step, from the very beginning of our journey, going everywhere we go, looking at everything we see, thinking everything we think: the cosmic mystery—within us?

13.3 Consciousness and the Unknown: Complexity vs. Mystery

Suppose I opened up your brain. I'd see neurons and the like. No pictures, no images. Just neurons! Now, while I'm looking at your brain, I'm having an image of it: I see neurons. But where are *those* images that *I* see? Are they in my brain? Well, but if someone opened up *my* brain and looked at it even as I was looking at yours, would they see an image of your brain in my brain? No, they would see only neurons.

The scientific picture of ourselves, which tries to paint physical, objective reality using physical, objective images, obscures the most crucial element in the entire realm of existence: the picturing itself and that which is doing the picturing—ourselves.

To search for God and cosmic mysteries is impersonal. It leaves us out of the picture. Now we are asking: What about us, this awareness of ourselves existing as conscious beings in the world, this "being aware" of our own existence? What *is* that and what are *we*? It is one thing to wonder about a physical universe consisting of space, time, and matter. It is quite another to wonder about a physical universe being somehow observed by someone within it—a conscious mind, aware of itself, of its own existence—that asks, "Who—what—am I? How did the consciousness thinking these very thoughts, this awareness, come to be? Why do *I* exist? What is the ground of *my* being?"

Suddenly the mystery is no longer out there but in here. In *where*? In *here*? *Where* is the "here"? Inside neurons, perhaps? It's very dark inside neurons. Does it seem dark to you right now? Inside atoms, perhaps? It's even darker inside atoms than it is inside neurons, since they are smaller than the smallest wavelength of visible light. (Who was it who said, "Let there be light," anyway, and what did that thing who said it look like, to itself, without any light?) There is no "hereness" inside neurons, there are just the atoms, no "hereness" inside atoms, just the . . . well, whatever it is down there (and what is *it* made of?). You need someone pointing to have a "here." What is this "hereness," this "nowness," pointing all around at everything but itself, of what does *it* consist?

Here suddenly we present ourselves with a phenomenon as surprising as it is eerie, in a manner suggestive of a cross between high courtroom drama and the Twilight Zone. The mystery isn't the universe, nor the Bible, nor the Shroud of Turin. The mystery is *you*.

I'm not talking now about unusual, extraordinary states of mind. Throughout the ages mystics have claimed to have certain sorts of uncommon mental states, sometimes implying thereby to have experienced direct union with God. But the phenomenon we are inquiring into here is not mystical states of mind that may or may not occur in the way the mystics claim and which mean what the mystics say they mean; the phenomenon, rather, is *ordinary* states of mind. And remember our purpose: Can we find, with accuracy and precision, a seed within ourselves that hints at the limitlessness of the ultimate mystery, in the sense we have defined it? That is, we are not now looking outside ourselves for evidence of the existence of God; rather, we are looking inside ourselves for evidence of the ultimate mystery.

Could it be that the most common of all experiences—in fact, what is necessary for any experience, our moment to moment, ordinary states of consciousness—provides reason for thinking that the ultimate unknown transcends all propositional frameworks that we could ever hope to bring to it?

Clearly, science has made progress in understanding what consciousness is, what makes it possible, and what makes it happen. Science has made progress in many areas that formerly were unanswerable unknowns: what makes stars burn via the proton-proton interaction, how trees get energy through photosynthesis, where babies come from, the structure of the benzene ring, how to make a light bulb, and a slew of other things. Indeed, in terms of understanding the human mind, we are not far from creating machines that think. Today's computers—electronic brains—are proof that we are making progress at least in terms of making machines that mimic what the mind does. This is something people of only a few generations ago could only fantasize about. There is no question that many formerly unanswerable unknowns regarding consciousness can today be answered by evoking a variety of scientific complexities involving the functioning of the human brain, analogies with computers, and so on. But what we are now pursuing is the possibility that if we are not exceedingly careful as philosophers, we shall unwittingly grow up as Marvin in the example above ultimately grows up: Once Marvin's mind receives an answer to the question

219

"Where do babies come from?" it successfully turns a questional attitude from "unanswered" to "answered." While this was an unanswered unknown, that mind had, within itself, contact with the mystery. Once "Where do babies come from?" is answered, that contact is broken. The question has been answered by science, which has a whole labyrinth waiting for Marvin, with which it will educate Marvin into an adult. Eventually the brief contact Marvin had as a child with the mystery will be broken, perhaps forever. It is a flaw within the rational mind which I call, "Hiding the Mystery Within the Complexity."

Consider the following story. Suppose we live in a different universe. We are the first surgeons ever to open up a living human head and actually have a look inside. We've believed for some time now that thinking happens somewhere in the head but we don't know what it is because we've never looked. We give Charly a local anesthesia, make our incision, and open up his skull. What do we see?

Floating inside Charly's head cavity we find one marble. It's a nice, round, hard, shiny steely with some wires attached. One wire goes to each eye, one wire to each ear, and one more connects the marble to the spinal cord where there are wires going to each of the fingers, the mouth, etc. Charly, by the looks of it, is a very simple machine.

We ask Charly how he feels. "Fine," he says. "Tell me what you see inside my head."

"We see a marble, Charly, connected with wires to your eyeballs and the other sense organs."

"Wow," says Charly. "So that's the seat of consciousness! At last, I know what the mind is. A marble."

This would be a very odd thing for Charly to conclude. Why? Well, suppose that having opened up Charly's head we found a round, ethereal, glowing light, spinning and dancing, a myriad of colors twirling dizzyingly. We might be astounded, shocked, and amazed, but now we *might* be willing to say, "At last, we've found the seat of consciousness: a spiritual atom the size of a diamond." What *might* prompt us to say this is that the seen object has just the sort of inexplicable mysteriousness that one might expect to find from an object responsible for the amazing phenomenon of consciousness.

Recall some traditional types of religious miracles—say a stone statue bleeds. It is the fact that the bleeding statue is made of stone that makes it so miraculous. If the bleeding statue were made of flesh and blood, and it bled, we should not be prompted to shout, "Yazoo!" We should say, rather, "Look, the statue made of flesh and blood is bleeding; somebody get a bandage to plug up the hole and keep the blood in so it doesn't make a mess."

But if the statue is really made just of stone, and it bleeds, it seems idiotic to conclude, on the basis of seeing blood coming out from between the graphite, that blood comes from graphite. One imagines God, up in heaven, who made the statue bleed to wake up the idiots from their dogmatic slumbers, looking down and wondering, "Where did I go wrong? Idiots! I made idiots!"

Well, but how much more ludicrous would the situation be, if *all rocks bled* and our human inquirer concludes, with the glowing satisfaction of scientific discovery, that, "No wonder the stone statue bled—*all* stone bleeds!" At this point God tosses the universe into a bottom drawer and says, "Forget it, I'm never making another one of these again."

Now ask yourself this: What is blood from a stone in comparison to *consciousness* from a stone? Before you answer, "But wait, it's not just one stone," let's *think*. Let's go back to our friend Charly who's just had his head opened up, revealing the presence of one shiny steel marble. Thoughts are not a shiny steel marble, any more than rocks are water or emptiness is solidity. They may ultimately allow of a theoretical explanation showing how it is possible that, from a different perspective, the activity of thought can be explained using the language not of mental things but physical things, such as their functional relations. Currently philosophers of mind debate the question of whether mental descriptions can be translated into physical descriptions. But we're not talking about whether mental descriptions can be translated into physical descriptions; they can. They can be translated, in fact, into theological descriptions. We're not even just asking whether mental representations can be shown, experientially, to consist just in physical activity, though here the answer might be "No." The question is whether we can locate, clearly and distinctly, an obscuring of the mystery within what is closest and most apparent to us so that we don't see it not because it isn't there but because, like the air, it is always there.

Mystics and scientific reductionists/eliminativists (who try to eliminate metaphysical entities, all the way from God to consciousness, from the world) have something in common, though in a complementary way. Mystics ultimately end up implying they can have an interpretation-free experience. The scientific reductionists/eliminativists ultimately end up implying that they can have an experience that is not an experience—*an experience-free experience!* Though we cannot further pursue the question here, there may be good reason to think that such implications, if they are sound, ultimately undermine both mysticism and reductionism.

In other words, the problem in the story above about Charly is not merely that there is one inactive stone and consciousness is an activity; if there are two stones bouncing back and forth, we should not be any more convinced that what we are seeing, when we see the two stones hitting each other, is the activity of consciousness. Add as many stones as you like; the mystery remains, although at some point the complexity will no doubt obscure it. (And adding little stones that orbit the big stones won't do the trick, either, except in the original sense of *trick*.)

When you look up at the sky on a clear night you see what to you looks like a constellation—say, Hercules. That constellation is *not* solid. It might look solid to a huge giant ten thousand times larger than the galaxy, but looking solid and being solid are very different. Similarly, if you shrink down to a size smaller than a water molecule, so that looking up you see various H_2O constellations, it would be very odd to point at those atomic constellations and to say, "There, see, there's wetness—that's what wetness consists of entirely, those little floating hardballs." *Wetness* does not—and cannot—consist *only* of little floating hardballs, not even a constellation of atoms, any more than *solidity* can consist only of a constellation of stars! *Looking solid* and *feeling wet*, what do *they*, themselves, consist of?

Let's again take a look back at the situation with Charly. If we find one steel marble inside his head and conclude on the basis of this that thoughts are made of steel, we should be laughed at for being idiots. How could one even *think* the thought, "Thoughts are made of steel!" And yet, look at what has happened. Here we are, floating on a rock in the middle of this Cosmos, supposedly having come into existence from nothing according to science and from God according to religion. Curious to find ourselves existing, we open up our heads and find not one marble but *many* marbles called "atoms." The marbles are strung together like beads on a string into worms called "neurons." It's all very, very complicated—too complicated to fully understand. But here comes the crucial, revealing missing link to the mystery.

The psychological state, *"too complicated to understand"*—let us call it "bewilderment"—is rather similar, in terms of how it feels psychologically, to the psychological state we above called *"the sense of amazement,"* the feeling evoked when an unknown—a questional attitude—warrants the opposite of maximal psychological confidence, maximal psychological insecurity: a state of awe. Earlier, we were careful to distinguish between the psychological attitude of insecurity and the cognitive questional attitude, "unanswered," or the stronger, "unanswerable." Now we are distinguishing, within the psychological attitude making up the unknowns (questional attitude plus insecurity) within the mind, two very different types of experiences. One comes from the top down. It's the feeling of being overwhelmed, psychologically, by complexity. The other comes from the bottom up, the feeling that even though everything is there, still there's something missing: an unanswerable unknown. I'm calling the first feeling "the sense of bewilderment," the second feeling "the sense of insecurity." When the first is at maximum, there is a state of utter confusion and incomprehensibility. When the second is at maximum, there is awe and wonder.

It is important to note that you might not be in awe of something that is really very mysterious, that is, there may be an unanswerable unknown lurking about in your framework which you have covered up with some answer that doesn't really work, or have obscured with a feeling of obviousness. Or you might be in a state of awe about something that is really not very mysterious—the Bermuda Triangle, for instance. What I call *rational awe* is a state of mind in which your psychological insecurity toward a question q is proportional to the degree of q's status as an unanswerable unknown.

Note, too, where the "too complicated to understand" feeling comes from: the complexity of scientific theory and concepts, such as "the brain is the cause of consciousness." We then—if we are not careful enough as philosophers—*confuse the psychological sense of insecurity which comes from the unanswerable unknown—the mystery—with the psychological sense of bewilderment which comes from complexity;* we may thus be led to believe that the cause of the sense of awe is the same as the cause of the sense of bewilderment. *It's the old bait and switch again, only in a different form.*

In other words, the crucial difference is this. There is the situation in which the conscious mind is overwhelmed by the amount and complexity of information and data; your concepts are stretched to the limit. If we think of your conscious mind as analogous to the RAM (random access memory) of a computer, psychological bewilderment would be akin to not having enough RAM to graphically represent some very complicated calculations; the brain—the hard disk and operating system—throws up an error message. It is not that the system isn't working properly, but that the work the system is doing cannot be represented on the screen. Thus, the sense of confusion and bewilderment tells us something about the "screen," that is, about the limitations of the conscious mind to sustain, all at once—i.e., in your RAM—what the system as a whole is doing. In other words, *confusion and bewilderment are merely a psychological representation of the limitations of our psychologies.*

The sense of awe and wonder, on the other hand, is something completely different. It too is a psychological representation—but not of the limitations of our psychologies. *Rational awe* is a psychological representation of the limitations of our entire propositional framework; it is what a hole in the conceptual framework *feels* like. This is not surface limitation; it is a limitation at the very core of our being. It cuts deep. It is a hole in the foundation.

Imagine we're in the village where the stone statue bleeds. Suppose there is a devil, too. The devil cannot erase the work of God. Nor can the devil originate miracles. All the devil can do is be a copycat and multiply God's miracles. Seeing the bleeding statue, the devil takes one of the villagers aside, gives him a white coat, and shows him how to make bleeding statues. Soon the village is full of bleeding statues. When people wonder how you can get blood from a stone, the villager in the white coat takes them aside and shows them how: by putting together certain kinds of stones, you can make blood happen. "But how do you get blood from a stone?" some inquisitive individual still wants to know. "Like this," says the fellow in the lab coat, controlling what he does not understand—the control being a clever substitute

224

for his inability to explain the unexplainable, mysterious, ultimate unknown.

So the thrust of my argument here is *not* that matter is not conscious! Imagine in the village in our story above, making the Argument from Blood and the scientist retorts: "But look, see, it is the stone itself that is bleeding!" We should say to him, "Yes. Precisely. Thank you very much."

"But look, see, it is the physical body itself, the brain, that is conscious!"

Yes. Precisely. Thank you very much.

13.4 What Is the Moral of This Story?

What is the moral of this story? Only this: Perhaps the reason the brain continues to sustain its religious openness with the idea of God, even though it lacks reasonable evidence—alas, perhaps even against the evidence—is that the concept of God is a way of keeping contact, at all costs, with the mystery. The No-Believer must therefore ask whether perhaps the brain, in some primordial sense, is "smarter" than its psychology or any part of its cognitive apparatus. After all, it is the human mind and the human mind alone that, as far as we know, can do something absolutely remarkable and incomprehensible: It can discover where babies come from—explain it, understand it, fix it when it goes wrong —and yet still remain in a state of awe and wonder about the existence of life. If we can understand the proper place of rational awe in our frameworks of understanding we can have a place for our answers and for the mystery, too. With each and every newborn child, as the sphere of our belief grows, the mystery can continue to live within us. In a state of rational awe we may venture to build not enclosures and citadels but vast infinite structures that open into the sky.

Perhaps, then, the proper place of the concept of God in our lives as we enter the next millennium will be to remind us, as we become wiser and wiser about all things, that ultimately we must not allow knowledge and the light of our own reason to blind us to the awe and mystery. The existence of religion in the human sphere may therefore ultimately be a philosophical warning sign from deep within the innermost corridors of the human brain: Those of you who draw nourishment from the fruits of the trees of knowledge, beware.

Don't break contact with the ultimate mystery, even when you think you are full. Even when you are full: Never break contact. Never.

Note

1. Ernest Nagel and James Newman, *Godel's Proof,* New York: New York University Press, 1958, p. 101.

What Is the Source of God?

WHAT COULD *THIS* QUESTION BE ABOUT?

If God exists and is the ultimate being, it cannot be about God. Regardless of whether God exists or does not exist, the concept of God arises and so now we ask, Why? Why God? What is the origin of this concept within us?

Presumably—God or no God—rocks and trees have no concepts of any kind, and therefore no such concept exists within them; there is no image netted among their atoms. If God created the universe and all its atoms, to keep the concept of God out of God's creation and thus keep us oblivious would surely be a small feat by comparison. Without the God-concept, regardless of whether God is real, neither the question nor the thought of God could ever even arise within us. But it did arise within us. How?

Either God put the question within us or else it arose naturally from within the brain. In either case, the concept is the effect of something within us. So let us look within.

A little girl walks for the first time into a church with her mother and father. She has by then already asked a million questions. No one taught her how to ask questions. They crop up naturally, like her arms, her hands, her fingers, the fingernails on her fingers. Picture your growth from when egg and sperm first met to this present moment; imagine playing back the tape and then running it fast forward so that you see the swelling from then to now and then continuing forward to your death, all in one minute. What would you see? Like the big bang, a dot expands and swells until it stops as you are now, expanding no more. And then, slowly, it begins to disintegrate, to fade. Now imagine that every life form that has ever existed is thus shown thrown forth from nothing to something: each and every thing stops at a certain border, and then fades, followed by the next thing, and then the next, from one-celled organisms to us, each shivering bubble thrown forth into the world, each one tossed just a little further.

And so likewise within the big bang there is the little big bang with the curly hair, and within that little girl there are tiny big bangs: questions! No one taught her how to ask. Her father and mother did not sit down with her and teach her how to ask questions, any more than they had to teach her how to make her cells divide; the DNA within her does not need any help from the adults whose desire set in motion the long chain of events leading up to the little girl with the big questions emerging effortlessly from within. Matter bubbles forth up to its present pause and then like leftover momentum the questions continue flying outward past the borders, cosmic vectors from the mind.

Unprompted she asks where she came from, where the world came from, where everyone and everything came from. The father answers. Or the mother answers. They say, "God." All things, including her, come from God. God created everything.

We have traced the question. What happens if we trace the answer? Did that too bubble forth from within, unprompted and unencumbered? The question comes from within but the answer comes from outside. The parents take the girl into the church into which they were taken by their parents. She sees a statue, a crucifix, stained glass.

At the other end of town, a little boy walks for the first time into a synagogue with his mother and father. On the other side of the Earth, another little boy enters a temple. In yet another country, a little girl sits inside an ashram.

Thus the mind is in each case presented for the first time with images which it is told, by its own parents, are of the ultimate parent, or ultimate parents, of everything. X, some image of God, enters the mind for the first time. What happens? Do the images pass through, unencumbered, as neutrinos from the sun pass continuously through you and the Earth and everything? God: creator of everything, your judge who sees everything you do; where did this concept come from? How did it originate?

The crucifix, the star of David, the statue of Buddha, of Krishna, and so on, we know where they originate. These are images of the conscious mind. But what about the concept, which would have had to precede the existence of the images? The images, passed down from the mind of one generation to another, are then thrust into the minds of the next generation, and then the next. Each time there is a marriage between that inner springing forth, the question, and the image, the answer. The children in the church, the synagogue, the temple, the ashram, did not choose the image. It imposes itself from the outside. Nor did they invent the question, which comes from the inside, any more than they invented their own bodies. The image flies inward to fill up the hole: "I am a Christian," "I am a Hindu," "I am a Buddhist," "I am a Muslim," "I have an answer," I am silenced.

But the tossing forth continues, in silence. And when the silenced girl becomes a silent woman and gives birth to another questioning child she will see that the question has not been silenced, that it cannot be silenced. It is like putting up your hand to stop a waterfall; the water doesn't mind, it doesn't care, it just goes around you thunderously laughing. And when you are thirsty it will not run from your lips, it will not judge you for having tried to stop it.

The water rolls over your tongue no matter what noises the mouth has made against it, it rushes inside to let you carve it up as you will. Here, have a piece of oxygen, two pieces of hydrogen. The body absorbs it, takes it exactly where it needs to go, delivering to the blood the oxygen it then ferries to the heart, which in turn dispenses life to each and every cell of the body.

Is it not the same with the whole of you? Light knocks against the eye and the eye reacts, ears bid welcome to all sound, the skin responds to every touch and all the signals quickly travel along myriad inner subways without maps, no one at the switches, arriving always and exactly on time to where then the brain trembles, and must tremble, just so. And then in this trembling with eyes open it knows to dream the world just so, and sends its own image of itself into it, the seen body without a head where this representation of the book you are reading is being held by those representations of your hands. Our concepts are the real antennas of the brain, the myriad eyes within, each one not just a looking-for, but already fine-tuned to a specific frequency.

Then from within itself comes a most curious need: a desire from the deep to know. It bubbles forth into the world and comes back unanswered, and from out of this aloneness the mind divines a question: What are you, world, and what am I, what is this unknown well from which we both have sprung? The image then rushes in to fill the hole, a symbol for everything and nothing, a surrogate other to stand in place of what is missing. What is the function of this? What is being accomplished? What purpose does it serve? To fill a need? But whence the need? From within? From without? The concept of God within us, what is it seeking, what is the hole that the image of God covers?

The mind springs forth. The world reaches in and the mind responds, the mind reaches out and the world responds. Experience is the great conversation.

So we ask: What then is the concept of God looking for? We are not now asking about the image that has been hung in place of something, the X that marks the spot. We are inquiring into the place itself that holds the image, the spot where it hangs. It is not even a question of the nail that holds the picture in place, but the wall itself—the entire framework of understanding—and the hole in it that has been made, that which holds both the picture and the nail: the awe, the mystery, the ultimate unanswerable unknown.

Inconclusive Unreligious Unscientific Unhistorical Unphilosophical Postscript

ONCE UPON A TIME IN A LAND FAR, FAR AWAY, MORE THAN TWENTY-FIVE centuries ago, a man named Thales was walking down a road with two friends, Anaximander and Anaximenes.

"Everything is made of water," he said.

They walked on for a bit.

"Everything is made of water," he repeated.

His two companions stopped and stared at him, perplexed.

"Water?" asked Anaximander.

"Water," said Thales.

"Everything?"

"Everything, yes. Everything is made of water."

"What about rocks?" asked Anaximenes.

"Even rocks."

"What about stars?" asked Anaximander.

"Even the stars." Thales paused. "Even us." He smiled.

They continued on. As they rounded a bend, Anaximander turned to his teacher, suddenly very perplexed. "That's it?"

Thales looked at his pupil. "That's it."

"Water . . . just water?"

"Yes." The old teacher nodded knowingly. "Everything is made of water."

"You're sure?"

"Oh, yes, I'm sure."

"Not *everything*," said Anaximander.

Anaximenes nodded. "I agree. Everything can't be just water! There must be something else besides water."

"Hmm . . . well . . ." suddenly, Thales stopped. "Actually, yes. The more I think about it, the more I see that I have left something out." He smiled yet again. "Also, everything is full of gods!"

The two looked at him quizzically and then they continued on for a bit until suddenly Thales stopped and shook his head.

"Isn't that amazing?"

The three looked at each other, smiled, and continued walking along the road together.

Some years after Thales's death, Anaximander and Anaximenes were walking down that same road. The younger one turned to the older and asked,

"You think the old man was right, Anaximander?"

"What about?"

"That everything is made of water."

"You forgot gods. Everything is made of water and everything is full of gods. That is what Thales said." Anaximander chuckled strangely. "Isn't it funny how you forgot about the gods."

"But do you think it's true?"

"Actually, I've been thinking." Anaximander looked up at the sky, at the horizon, at the cypress trees along the road, at the road itself, and then at his own hand. "The indeterminate boundless. Everything is made of the indeterminate boundless." Anaximander smiled. "Isn't that amazing?"

They walked on.

Several years later, Anaximander had died. Anaximenes was walking alone down that same road. A pupil came and greeted him.

"Where are you going, Anaximenes?" asked the young man.

"Nowhere."

"Nowhere?"

"Just walking."

"May I walk with you?"

"What's on your mind?"

"I was thinking."

Anaximenes nodded knowingly. "What about?"

"Everything."

"What about everything, Pythagoras?"

"What is it?"

"What is what?"

"This!"

"This?"

"All this," said Pythagoras. "All these things—what are they? How did they come to exist? What are they made of? What is everything?"

"I see." Anaximenes paused. He was old and tired. He leaned against the tree. He ran his hand along the bark. "Air," he said. He picked up a stick that was lying by the side of the road and tossed it cautiously, insecurely, through the air into the nearby river. "Air," he repeated. "Everything is made of air."

The young man offered the old man his arm.

The old man looked into his pupil's silent eyes. "Isn't that amazing."

Together they walked on down the road.

Many years later, Pythagoras was an old man walking down that same road. When he passed by the bend near the river, he sat on a stump that used to be a tree. He picked up a guitarlike instrument, which he had invented, and began to strum. His students huddled quickly around, realizing that the old master was about to speak. He waited until all eyes were upon him. "After many years of thinking, I have finally come to an inexorable conclusion." With a gesture of his hand, Pythagoras made a big circle. "Everything is made of numbers!"

The group sat there for a long time in silence, with only the sound of the river and the air and the first chords ever to be played in the world tickling their ears. Pythagoras sighed deeply.

"Oh, well," he said, putting down the instrument. He rested for a while longer and then staggered up from the old tree stump toward the road, the instrument strapped across his shoulder. The students started after him.

"Never mind," said the old man. "I want to walk alone a while. I want to think."

Pythagoras walked alone up the road. After a while he heard footsteps behind him. He stopped, turned and waited for the fellow to catch up. It was one of the students.

"Wait, Pythagoras."

"What is it?"

"May I walk with you, teacher?"

"I am tired. I want to think. Tell me what you want."

"Numbers, you said."

"Yes. Numbers."

"Everything is made of numbers?"

Pythagoras made a slow circle with his cane through the air and then, pointing between the young man's eyes, said, "Everything, yes. Everything is made of numbers." Pythagoras smiled. "What do you think, Heraclitus? Isn't that amazing?"

Years passed. One day, Heraclitus was walking down that same road with some students. One of them turned to him.

"May I ask you something, Heraclitus?

"What?"

"Well, I was thinking, teacher. You know how you said that everything is made of fire?"

"What about it?"

"The other day you said not fire but change. Everything is change, you said. Yesterday you said everything is made of chaos. Nothing fixed, nothing permanent—"

"Those are some of the things I said, yes. Why are you telling me what I said? I know perfectly well what I said. Do you have a question?"

"Well . . . change, fire, chaos—which is it? Which one of those things?"

"It's not any one of those things," said Heraclitus. "It's all of those."

"At the same time?"

"Yes."

"But then everything is . . ."

"Everything is what, Parmenides?"

The student shrugged. "Everything is . . . many?"

"Everything is many. Yes."

"I see." Parmenides nodded.

The old man offered the young man his arm for support. "Isn't that amazing?"

One night, Parmenides was walking down that same road with a pupil. They had been walking for some time in silence, when his student finally stopped. "So what is this important thing you have to tell me, Parmenides? What was it you realized, that you had to get me up in the middle of the night to go walking down this deserted road?"

Looking up into the starry night, Parmenides swept his hand across the milky way. "See all that?"

"Yes, I see it, I see it!"

"What do you see, Democritus?"

"The moon. The sky, full of stars. The universe."

"Everything is one."

"But what about all that vast empty space between the stars, between us and everything?"

"There is no empty space," said Parmenides. "Existence is completely full. It is all one permanent, indivisible, impenetrable, immovable, eternal whole."

Democritus stared up at the points of light. Suddenly, directly above them, a meteor flashed, moving quickly across the entire sky.

"All is one," echoed Democritus. A smile spread slowly across his face.

"Yes," said Parmenides. "Isn't that amazing?"

Some years later, after Parmenides had died, Heraclitus was walking down the road with his students. He paused next to a tree stump and sat down.

"I have something very important to tell all of you," he said.

"What is it, Democritus?"

"Everything is made of atoms." He smiled. "Isn't that amazing?"

As years became centuries, many people walked down that road. In the middle ages, one teacher turned to his pupil and said, "The space you see between the road, the trees, and the river—there really is no space, it is all filled up with matter. Isn't that amazing?"

"It is," said his pupil, and they continued walking.

During the Renaissance, a fellow stood lecturing in the middle of the road, pointing at everything, "All this empty space between things—incredible. The ancient Democritus was truly right! Everything is made of atoms. The universe is mostly empty space with numerous tiny atoms. Everything—the trees, the road, us—everything is made of atoms!"

"Little atoms doing all this by themselves?"

"Atoms and nothing else!"

"Amazing."

At the same time, on another part of the road, a small group sat on the grass between the road and the river, listening to their teacher.

"There is no matter," said the teacher. "There are no atoms. Everything is made of mind. All this what you see is just the mind."

"Amazing," one of the students said.

And so it went on, century after century. Today, that road is still there. Parts of it are overgrown but it winds through many places. The people are different and the voices are different and what they say is different, sometimes from day to day, sometimes even on the same day.

Recently, an old man with silver hair happened to pause a while at the stump on the side of the road worn smooth by all the rumps that have rested on it, since it is such a good place to lecture from. Sitting there, he declared:

"Everything is made of quarks!"

"Everything?" a pupil asked.

The old man nodded. "Everything."

The student helped the old man up.

"Yes," said the old man, and together they walked on down the road. "It really is amazing."

To forget this road is easy because it is always there. To find this road is equally as easy. You need only remember.

Walk.

Think.

Be amazed.

INDEX

Index

Index